RIGHT THINKING
IN A
CHURCH
GONE
ASTRAY

NATHAN BUSENITZ
GENERAL EDITOR

HARVEST HOUSE PUBLISHERS
EUGENE, OREGON

RIGHT THINKING IN A CHURCH GONE ASTRAY

Copyright © 2017 Nathan Busenitz
Published by Harvest House Publishers
Eugene, Oregon 97402
www.harvesthousepublishers.com

ISBN 978-0-7369-6675-7 (pbk.)
ISBN 978-0-7369-6676-4 (eBook)

Library of Congress Cataloging-in-Publication Data

Names: Busenitz, Nathan, editor.
Title: Right thinking in a church gone astray / [edited by] Nathan Busenitz.
Description: Eugene, Oregon : Harvest House Publishers, 2017. | Includes
   bibliographical references.
Identifiers: LCCN 2016048379 (print) | LCCN 2016051070 (ebook) | ISBN
   9780736966757 (pbk.) | ISBN 9780736966764 (ebook)
Subjects: LCSH: Christianity and culture. | Church.
Classification: LCC BR115.C8 R57 2017 (print) | LCC BR115.C8 (ebook) | DDC
   261—dc23
LC record available at https://lccn.loc.gov/2016048379

Printed in the United States of America

17 18 19 20 21 22 23 24 25 / BP-SK / 10 9 8 7 6 5 4 3 2 1

Contents

SECTION III:
The Church and the Great Commission

Foreword

JOHN MACARTHUR

The world is getting worse.

Read the morning paper, turn on the evening news, or log on to your favorite news website at any point in between, and you're certain to catch a glimpse of the chaos that characterizes contemporary society. Biblical principles and Christian moral values are under assault like never before in recent history. What Scripture identifies as sin, modern culture celebrates under the guise of personal liberty. Meanwhile, those who boldly proclaim biblical truth are mocked as being intolerant, ignorant, and irrelevant.

The downward spiral taking place in America and other western societies is articulated by the apostle Paul in Romans 1:18-32. In that passage, Paul explains how the judgment of God affects those who reject Him. Having suppressed the truth in unrighteousness, they are without excuse. Therefore, God gives them over to degrading passions, including nature worship (verse 25) and homosexuality (verses 26-27). A society under divine judgment begins to self-destruct as God allows rebellious people to run headlong into sin. As Paul explains,

> God gave them over to a depraved mind, to do those things which are not proper, being filled with all unrighteousness, wickedness, greed, evil; full of envy, murder, strife, deceit, malice; they are gossips, slanderers, haters of God, insolent, arrogant, boastful, inventors of evil, disobedient to parents, without understanding, untrustworthy, unloving, unmerciful; and although they know the ordinance of God, that those who practice such things are worthy of death, they not

only do the same, but also give hearty approval to those who
practice them (Romans 1:28-32).

Paul's words, penned two millennia ago, provide a fitting description
of the state of American culture today. It is no longer a question about
whether or not America will fall under God's judgment. The reality is
that such judgment has already begun.

People often ask me if I'm surprised by the accelerated rate of cultural deterioration taking place. My answer to them is simple. The
New Testament teaches that the world will grow increasingly worse
before the Lord returns. So no, I'm not surprised, nor am I overly concerned. The Lord Jesus told His disciples that they would be hated by
the world. Those who follow Jesus should not be shocked or dismayed
if they are persecuted by an unbelieving society. Their hope is not in
this world anyway. They know they will one day see their Savior face
to face. When He comes back to this earth, He will make all things
right. That is their blessed hope.

So I'm not shocked by secular culture's precipitous decline. But
there is one trend I find both surprising and deeply concerning—
namely, the downward trajectory of the church. If there were ever a
time when the church needs to distinguish itself from the world, standing firm in its commitment to biblical truth and sound doctrine, this
is that time. Rather than succumbing to secular pressures, or camou-
flaging itself to blend in with the world, the church ought to be boldly
shining the light of the gospel into the kingdom of darkness. Now is
not the time for compromise, but for courage and conviction.

Sadly, the broader evangelical church finds itself unprepared for the
storm clouds of persecution gathering on the horizon. The net effect
of weak theology, shallow preaching, syrupy sentimentalism in worship, and a consumer-driven approach to ministry has left the church
vulnerable and infirm. Too many preachers are more concerned with
being popular than with rightly dividing the Word of truth. Too
many Christian universities care more about federal funding than
they do about upholding biblical morality. Too many seminaries are

abandoning their evangelical heritage to maintain a façade of intellectual respectability. And too many churches are nothing more than glorified youth events, designed to draw a crowd but devoid of the biblical qualities that define a church. In many ways, the evangelical church has gone astray.

When the Lord Jesus addressed the churches of Asia Minor in Revelation 2–3, He commanded those congregations that had strayed into apathy, worldliness, and false teaching to repent and return (Revelation 2:5, 16, 22; 3:3, 19). Churches today ought to heed that same warning. As Christ Himself repeatedly states, "He who has an ear, let him hear" (Rev. 2:7, 17, 29; 3:6, 13, 22). Those who fail to listen will face His hand of discipline.

The church today is in need of a serious wakeup call. *Right Thinking in a Church Gone Astray* not only provides that wakeup call, it also offers a biblical framework for how to evaluate some of the key issues in contemporary evangelicalism. The book's contributors are men whom I trust, having worked alongside all of them in ministry at either Grace Community Church or The Master's University & Seminary. Hence, I heartily recommend this resource to both church leaders and laypeople looking to honor Christ and think biblically in spite of the confusion that persists both inside and outside the church.

The world is indeed spiraling down at breakneck speed; and to a significant degree, the church is going with it. Nonetheless, believers can rest in knowing that Christ promised to build His church, declaring that the gates of death and hell would never prevail against it (Matthew 16:18). Though dark days may be on the horizon, at least for the church in America, the true church of Jesus Christ will never be defeated or destroyed. All who belong to Him will triumph, even in death. The present may seem bleak, but the future remains glorious.

As believers, our hope is not diminished. When this life is over, we will gather with all the saints of every age to worship the Lamb around His throne. In the meantime we need to arm ourselves with biblical truth and right thinking as we press on for the glory of Christ and the advance of His kingdom. This book will help you do exactly that.

SECTION I:

THE **CHURCH**
AND **CONTEMPORARY**
ISSUES

CHAPTER 1

When the Church Goes Astray

Evangelicalism's Misguided Quest for Popularity and Prestige[1]

NATHAN BUSENITZ

Over recent decades, evangelicals have sought to influence society through academic respectability, political activism, and cultural accommodation. Sadly, when this quest for influence has been prioritized above gospel faithfulness, it has had devastating consequences—leading to doctrinal compromise and a diminished testimony to the lost. This chapter calls Christians to remember that God measures success not in terms of popularity or numbers, but in terms of faithfulness to Him.

Since its inception, the American evangelical movement has been characterized by an enthusiastic quest for greater influence in society. "New Evangelicalism," as it was called in the 1940s, was marked from the outset by a desire for a louder voice, bigger platform, and more prestigious position in American culture than had been afforded its predecessor: the fundamentalist movement of the 1920s and 1930s. In order to achieve higher levels of influence, evangelicals sought to make their movement academically respectable, politically powerful, and culturally relevant.

Generally speaking, evangelical influence is a good thing. Historically, the word *evangelical* comes from the Greek word, *euangellion*, which means "gospel." All believers want to see the gospel message have greater influence in the world. That is the heart of the Great Commission—to proclaim the good news of salvation to people from every nation, tribe, and tongue. Insofar as "evangelical influence" means influence for the gospel, it represents a positive development. But when evangelicals become so focused on gaining academic prestige, political clout, or cultural popularity that they compromise the purity of the gospel in the process, then the quest for influence inevitably leads to disaster.

In his article "The Myth of Influence," Robert Godfrey explains how the quest for influence can lead to problems. He writes,

> For a long time, I have felt that the cause of biblical Christianity has been undermined in our time by sincere people who engage in unbiblical activities for the sake of being an influence. The sad and ironic result of those actions has been harm to the cause of Christ and little or no good influence has actually occurred. The myth of influence seduces Christians into believing that by compromising important theological truths more people can be influenced for Christ.[2]

He continues,

> I am not opposed to the idea of trying to be an influence... Christians should hope, pray, and work to be a godly influence wherever they can in this world...The danger comes, however, when Christians adopt a notion of influence derived from the world of politics or business. That world sees influence in relation to power, money, numbers, and success. Compromise, cooperation, and intentional ambiguity are all methods used to achieve influence in this world. But should Christians adopt strategies and set goals that compromise basic elements of their faith in the name of influence?[3]

From a biblical standpoint, the answer to that question is clearly no. Yet the temptation to compromise for the sake of influence is alive and well in the modern church. As a result, the quest for influence is sometimes used to justify compromise. For example, the abandonment of core evangelical beliefs, like the inerrancy of Scripture, is excused as long as it gains credibility with the secular academy. Cooperation with unbelievers, including Roman Catholics and Mormons, is applauded provided it achieves the desired political outcome. And worldly methods in the church are justified as long as they seem culturally relevant and draw large crowds.

Such examples may be prevalent in contemporary evangelicalism, but they illustrate a fatally flawed way of thinking—one that prioritizes *influence* over *faithfulness*. Scripture's priority structure is precisely the opposite. *Faithfulness* is the true standard of success (Matthew 28:21, 23). Those who have success are those who are faithful to the Lord and His Word (cf. Joshua 1:7-8; Psalm 1:1-3). They refuse to compromise their commitment to the truth, even if doing so makes them unpopular or seem out of touch.

By way of illustration, consider the difference between two Old Testament prophets, Jonah and Jeremiah. Jonah was a man who had great influence. His ministry had incredible numeric results; yet he often exhibited a lack of faithfulness. On the other hand, Jeremiah's ministry had almost no visible fruit, even though he remained true to his calling. From the world's perspective, Jonah seemed to have greater success. But from God's perspective, Jeremiah's ministry was far more successful than Jonah's. Jeremiah prioritized faithfulness over influence. So did the apostle Paul, and every other notable hero of the faith throughout Scripture. But contemporary evangelicalism, to its own demise, has gotten this backward in many cases.

The New Testament indicates that the gospel will be viewed as foolish by secular society (1 Corinthians 1:18-25). It expressly warns believers not to partner in any spiritual enterprise with unbelievers (2 Corinthians 6:14-18). And it repeatedly admonishes the church to avoid worldliness (Ephesians 5:3-12; James 4:4; 1 John 2:15-17). Nonetheless, many evangelicals ignore these biblical truths in their quest to gain influence through academic, political, and culturally-relevant means.

In this chapter, we will briefly survey three arenas—the academic, the political, and the cultural—in which contemporary evangelicalism has, at times, prioritized influence over faithfulness.

The Quest for Academic Prestige

New Evangelicalism began in the 1940s, when a younger generation of fundamentalists distanced themselves from fundamentalism because they felt it was too critical, isolationistic, and anti-intellectual. They remained committed to the fundamentals of the Christian faith, but wanted to present them in a more gracious and academically credible way. So in April 1942, a group of 147 leaders met in St. Louis to found a new organization called the National Association of Evangelicals for United Action. A year later, the name was shortened to the National Association of Evangelicals. The first president was Harold John Ockenga, a pastor from Boston who later cofounded both Fuller Theological Seminary and Gordon-Conwell Theological Seminary.

Historian George Marsden, commenting on the state of American fundamentalism when Fuller Seminary was founded, writes,

> By 1947 fundamentalism seemed a cultural and intellectual wasteland…Fundamentalist leaders, despite far larger constituencies than America's secular self-image would admit to, felt keenly their lack of respect at the centers of culture. Academia was especially tightly closed. Only rarely did a bona fide conservative Bible believer gain a significant university position…Universities were crucial to the future of the nation, and fundamentalist evangelicals could point to no nationally recognized scholar who spoke clearly for their cause.[4]

The founding of Fuller Theological Seminary in 1947 was intended to be a response to all of this. Charles Fuller himself exclaimed that it would be the "Caltech of the evangelical world."[5] But the desire for scholastic respectability came at great cost, as the seminary eventually abandoned the doctrinal moorings of its founders to embrace more progressive positions. Core evangelical principles, like biblical inerrancy, were discarded for the sake of acceptance by the academy. As Godfrey explains:

> The most tragic consequence of the myth of influence is that those who embrace it often end up being influenced by the world rather than being a good influence on the world. For example, Fuller Seminary in its efforts to be more influential

by moving beyond its own fundamentalist roots has abandoned basic evangelical doctrines such as the inerrancy of Scripture.[6]

Marsden similarly observes:

At the School of Theology the new curriculum of the 1960s reflected the neo-evangelical intellectual agenda of being distinctly evangelical while at the same time producing scholarship so scientific that everyone would have to listen to it…A small incident from the mid-sixties was later reported by a number of alumni as encapsulating the academic ethos of that time. A student noticed that the seminary's sign could be much improved with a small scribal emendation. For several days it read, appropriately, FULLER THE LOGICAL SEMINARY.[7]

The seminary's original faculty held to biblical inerrancy. But that watershed doctrine was abandoned as the school began to prioritize human reason and academic influence above its historic commitment to Scripture. Iain Murray recounts Fuller's doctrinal decline with these words:

David A. Hubbard was made president [of Fuller] in 1963, despite the fact that he also needed to reinterpret the seminary's stated position on Scripture. Under Hubbard, Fuller Seminary moved into the mainstream of the American churches…But it was at the cost of Scripture. Hubbard came to represent his predecessors' beliefs on inerrancy as "the gas-balloon theory of theology. One leak and the whole Bible comes down." By 1982 it is said that only about 15 percent of the student body in the school of Theology held to the conviction of the seminary's founders on inerrancy. In Carl Henry's words, Fuller Seminary "moderated its initial biblical commitments and became infatuated with numbers."[8]

The doctrinal shift that took place at Fuller Seminary illustrates what can happen when evangelicals exchange biblical principle for the seduction of secular scholarship and academic prestige. In the early 1970s, Martyn Lloyd-Jones warned against this very problem:

> The true evangelical is not only distrustful of reason, but he is also distrustful of scholarship...The evangelical starts from the Scriptures. He also reads the history of the church, and there he finds that the history proves what has been emphasized in the Scripture, that when men trust to [human] reason and to understanding they go astray...The sum of all I am saying is that the evangelical distrusts scholarship and is watchful of it. That does not mean that he is anti-intellectual; it does not mean that he becomes obscurantist; but it does mean that he keeps reason and scholarship in their place. They are *servants* not masters.[9]

The myth of academic influence still tempts those who teach at evangelical universities and seminaries to weaken their commitment to Scripture. Mark Noll's book *The Scandal of the Evangelical Mind* called evangelicals to leave behind the "intellectual disaster of fundamentalism"[10] and get with the times. In particular, Noll challenged evangelical scholars to jettison what he considers to be the intellectual embarrassment of creation science.

The issue of creationism has been at the forefront of fundamentalist and evangelical debate ever since the Scopes Monkey Trial of 1925—when a Tennessee high school teacher named John T. Scopes was prosecuted for teaching evolution in the classroom. The case received national attention, and was seen by many as a showdown between fundamentalism and modernism, between the Bible and science. Though the fundamentalists (represented by prosecutor William Jennings Bryan) won the trial, they lost in the court of public opinion. As a result, fundamentalism became an object of derision by the academic elite in American society.

Today, evangelicals are still being told that unless they relinquish young earth creationism and embrace forms of evolution, they will never be taken seriously by the scientific community.[11] Many believe the only way to rescue Christianity from the ridicule of secular skeptics is to reinvent the Genesis account by turning days into ages or inserting gaps into the white spaces. Ironically, such attempts to rescue evangelicalism often end up attacking it. As Murray points out,

> Evangelicals who step into situations where it is professionally unacceptable to teach the infallibility of Scripture come under immense pressure to show that the difference between them and their non-evangelical colleagues is not as great nor as serious as the Bible says it is. And where the desire to share the intellectual respectability associated with "modern scholarship" is strong, we should not be surprised if a less "rigid" view of Scripture soon comes to be espoused. In some cases, as we have seen, the process may well end with men criticizing the very evangelical Christianity which, it seemed, they once wished to see re-established.[12]

Much more could be said about these specific matters—but the point remains: When evangelicals prioritize *popular influence* over *biblical faithfulness*, they inevitably find themselves abandoning historic evangelical principles (like the inerrancy of Scripture) for the sake of academic respectability. Fuller Seminary is one such example of that downward trend. The current debate over origins is another.

To be clear, we would affirm that evangelicals ought to be diligent in their academic undertakings, aiming for excellence in their intellectual pursuits. At the same time, there will often come a point when the wisdom of God will be deemed foolish by the world. It is at that point where one must choose whether faithfulness will be prioritized over academic accolades. Whenever evangelicals have chosen academic respectability over doctrinal faithfulness, the results have been tragic.

The Quest for Political Power

Politics represents a second area in which modern evangelicalism has sometimes forfeited faithfulness for the sake of influence. For at least the last five decades, American evangelicals have been fixated on politics. The landmark *Roe v. Wade* Supreme Court decision of 1973; the 1976 election of Jimmy Carter, a "born again" President; the founding of Focus on the Family by James Dobson in 1977; the establishment of the Moral Majority by Jerry Falwell in 1979; the zenith of conservative politics during the Ronald Reagan administration in the 1980s; the forming of the Christian Coalition with Pat Robertson in 1989; the election of George W. Bush in 2000 and his re-election in 2004—factors like these have fueled the evangelical political machine over the years. Today, many in the church are still convinced that God is calling them to make a difference in the public square. As a result, they remain as enthusiastic about politics as ever.

Certainly, it is appropriate for evangelicals to be a prophetic voice in society. The Bible is clear that life begins at conception and therefore abortion is murder, that homosexuality is a sin, that capital punishment is a reasonable consequence for certain crimes, and that those who do not work should not eat. These biblical values will inevitably impact the way believers think about political issues. It is right for pastors to preach and teach those biblical values, and for the church to proclaim them in its role as the conscience of our nation. Christians are called to be salt and light, and at times that command may have political implications. Even so, the church must not allow its quest for political influence to override its commitment to gospel faithfulness.

Yet that is precisely what has happened. Evangelicals have partnered with Roman Catholics, Mormons, and other aberrant groups in order to gain political influence. In so doing, they have sacrificed the clarity and integrity of the eternal gospel on the altar of temporary political gain. When a common social or political agenda is prioritized over gospel faithfulness, the line between true and false forms of Christianity can easily get blurred. Consider the words of Mark Noll and Carolyn Nystrom in their book *Is the Reformation Over?*

> America's fundamental social concerns [like abortion and
> the economy] have contributed a great deal to the withering

of old interreligious antagonisms. Political debates on these issues, particularly controversy concerning how moral beliefs are to shape education, regularly reflect the passionate commitments of Americans from all points on the religious compass...In this new situation, Catholics and evangelicals often find themselves arguing the same or similar positions on public issues.[13]

According to Noll and Nystrom, common *socio-political* interests shared by Protestants and Catholics are undoing the *doctrinal* divisions that defined the Reformation. That shift is only possible because many modern evangelicals have placed greater weight on political influence than on doctrinal orthodoxy.

There is also the question of whether or not evangelicalism's involvement in politics has made any lasting difference. Perhaps it has slowed the tide of moral decay in America, but it has been unable to stop it. Any political gains that have been made along the way have only been short-lived. As Cal Thomas and Ed Dobson, former insiders in the Religious Right, observe:

> The impotence and near-irrelevance of the Religious Right were demonstrated on the day William Jefferson Clinton was inaugurated. Clinton's first two acts as president were to sign executive orders liberalizing rules against homosexuals in the military and repealing the few abortion restrictions applied under presidents Reagan and Bush. With a few pen strokes, Bill Clinton erased the little that the Moral Majority had been able to achieve during its brief existence. The tragedy was not the failure to succeed, but the waste of spiritual energy that would have been better spent on strategies and methods more likely to succeed than the quest for political power.[14]

More recently, the Supreme Court's landmark *Obergefell v. Hodges* decision in June 2015, which legalized gay marriage across the nation, provides a prime example of how attempts to legislate morality in

America often fail. Viewed from an earthly perspective, that reality can be deeply disheartening. But believers should not be surprised nor become discouraged. Society will grow increasingly worse until the Lord Jesus Himself returns.

When we look to the New Testament, we see Christ commissioning the apostles not to go and make political changes in the world, but to make disciples through the preaching of the gospel. We see the apostle Paul, the great first-century missionary, telling his readers to submit to the government while trusting and obeying the Lord. Believers' hope for the future comes not from being able to vote, but from knowing that the Judge of all the earth is sovereign over the affairs of every government.

Sadly, evangelicalism's preoccupation with politics has resulted in an identity crisis of its own making. In the minds of many people, both inside and outside the movement, evangelicalism is no longer primarily associated with defending and declaring the truth of the gospel. Instead, it is more closely connected to socially conservative politics and attempts to legislate morality.[15] While it is true that social issues are important, evangelicalism should not be defined chiefly by its political interests. Rather, it ought to be defined first and foremost by a faithful commitment to proclaim, protect, and live out the gospel of Jesus Christ.

The Quest for Cultural Relevance

Beyond the academy or the political action committee, the quest for influence has also left its mark on the American evangelical church. As congregations reach out to their communities, they rightly want to make an impact within their local sphere of influence for the sake of the gospel. But again problems arise when that desire for influence overrides the commitment to gospel faithfulness.

One of the most well-known examples in recent evangelical history is that of Billy Graham. Though he was brought up in fundamentalist circles, Graham adopted a ministry model for his evangelistic crusades that was decidedly antifundamentalist. Whereas fundamentalists made it a point to separate from apostate movements like liberal

Protestantism and Roman Catholicism (based on passages like 2 Corinthians 6:14-18), Graham took the opposite tack. He welcomed
nonevangelicals to participate in his crusades. As Godfrey explains,

> The problem, however, was not just that Graham increas-
> ingly had liberal Protestants and Roman Catholics on his
> platform and committees, but that he sent inquirers back
> to those churches...As a matter of conviction, he wanted
> his work to serve the churches, but he also wanted to be
> an influence by having many churches involved and having
> large numbers attend the meetings. Cooperation with liberal
> Protestants and Roman Catholics was designed to increase
> the influence of the ministry with the aim of seeing more
> people converted.[16]

Graham's desire for greater evangelistic influence was noble, but it
crossed the line of compromise when he began to partner with those
who denied the true gospel. Speaking of the Billy Graham Evangelistic
Association (BGEA), Iain Murray writes:

> The reason why the BGEA decided to co-operate with liber-
> als and other non-evangelicals was never set out in terms of
> principle. The fact is that the policy was seen as a necessary
> expedient designed sincerely for the best end, namely to gain
> a wider hearing for the gospel. Crusades depended upon
> crowds and in the Graham story there is an almost ever-
> present concern for maintaining and increasing numbers.[17]

Greater influence, in terms of larger numbers of people, was so heavily
prioritized that Graham's commitment to gospel purity began to erode.

This cooperative approach eventually led Graham to affirm Roman
Catholics as fellow Christians,[18] and to say things that sounded almost
universalistic. In a 1997 interview with Robert Schuller, the aging
evangelist made a startling statement. He said,

> [God] is calling people out of the world for his name, whether
> they come from the Muslim world, or the Buddhist world

or the non-believing world, they are members of the Body of Christ because they have been called by God. They may not know the name of Jesus but they know in their hearts that they need something they do not have, and they turn to the only light they have, and I think that they are saved and they are going to be with us in heaven.[19]

Graham's gradual move from fundamentalism to a far-reaching ecumenism illustrates what can happen when the quest for influence supersedes a commitment to faithfulness. In seeking larger audiences, the lines of gospel exclusivity began to be erased.

Around the turn of the millennium, a similar trend was seen in the market-based methodologies of the seeker-driven church. Pastors started to think of themselves as CEOs, their churches as corporations, and their congregants as customers. Success was measured in terms of numbers, and church-growth gurus developed multistep programs that were virtually guaranteed to increase the size of any church. David Wells reflects on that market-driven approach to ministry:

> Inspired by the corporate world, modeled after some of its successes like Disneyworld, and directed by Barna's polling numbers, the church set about selling itself and its gospel. What has happened is that the consumer model on which it was based reduced Christianity to just another product and its buyer to another sovereign consumer. In no time at all, Christianity was dancing to the tune of consumer desire, and the major casualty was biblical truth.[20]

The market-driven church was followed by the emerging church movement, which pointed out the superficiality of its predecessor and called for authenticity, conversation, and cultural relevance. The emerging church did not last long on the evangelical scene. But it left in its wake a wave of enthusiasm for "contextualized" approaches to ministry. Mark Dever articulates the modern sentiment before offering an important warning:

The concern is what our outreach should be like; the buzz-word is "contextualization." Many writers and pastors seem to begin with the assumption that the gospel appears irrelevant to people today...As a result, we stress similarities [with unbelievers] in an attempt to help them feel at home, understood, and cared for when they are among us...[Many pastors think that] the more similar we appear to those we are trying to reach, the more the gospel will appear relevant to them, and therefore the more successful we'll be at reaching them. We must beware here. A concern for evangelism, unmoored from the important revealed truth of Scripture, has often been the pathway to theological liberalism.[21]

Whether it leads to theological liberalism or moral libertinism, the reality is that contextualization can easily be abused. In some churches, it provides a convenient justification for imitating the world. Coarse jesting from the pulpit, sexually explicit sermons, the abuse of Christian liberty—these and similar antics are all excused in the name of building bridges to the lost. But that kind of ministry mindset is both spiritually dangerous and ultimately ineffective. To use sinful methods to reach sinners is self-defeating, and brings a reproach on the holy name of Christ. Yet such methods are often excused under the guise of trying to make the gospel relevant to those in modern culture.

A key passage in this regard is 1 Corinthians 9:19-23, where Paul explained that he was willing to make whatever sacrifices were needed to reach different types of people with the gospel. In verse 22, Paul said, "I have become all things to all men, so that I may by all means save some." Those words are sometimes used to defend an evangelistic approach that appeals to unbelievers using morally questionable methods. But that is actually the opposite of Paul's point. He is not teaching that the end justifies the means, as though worldly methods (or an abuse of Christian liberties) should ever be used to create common ground with unbelievers. Rather, in the broader context, his point is that he *restricted* the use of his Christian liberties, if such was necessary, to reach those whose consciences were more strict (and therefore weaker) than his own.

From both the context of this passage and his other epistles, it is clear that Paul would never sanction the use of carnal conduct, coarse humor, or crass speech to build bridges to the lost. Along with the other biblical authors, he consistently exhorted his hearers not to embrace the corruption of the culture, but rather to distance themselves from it. A survey of pertinent passages (like Romans 12:2; Colossians 3:5-8; 1 Thessalonians 4:3, 7; Ephesians 5:3-10; Titus 2:6-8, 11-12; James 1:27; 4:4; 1 Peter 1:14-16; 1 John 2:15-17) demonstrates that an emphasis on holiness in the midst of secular culture is not legalistic, it is biblical.

While it is true that believers minister within a cultural setting, there will inevitably be certain aspects of the culture they cannot embrace or celebrate. They are called to be *in* the world, but not *of* the world. As children of light, Christians do not reach those trapped in darkness by shrouding their light and acting like darkness; rather, they reach the world by shining brighter and brighter in holiness (Matthew 5:14-16). The Bible is clear: The church has its greatest impact on the world not when it becomes like the world, but when it stands in counter-distinction to it.

Making It Personal

As we have seen, when evangelicals prize influence and popularity over faithfulness to the gospel, the results are spiritually destructive—whether in the academic arena, the political sphere, or the local church. But while it might be relatively easy to point fingers at the evangelical movement as a whole, it is much more difficult to examine our own hearts and motives. The sin of pride presents an ever present danger. So we must continually ask ourselves: Are there areas in our hearts, lives, or ministries in which we have been tempted to prioritize influence (in terms of respectability, relevance, or numeric results) over faithfulness to Christ and His Word?

Scripture defines true success as faithfulness to the Lord. The apostle Paul articulated that truth this way: "Therefore we also have as our ambition, whether at home or absent, to be pleasing to Him" (2 Corinthians 5:9). Every believer's primary duty is to love and obey our heavenly King (cf. Mark 12:30; John 14:15). Consequently, *faithfulness* to Him should always be the priority. If we remember that truth and live in light of it, we can look forward to that future day when we will hear our Lord say to us, "Well done, my good and *faithful* slave. Enter into the joy of your Master" (cf. Matthew 25:21).

CHAPTER 2

Rock-Star Religion

Countering the Church's Celebrity Culture

TOM PATTON

From Hollywood to reality TV, the cult of celebrity pervades secular society in America. The church has not been immune to the effects of that influence. Even many pastors have embraced the quest for celebrity status, using social media as a way to elevate their personality-driven platform. In so doing, they have often lost sight of the biblical qualifications and characteristics that ought to define their perspective on ministry. This chapter represents a timely reminder to those who would prioritize their own fame over Christ's glory.

On March 4, 1966, an article appeared in the *London Evening Standard* that ignited one of the most shocking controversies in journalism history. Reporter Maureen Cleave had been conducting an interview for her newspaper entitled "How Does a Beatle Live? John Lennon Lives Like This" when she asked the famous musician about the current state of religion in England. She quoted Lennon as saying, "Christianity will go. It will vanish and shrink. I needn't argue about that. I'm right and I'll be proved right. We're more popular than Jesus now." [1] A shock wave immediately reverberated throughout the room; John Lennon had just claimed his celebrity status was greater than Jesus Christ's.

Across the Atlantic lives a woman by the name of Marcy Braunstein, a professing Christian from Pittsburgh, Pennsylvania, who has dedicated much of her life to following the rock star Rod Stewart. In fact, she has dedicated an entire room of her home with what she estimates to be around $25,000 worth of memorabilia devoted to the singer. She calls it "the Rod Room." While being interviewed for a book on the phenomena of fame in America, she confessed, "I wish that I were as passionate about Jesus, and the life of Jesus and everything Jesus said when He was on this earth as I am about Rod. I do worry about that. I worry that I'm worshiping the celebrity of Rod."[2]

In Atlanta, Georgia, a movement has started devoted to the worship of pop star Beyoncé. It is called The National Church of Bey. According to church leaders, they gather every Sunday to sing their goddess's songs and mutually praise her supposed divinity. As their website states, "While we do not believe Beyoncé to be the Creator, we recognize that she still sits among the throne of gods."[3]

Whether it be John Lennon, Rod Stewart, or Beyoncé, these examples illustrate the extreme lengths to which a culture obsessed with celebrity can go. Devotees from all walks of life find themselves praising the sirens of iTunes and the idols of YouTube in ways that boggle the mind. Now, due to the dramatic rise of social media, accessibility to these popular demigods has become more pervasive than ever before. Today we live in a culture that is inescapably engulfed in a kind of celebrity where fame is its own religion.

Celebrity in the Culture

A number of underlying forces have fueled the current cultural frenzy. Though man has always worshiped the creature over the Creator (Romans 1:25), recent developments have propelled this idolatry with more fervor than ever before. In fact, the very concept of celebrity has morphed as media and technology have advanced at lightning speed. The result has been a new brand of religion. Hence, it is crucial for Christians to understand the shift that has taken place so they can resist the seduction represented by the cult of celebrity.

Celebrity in the Past

In his 1828 dictionary, Noah Webster defined the word *celebrity* in these terms: "fame; renown; the distinction or honor publically bestowed on a nation or person, on character or exploits; the distinction bestowed on whatever is great or remarkable, and manifested by praise or eulogies." A careful examination of this definition tells us that the word *celebrity* was once connected to the concept of greatness attained through remarkable deeds. In the past, being a celebrity implied that the person had performed some heroic act or extraordinary accomplishment.

When historians look for examples of celebrity in the ancient world, many begin with Alexander the Great and his colossal exploits. Alexander was tutored by the Greek philosopher Aristotle at the age of 16, came to the throne at the age of 20, ruled the majority of the known world by the time he was 30, and remained undefeated in battle till his death. He was one of the greatest military geniuses of all time. Clearly, his fame was that of extraordinary achievement.

To ensure that these accomplishments would never be forgotten, Alexander created his own media coverage by inviting artists to his battles to paint pictures of his victories. He commissioned all statues and coins of his day to be engraved with his own likeness, an ancient custom generally reserved for divine figures. That way, whenever money was exchanged, every man, woman, and child in his empire was exposed to the likeness of the celebrity king to whom they now owed allegiance. This was one of the earliest examples of media (albeit in the form of currency and art) fueling someone's celebrity status. Alexander the Great was not only a bigger-than-life commander and king, but he was also an amazingly shrewd publicist who guaranteed that the fame generated by his accomplishments would never be forgotten.

King Solomon of Israel was by far the wisest and most strategic ruler of his time, predating Alexander the Great by more than 500 years. The Bible records his celebrity status with these words: "Now when the queen of Sheba heard about the fame of Solomon concerning the name of the LORD, she came to test him with difficult questions" (1 Kings 10:1). Interestingly, Solomon's renown was spread merely by means of oral and written communication. His likeness on coins or statutes was not permitted due to the Jewish belief that such practices violated the second commandment. Therefore Solomon's fame, which was associated with his great achievements, was transmitted by mouth and by pen. Given the limited means of communicating such ancient celebrity, the ubiquitous spread of his fame throughout the ancient world becomes even more astonishing.

Celebrity in the Present

Through the invention of electronic media, people now have the ability to gain notoriety on the world stage without the necessary inconvenience of actually having to accomplish anything. It doesn't matter if you're talented or terrible, gifted or graceless—celebrity can be bestowed upon any who seek it. Fame used to be connected to honor and achievement. Now it has morphed into what might be called the "new celebrity"—a category in which people achieve celebrity status simply for being seen on a screen. In the place of great accomplishments or valiant acts, fame and celebrity in today's world are more often linked to acts of trivial amusement and shocking sensationalism.

More than four decades ago, cultural historian Daniel Boorstin issued his now-famous proclamation on celebrity. A celebrity, he wrote, is a "person who is known for his well-knownness." In other words, celebrities are famous for being famous.[4] Author Neal Gabler refined the definition of celebrity to refer to "those who have gained recognition for having done virtually nothing of significance."[5] This phenomenon has been called the "Zsa Zsa Factor" in honor of Zsa Zsa Gabor, whose brief movie career catapulted her into a much more enduring career of celebrity. Gabler defines the celebrity of today as "human entertainment," by which he means a person who provides entertainment by the very process of living.[6]

While celebrity was once bestowed upon those of outstanding ability, now celebrity can be granted to anyone who merely considers themselves deserving of the title. People today can be famous for being self-congratulating iconoclasts who glory in the most pedestrian aspects of their own humanity. Our culture worships those who remind them of themselves. In fact, some call the cult of celebrity "the new polytheism."[7]

Due to the accelerated spread of images and information through social media, the "new celebrity" has become a platform for celebrating narcissism and exalting the new polytheism of hero worship. Once the basis for becoming a celebrity shifted from accomplishment to mere entertainment—from doing something great to simply being known—achieving celebrity status became possible for anybody. Now anyone can be a rock star, whether or not he can play a note. Audiences no longer require quality content; they only demand an amusing spectacle.

Celebrity in the Church

Because the contemporary church exists alongside the most media-driven culture of all time, it has become increasingly vulnerable to the influences of society's infatuation with entertainment and celebrity. Given the environment in which we live, it would be all too easy for believers to compare the quality of their pastor's preaching to a late-night stand-up monologue. Instead of recognizing the need for biblical teaching that may call for sober introspection, they may find themselves desiring to have their ears tickled. Rather than longing for exhortation and edification, they may long for entertainment. Therefore the church must continually guard itself against the intense gravitational pull of our celebrity-driven culture.

Celebrity in the Pew

From the beginning of the church's existence, there have always been those who align themselves with "Christian celebrities." In the first-century congregation at Corinth, some identified themselves so closely with certain teachers that it caused division in the church. The apostle Paul called the Corinthians spiritual infants due to their devotion to men such as Apollos, Cephas, and even himself by calling them spiritual infants (1 Corinthians 1:11-13; 3:1-7, 21-23). They valued human personalities over divine truth.

Though Paul's correction is surely appropriate, it is understandable why some of the Corinthian believers were in awe of such notable men. Apollos was a great orator, mighty in the Scriptures, and eloquent in his teaching. Paul was an apostle, a profound theologian, and a missionary extraordinaire. Cephas (or Peter) was also an apostle, the leader of the twelve, and the powerful preacher of Pentecost (Acts 2:14-36). All three of them taught the truth; all were godly men who loved the Lord Jesus. But the believers in Corinth, in their immaturity, began to attach themselves to whichever teacher they fancied as their favorite. At some point, they had begun to prioritize *personalities* over *truth*. Instead of listening for Scripture they began listening for spectacle. They had unwittingly turned their Christian leaders into celebrities.

It is helpful to note that the Corinthian believers were converts from Greek and Roman paganism. Therefore even after they were saved, many in the church still struggled with the built-in propensity to worship men as gods. They were plucked out of a culture that was accustomed to turning great men into idols.

We find evidence for this kind of idolatry in Acts 14, when Paul and Barnabas preached in the city of Lystra. There they encountered a man who was lame from birth. Paul commanded him to stand up, and he was instantly healed (verse 10). When the crowd of bystanders saw what had happened, they responded by hailing Paul and Barnabas as if they were Greek gods (verses 12-15). Luke recounts the story:

> When the crowds saw what Paul had done, they raised their voice, saying in the Lycaonian language, "The gods have become like men and have come down to us." And they began calling Barnabas, Zeus, and Paul, Hermes, because he was the chief speaker. The priest of Zeus, whose temple was just outside the city, brought oxen and garlands to the gates, and wanted to offer sacrifice with the crowds (verses 11-13).

As that account illustrates, the proclivity to elevate mere mortals to divine status permeated the Greco-Roman culture. Therefore, in response to the situation at Corinth, Paul commanded the church to stop favoring one teacher over another (1 Corinthians 1:11-13). By doing so, the Corinthian believers were not only dividing the church, they were robbing Christ of the glory that exclusively belongs to Him.

Commenting on the situation in Corinth, John Calvin remarked, "Those that extol men above measure, strip them of their true dignity. For the grand distinction of them all is…that they gain disciples to Christ, not to themselves." [8]

Fast-forward to today. The tendency to turn spiritual leaders into "Christian celebrities," promoting one above another in a sectarian way, is still alive and well. Many modern evangelicals instinctively want their pastor to be on the big screen. In their minds, his fame validates their church; his celebrity status confirms that they too are a celebrity congregation. And so they welcome any media mirage that makes their pastor seem like a rock star in spite of the fact that celebrity status is not the biblical measuring rod of a successful ministry.

This is not to say that church members should fail to honor their pastors as leaders. The Bible is clear; people in the pew ought to show gratitude to those who have ministered the Word to them and shepherded them in the faith (Hebrews 13:7). Scripture instructs believers: "Obey your leaders and submit to them, for they keep watch over your souls as those who will give an account" (verse 17). The apostle Paul said that those who labor faithfully in preaching and teaching are worthy of "double honor" (1 Timothy 5:17) and are to be respected and esteemed highly in love (1 Thessalonians 5:12-13).

Clearly, church members should work hard to encourage and show respect to their pastor for his work in the ministry. But if they are to heed the lesson of the Corinthian church, they will remember that spiritual leaders should not to be turned into celebrities. Rather than being flattered as up-and-coming stars, pastors need to be protected from the danger of pride as they humbly seek to serve the sheep (1 Peter 5:1-4).

Celebrity in the Pastorate

Moving from the pew to the pulpit, pastors also need to resist the temptation to think of themselves as celebrities, which is nothing less than pride. That temptation sometimes arises in the form of discontentment regarding the flock God has given them to shepherd. When seeds of discontentment begin to take root, the result is often a change in motivation and focus—away from Christ-honoring church ministry and toward a self-exalting infatuation with things like the number of YouTube hits, Twitter followers, or Facebook friends one has. Though the word *celebrity* might never be used, the sin of self-promotion is alive and well in many an American pulpit.

To be sure, there are some in our day to whom God has given great influence, even beyond their own flock. Like the Charles Spurgeons and George Whitefields of yesteryear, these ministers of the gospel have committed their lives to the bold proclamation of God's Word. Their motivation is not to garner fame, but only to be faithful. They are humble men whom God has chosen to elevate by giving their ministries worldwide influence. In response, we should be thankful that God has richly blessed their work. But we should also remember that they represent the exception, not the rule.

As we seek to please Christ in whatever sphere of influence He has given us, we must be careful to examine our motives and ambitions (2 Corinthians 5:9). The old saying "The best of men are men at best" is one that applies even to pastors and church leaders. Therefore, it is essential for them to recognize and resist the temptation to seek fame for themselves rather than Christ. The growing influence of "the cult of celebrity" in the American church is due, in large part, to pastors who have turned a blind eye to the root of pride in their own hearts (cf. Jeremiah 45:5).

But how can pastors combat this tendency toward self-exaltation, both in themselves and in celebrity-smitten congregations? A fundamental answer would be to examine what God's Word teaches about pride, humility, and the qualifications for spiritual leadership. In addition, pastors ought to be aware of the cultural influences that promote the cult of celebrity so that they can defend themselves and their people against it.

Wanting to Be Like the World

Pastors need to recognize that their people are constantly being bombarded with the cult of celebrity that pervades American society. It comes in the form of movies, television shows, trending Twitter topics, and even supermarket tabloids. In secular culture, this kind of starstruck hero worship seems normal. But when Christians imbibe that same perspective and bring it with them to church on Sundays, the results can be damaging.

The church, in many ways, has followed the world's lead by creating its own brand of celebrities—from pastors to musicians to Christian actors. In that regard, modern evangelicalism might be compared to the nation of Israel in the days of Samuel. The Hebrew people desired a king for themselves not because they needed a human monarch, but simply because they wanted to be like the pagan nations around them.

Prompted by the people, the elders of Israel approached Samuel with the following request: "Behold you have grown old, and your sons do not walk in your ways. Now appoint a king for us to judge us like all the nations" (1 Samuel 8:5). They wanted a celebrity leader whom they thought would legitimize them in the eyes of the surrounding nations. It was not enough for them that God Himself was their true king, or that Samuel was His appointed prophet. Wanting to be like the world, they redirected their focus from God to a mere man. That is why God told Samuel, "They have not rejected you, but they have rejected Me from being king over them" (verse 7). What a tragic day for God's chosen nation!

Pastors must resist the temptation to give in to pressures, whether from the congregation or from elsewhere, to make the church more like the world. For believers, and especially spiritual leaders, worldliness must be resisted on every front. As James warned his readers, "Do you not know that friendship with the world is hostility toward God? Therefore whoever wishes to be a friend of the world makes himself an enemy of God" (James 4:4). The apostle John offered a similar admonition:

> Do not love the world nor the things in the world. If anyone
> loves the world, the love of the Father is not in him. For all

> that is in the world, the lust of the flesh and the lust of the
> eyes and the boastful pride of life, is not from the Father,
> but is from the world. The world is passing away, and also
> its lusts; but the one who does the will of God lives forever
> (1 John 2:15-17).

In light of such warnings, pastors must protect their people from the poison of worldliness by faithfully feeding them with the pure milk of the Word (cf. 1 Peter 2:1-3).

Wanting to Have Their Ears Tickled

A culture of celebrity can also arise in churches where entertainment is prioritized over sound exhortation. In a society characterized by an insatiable desire to be entertained, people are constantly looking for amusement, diversion, and fun. Far too many preachers are happy to accommodate, falling into the very trap that Paul warned Timothy to avoid:

> The time will come when they will not endure sound doctrine;
> but wanting to have their ears tickled, they will accumulate for
> themselves teachers in accordance to their own desires, and will
> turn away their ears from the truth and will turn aside to myths.
> But you, be sober in all things, endure hardship, do the work of
> an evangelist, fulfill your ministry (2 Timothy 4:3-5).

Faithful pastors preach the Word "in season and out of season" (verse 2); they do not cater to the changing whims of whatever might be popular. Their goal is to be diligent workmen who are approved by God (2 Timothy 2:15), not eloquent entertainers applauded by men (cf. 1 Corinthians 1:17).

Most pastors know full well that biblical truth is no laughing matter. Yet they still are tempted to accommodate their messages to fit their congregation's felt need for humor and amusement. A growing number can't seem to resist turning their sermons into stand-up routines. Unfortunately, the badge of clerical comedy has become their trademark. But that is not the trademark of faithful preaching.

In contrast to this growing trend in evangelicalism, the Bible's presentation of divine truth is characterized by sober-mindedness. From the account of creation to the vision of the Apocalypse, the Bible is quintessentially a serious story. There is nothing funny about sin, salvation, or sanctification. Nor is there anything laughable about heaven and hell, Satan and demons, suffering and sacrifice, or fire and fools.

To be clear, it is not that humor should always be avoided in preaching. There are times when it is appropriate, if used in moderation. Yet because the superficiality of our culture is in such dire opposition to the seriousness of the Scriptures, pastors ought to employ humor with care. If the motivation is simply to entertain—or if it focuses the attention on the personality of the preacher rather than the truth of the text—humor in the pulpit has the potential to do more damage than good.

To Christ Alone Be All the Glory

The cult of celebrity saturates modern society, spurred by the advance of social media. That is why the church must be diligent to protect itself against the temptation to exalt human leaders above Christ. After all, believers must not bring the idols of the culture into the church.

The only one worthy of universal fame is the Lord Jesus. He came to earth in humility, and having accomplished the work of redemption, returned to heaven triumphant as the King of kings and Lord of lords (cf. Philippians 2:5-11). As members of His body, believers must never allow their high esteem for earthly shepherds to overshadow their worship and adoration for the Chief Shepherd. One day, we who know and love the Lord Jesus will join with the saints of all the ages, passionately proclaiming words of praise to our great God: "To Him who sits on the throne, and to the Lamb, be blessing and honor and glory and dominion forever and ever" (Revelation 5:13). May that be our heartbeat, both now and for eternity!

CHAPTER 3

The Crescent and the Cross

Engaging Muslims for the Sake of the Gospel

WILLIAM D. BARRICK

With more than a billion adherents, the religion of Islam represents a major geo-political force in the world today. Many in Western society view followers of Islam with suspicion and fear. But in light of the Great Commission, how should Christians respond to Muslim people? On one hand, the errors of Islamic teaching must be confronted and rejected. On the other hand, those trapped in false religion desperately need to hear the good news of salvation in Jesus Christ.

Armed black-garbed men with black bandanas across their faces marching orange-jumpsuited men along the seashore in Libya. The flash of knives as Christians clad in the orange jumpsuits are assassinated by the black-garbed figures. A diatribe and the waving of the black flag of ISIS. These images have become all too familiar on our television screens and in our news magazines. Conflict dominates our thinking when it comes to describing relations between Islam and Christianity—conflict created by radical Islamic terrorists.

Too often the Christian community responds with fear and allows that fear to silence their sharing of the message of the gospel of Jesus Christ. Blood in the sands of the Middle East closes the mouths of many Christians who should speak of the blood Jesus Christ shed to redeem sinners.

What is the solution? How can we encourage believers to witness boldly to Muslim neighbors and go to Muslim lands with the gospel? How can we continue to engage Muslims for the sake of the gospel? The solution is found within the pages of Scripture itself. With that in mind, let's look at Luke 5:17-26.

Christ's Own Teaching and Example

As new missionaries in Chittagong, Bangladesh in 1981, my wife and I faced our first season of political unrest and uncertainty. Army officers assassinated President Ziaur Rahman in the government house in Chittagong. For several years we had to live with the imposition of martial law, during which we were often confined to our homes for a number of days. Another missionary and I decided to walk out into the nearby section of shops along one of the city's key highways. Soldiers sat in sandbagged machine gun nests atop flat-roofed buildings. We walked past a barbed-wire enclosure housing a company of soldiers. That's when we decided that we should not attempt to return along the same route by which we had come. We certainly did not want to be accused of spying.

The route we took meandered through our section of the city. Near home we heard the call to prayer at a neighborhood mosque. As we approached, we noted that it housed a madrassa (a school). We could hear the children reciting their lessons. Stopping, we inquired about the possibility of coming back sometime to photograph the madrassa and its students. The madrassa's leader said that he must first speak with his father, who was head of the mosque.

After we received the invitation, we arrived to take our tour, cameras in hand. The leaders of the madrassa were friendly and hospitable. After we had taken pictures of the students learning Arabic, the madrassa's head invited us to stay for tea—a common practice in Bangladesh. He conducted us to a room with a bamboo mat on the floor. As we took our seats on the mat, the students entered. The administrator explained that it was time for the daily reading of the Qur'an with the students. He directed an older student to bring the Qur'an. The student retrieved it from a shelf, unwrapped it from a cloth, and brought it to the small wooden reading stand positioned in front of the administrator.

Suddenly an older man entered the room and inserted himself between the madrassa's leader and myself as he took his seat on the mat. He asked me, "Are you the one who gave this Injil Sharif [New

Testament] to my son?" He held the book out so there would be no mistake about what he meant.

"Yes, sir. I gave it to your son." My missionary companion and I began to feel a little uneasy, wondering if conflict was brewing.

"Well, you didn't give me one!"

"I will be very happy to give you one. In fact, I will give you one that is more nicely bound than this one."

"Can you read this book?" Although we were conversing in Bengali, he must have been uncertain as to whether I could also read the Bengali script.

"Yes, sir. I can read it."

"Read it for us now." With that, he waved a hand and instructed the Qur'an to be taken from its reading stand, rewrapped, and returned to the shelf.

"May I choose the portion of the Injil to read?"

"Certainly."

The text I selected was Luke 5:17-26. Everyone listened intently as I read. When I started to close the book after reading verse 26, the older gentleman (the leader of the mosque) snatched it from my hands. The other missionary and I thought, *Oh, now we've done it.* However, he picked up where I left off—he read aloud verses 27-39 before he stopped, closed the book, and gave directions to bring us tea and cookies. What a door the Lord had opened! Those students and the leaders of the mosque and the madrassa heard the words of Christ read in their midst—in place of the daily reading of the Qur'an. I discussed the gospel of Jesus Christ on many occasions with the sons of the mosque's leader.

Why choose Luke 5:17-26? Let's look at the text and discover the lessons it revealed to the madrassa's students and teachers.

Power

First, "the power [Greek, *dunamis*] of the Lord" (verse 17) accomplished its work in the situation that Luke describes. It was not the power of men (cf. Romans 1:16). Only the power of God in the gospel possesses the authority and force necessary to convert anyone. No one comes to Christ apart from God's power. No cleverness in preaching or witnessing can save anyone. The new birth comes only through the Word of God (James 1:18; 1 Peter 1:23). Therefore, the most powerful action we can take in any setting involves the simple reading of God's Word. Indeed, as the apostle Paul wrote, "So faith comes from hearing, and hearing by the word of Christ" (Romans 10:17).

Partnership

Second, the men who were bringing their friend to Jesus exhibited partnership in their compassion for a fellow citizen (Luke 5:18). The Muslim *ummah* (greater community) maintains its unity in more ways than any disunity (Islam has approximately 72 different factions). Muslims have a sense of community. They might fight against one another, but they stand united when someone outside their community attacks a Muslim brother. In addition, they also show compassion for one another. Our experiences in Bangladesh proved that God uses Christian acts of compassion to get the attention of Muslims and provide open doors for presenting the gospel of Christ. Do not let radical Islamic terrorists color your view of all Muslims.

The People

Third, people crowded into the home to hear Jesus (verse 19). Such crowds are reminiscent of conditions one can witness in many Muslim nations today: Indonesia, Bangladesh, Nigeria, and Malaysia. These countries are densely populated. During our 15 years in Bangladesh we never lived in any neighborhood that had less than 48,000 people per square mile. Sometimes 12 or more family members would make their residence in a small two-room apartment or jungle hut. Those in the madrassa could identify with the conditions described by Luke.

Persistence

Fourth, persistence marked the men who found a way to help their brother (verse 19). Like everyone else, Muslims are fallen sinners in need of salvation through Jesus Christ, and they can be just as persistent in following the error of their religion. However, if you can get one of them to consider Jesus and read the Scriptures, they will do so with determination. When I gave a New Testament in Bangladesh to someone who was illiterate, he would take it home and ask his school-age children to read it aloud to the family. Sometimes their neighbors would gather outside their open windows to listen. For Muslims, such persistence is a product of the basic characteristic of Islam: submission to Allah's will. *Islam* does not mean "peace"—such an interpretation comes through errant political correctness in our society post-9/11. Rather, *Islam* means "submission," and *Muslim* means "one who is submitted." For Muslims, submission to the will of Allah is the driving force in their lives.

During our time in Bangladesh, I would fill a shoulder bag with New Testaments and gospel tracts and walk the winding, crowded streets of old Chittagong. Men would ask questions about who I was and what I was doing in Bangladesh. When I began conversations with them concerning Isa (the Muslim name for Jesus), they often invited me into a nearby tea shop and would serve me tea and cookies or other treats as we talked. If I gave them a New Testament, they would throw away any cigarette they might be smoking, wipe or wash their hands, take the book, kiss it, clasp it close to their breast, and thank me for giving them what they had often heard about but had never seen. No matter what the outcome of our conversation, no one left the New Testament or gospel tract behind—even if they left me with the bill for the tea and treats. I learned to save to the last any reference to Jesus (Isa) being God. At that point, conversation with any Muslim ended. Their reverence for the New Testament arose out of a desire to submit to Allah's will—they believed that the Injil consisted of divine revelation, even if they believed that Isa was merely a great human prophet.

The Priority
Fifth, note the priority from the divine viewpoint (verse 20). Jesus

forgave the man's sins rather than healing him. Clearly, God's purpose in the situation differed from man's. Jesus knew that the man needed more than physical healing. The paralytic's friends were focused on his physical condition; Jesus focused on his spiritual condition. Our aim ought to be the same. The persecution and martyrdom of Christians is not new to ISIS. In Acts we read that the early church faced the same kinds of perils—and none of those came from Islam, which originated nearly 600 years later.

Back then, it was Jewish religious leaders who killed Christians (Acts 8:1-2), as well as Roman soldiers. That persecution scattered believers and sowed the seed of the gospel far and wide, bringing about the evangelization of peoples inside and outside Roman-controlled Palestine. We forgive our persecutors because God, through Christ, first forgave us (Matthew 5:43-48; Luke 6:35; Ephesians 4:32). Indeed, we must follow the example of Jesus (Luke 23:34).

Polarization

Sixth, polarization took place (Luke 5:21). The Jews' religious sensitivities led them to condemn what they believed to be blasphemy. *Only God can forgive sins!* Muslims react to Christ in much the same fashion today. Nothing speaks louder to them about the deity of Christ than that He claimed the authority to forgive sins. In Islam, no one can be certain of obtaining forgiveness for sins. Muslims recognize that forgiveness is something only God can do, but in Islam, such forgiveness is entirely based on a person's works. Missing one time of prayer could cost a Muslim thousands of years in purgatory before he or she can enter Allah's presence. Only the dead can discover whether Allah has forgiven them. The absence of a clear teaching about forgiveness in Islam does not mean that Muslims do not long for forgiveness. To the contrary, it is exactly what they desire.

The Proposition

Seventh, Jesus offered a proposition (verse 23). Note that Jesus challenged the people's thinking—He was "aware of their reasonings" (verse 22). Yes, Jesus displayed His deity not only by His words, but by the way He knew their unspoken thoughts. Therefore He presented them with both a logical conundrum and the declaration of His authority: "so that you may know that the Son of Man has authority [Greek, *exousia*] on earth to forgive sins" (verse 24).

The Product

Eighth, the product of this encounter consisted of the people glorifying God and giving evidence of religious awe (verse 25-26). A right understanding of who Jesus is and what He came to do produces the same two outcomes today among Muslims who come to Christ through the gospel. Muslim converts are among some of the most devoted and fearless witnesses for Christ. They have submitted themselves to the will of the true God through Jesus Christ and persist in faithfully proclaiming the message of divine forgiveness. They have experienced a radical change and are willing to die for their faith in Christ.

Characteristics of Islam

The Muslims' attitude of submission leads to fatalism, submission to *kismet* (divinely predestined fate). Fatalism is so ingrained in their thinking that they feel helpless when faced with the catastrophes that we experience in this fallen world. Whether it is death, fire, earthquake, flood, or typhoon, they believe it is Allah's will, and they can do nothing about it. It leads to a loss of hope. Hope is something a Muslim desperately needs but cannot find in Islam except by means of death during pilgrimage to Mecca or death in *jihad*.

Muslims view life through a theocentric lens. This shows up in their daily conversation with statements like "Inshallah," meaning "If Allah wills" (cf. James 4:13-15), or "Bismillah," meaning "In Allah's name." This stands in stark contrast to the materialistic orientation of most Americans and Europeans, even if they claim to be Christian. This mindset presents a great opportunity for Christian witness. The fact Muslims are theocentric does not mean that they are not as equally self-centered as people in any other culture—they are fallen creatures too. If someone approaches us on an American street and speaks about God, we tend to treat them as either crazy or a religious fanatic. Our society is not as open to the discussion of theological topics as societies dominated by Islam.

In fact, our Muslim friends share many biblical concepts with us. As Samuel Shahid explains,

> Both Christians and Muslims believe that God created the world in six days, and that there is a hell and a heaven, angels and devils. They believe in all the prophets of the Old and New Testaments, the virgin birth of Christ, the Second Coming of Christ, the Resurrection, and the Day of Judgment.[1]

Muslims often confuse these concepts with unbiblical content. Having a theological idea in common does not guarantee accuracy nor total agreement. However, the commonality provides ground upon which to engage in a gospel-oriented conversation.

Muslims view Islam as the final revelation from Allah and the Qur'an as the book containing the authorized divine updating of the Old and New Testaments. In other words, Muslims believe that the Taurat of Moses, Jabur of David, and Injil of Jesus have been superseded by the Qur'an. Popular Muslim belief holds that the Old and New Testaments have been corrupted and have been abrogated. We need to explain that the original language of the Taurat (Torah), Nobira (Prophets), and Jabur (Psalms) was Hebrew, and that the original language of the Injil (New Testament) was Greek. Therefore, our English Bibles are just translations—like the many translations of the Qur'an. As the Muslim appeals to the original Arabic of the Qur'an, so does the Christian appeal to the original languages of Scripture.

Compassion for Muslims

Abandon All Hope[2] is the title of a documentary on Afghanistan and the Taliban. The title is not an exaggeration. Muslims lack real, certain hope spiritually and seek it by earthly means. In the midst of wars in the Muslim world, Muslims despair of life. Radical extremists among them have turned their existence into a living hell upon earth. The actions of those extremists make victims of everyone who disagrees with them—whether Christian, Buddhist, Hindu, Jew, or Muslim.

In 1 Peter 3:15 we read, "Sanctify Christ as Lord in your hearts, always being ready to make a defense to everyone who asks you to give an account for the hope that is in you, yet with gentleness and reverence." What are we doing to bring hope to Muslims? We cannot consider this merely optional—it is a demand of the gospel itself (Matthew 28:19). One of the reasons Muslims find the gospel of interest rests in the fact that it offers hope and the forgiveness of sins.

Every chapter (sura) except one (the ninth) in the Qur'an commences with "In the name of Allah, the gracious, the merciful." The Muslim concept of mercy relates only to Allah's benevolence or providential care, not his gracious mercy in not punishing people as they deserve. Muslims believe that men and women cannot have a close relationship with Allah—he is too distant and impersonal, too powerful and sovereign. For them, forgiveness is earned, not granted. Allah's forgiveness is inscrutable—he forgives whom he will. In Islam, no one can be certain of salvation until the Day of Judgment. Reasons for this conception involve the absence of any example of a direct confession of sin in the Qur'an (compare that to biblical passages like Psalm 51:4) and the fact that Islam possesses no developed personal analogies like Hosea or the prodigal son.

Conflict with Islam

Islam and biblical Christianity manifest different worldviews and conflicting concepts of each other. Nearly as much misunderstanding exists between these two viewpoints as material differences. To the Muslim, being a Christian is tantamount to living a lascivious lifestyle immersed in drugs, alcohol, and all forms of immorality. Therefore, Muslim parents mourn when their children convert to Christianity, because they believe their children have thrown off all moral restraints.

Most Muslims believe that degenerate cultural influences through television, movies, and music threaten their nations and their faith.

We must use this Muslim conception as an opportunity to explain how our Western (so-called "Christian") culture is really not Christian at all. In fact, the West has as much need of the gospel of Christ as any other group of people on the planet. Our culture is as distasteful to us as it is to Muslims. The common Muslim's concept of *jihad* consists more of personal spiritual warfare rather than going to war against the infidels. Radical Muslims still hold to a physical jihadist concept because they have focused on establishing their caliphate through military aggression. Just taking the time to explain that biblical Christians also "wage war" spiritually can provide amazing opportunities for witnessing about the gospel of Christ. Expounding a text like 2 Corinthians 10:3-6 establishes a bridge to the gospel.

The following chart presents a brief analysis of the conflict of worldviews between Islam and Christendom:

Comparative Worldviews

Concept	Muslim	"Christian"
Unity	emphasized—*umma*	only if pragmatic
Time	respect past	orientation to future
Family	solidarity	individualistic
Peace	integration, external	contentment, internal
Honor	all-important	not the priority
Status	family, name, age	wealth, accomplishment
Individualism	subordination to group	independence a priority
Secularism	totally unacceptable	largely acceptable
Change	undesirable	desirable
Efficiency	little or no concern	imperative

Christian Witness to Muslims

The acronym F-A-C-T-S offers a convenient outline for key concepts that ought to influence our witness to Muslims. These letters represent: Forgiveness, Assurance, Compassion, Time, and Scripture.

First, as I've already mentioned, Muslims deeply desire forgiveness for their sins. A lack of focus on this aspect of our faith leads to a weak and ineffective gospel witness. Every time we observe the Lord's Table (communion), we give testimony to the fact that the grape juice or wine represents Jesus' declaration: "This is My blood of the covenant, which is poured out for many for the forgiveness of sins" (Matthew 26:28). Jesus instructed His disciples that "repentance for forgiveness of sins" should be "proclaimed in His name to all the nations" (Luke 24:47; cf. Ephesians 1:7). Because our salvation comes by faith, not by our works (Ephesians 2:8-9; Titus 3:5), we could also say that the *F* in the acronym F-A-C-T-S stands equally for faith.

Second, assurance is what Muslims completely lack. They do not believe that anyone can know of salvation or forgiveness of sins in this life. When we speak of our assurance of salvation, they question it but desire it for themselves. Preparing ourselves with a sound exposition of 1 John 3:18-24 can be used by the Spirit of God in regenerating non-Christians, including Muslims.

Third, what Muslims need as evidence of our own Christian faith includes our consistent practice of Christian compassion (cf. 1 John 3:16-18). Every convert from Islam that I met in Bangladesh bore witness to how their attraction to the gospel by the Spirit's work within them was often accompanied by an act of compassion or kindness by a Christian.

Fourth, time is what it takes for an effective witness. It takes time to demonstrate true compassion, to get beyond all the false concepts and suspicions, and to build trust. Even after three terms of service in Bangladesh, we found some Muslim friends still convinced that we were paid to be missionaries by the US government and were really CIA agents. Such misconceptions cannot be overcome quickly. It takes time to respond to Muslims' sincere questions and to ask them key questions related to the gospel message. We need to ask the following questions, listen patiently and compassionately to their responses, and interact with them by referring them to what God says:

- What is sin?

- How does sin affect one's relationship to God?

- How do you obtain forgiveness for your sins?

- What does the Qur'an say about how we should forgive others when they sin?

- What does the Qur'an say about whether your sins are forgiven?

- How can you know that your sins have been completely forgiven?

Fifth, Scripture must be the spiritual weapon we bring to the spiritual battle in proclaiming the gospel of Christ. Without Scripture, nothing can happen (Romans 10:17).

Muslims Need Christ as Well

How then should we proceed to witness to our Muslim friends and neighbors—even to any who might be our enemy? Encourage each one to read God's Word for themselves and to ask questions about what they have read. Where should they begin their reading? Suggest to them that they begin with the Gospel of John. Explain that it opens with an account of creation itself. Tell them that the Gospel of John contains the teachings of Isa (Jesus).

One man to whom I had given a New Testament returned to my home a number of times to ask questions about what his children were reading to him from the Gospel of John. One morning he came at 7:00. He said, "I have a question about what the Injil says about Isa."

"What does the Injil say that raises this question in your mind?"

"Did Isa really do the things that the Injil says He did?"

"Yes. What is it that you are wondering about?"

"Isa must be the greatest prophet. He did things even our prophet never did. Isa raised a man from the dead!"

This man had his eyes opened, not through human arguments, but by reading the New Testament for himself. Remember the first point in Luke 5:17—that forgiveness comes by the power of God, not the power of persuasive speech. Nothing but the Word of God creates saving faith and brings about the new birth.

It is important that we as Christians demonstrate unconditional love toward our Muslim friends and neighbors. Show compassion for them. Be hospitable to them. Spend time with them. And, finally, be faithful to pray fervently for them in your private prayer time. Never treat Muslims any differently than anyone else who needs the gospel concerning Christ.[3]

CHAPTER 4

When Truth Meets Love

The Church's Response to Homosexuality

ALEX MONTOYA

One of the church's greatest challenges in the twenty-first century involves how to respond to the homosexual movement. A number of liberal Christian groups have embraced gays and lesbians with open arms, celebrating homosexual marriages and ordaining homosexual pastors. On the other end of the spectrum, some hyper-fundamentalists have responded with anger, organizing vitriolic protests and stirring up feelings of hatred. Clearly, neither option represents a biblically balanced approach to this important social issue. So how should the church respond to the homosexual movement? This chapter seeks to answer that question with both biblical fidelity and Christian charity.[1]

Without question, the church faces a major issue on how to respond to homosexuality in society and in the church. The church must rise to meet the challenges before it is rendered powerless by its apathy or before it is persecuted to inactivity for its lack of earnestness in stemming the tidal wave of moral corruption that began with the sexual revolution of the 1960s. She must heed the words of Scripture:

> This you know with certainty, that no immoral or impure person or covetous man, who is an idolater, has an inheritance in the kingdom of Christ and God. Let no one deceive you with empty words, for because of these things the wrath of God comes upon the sons of disobedience. Therefore do not be partakers with them; for you were formerly darkness, but now you are Light in the Lord; walk as children of Light (for the fruit of the Light consists in all goodness and righteousness and truth), trying to learn what is pleasing to the

Lord. Do not participate in the unfruitful deeds of darkness, but instead even expose them; for it is disgraceful even to speak of the things which are done by them in secret. But all things become visible when they are exposed by the light, for everything that becomes visible is light (Ephesians 5:5-13).

Do you not know that the unrighteous will not inherit the kingdom of God? Do not be deceived; neither fornicators, nor idolaters, nor adulterers, nor effeminate, nor homosexuals, nor thieves, nor the covetous, nor drunkards, nor revilers, nor swindlers, will inherit the kingdom of God. Such were some of you; but you were washed, but you were sanctified, but you were justified in the name of the Lord Jesus Christ and in the Spirit of our God (1 Corinthians 6:9-11).

The context today is much like it was in the Corinthian church. What God said to them is exactly what the contemporary church needs to hear. We must hear and we must act. Just as the Corinthian church needed to respond to the moral corruption of its day, so the church today needs to take a stand.

Consider the attitudes that paralyzed the Corinthian congregation in its need to respond properly to the immorality it was facing. The Corinthian Christians were ignorant, deceived, arrogant, and apathetic to the moral corruption within the church. The church today has the same problem. It is ignorant of the biblical mandate; it is being deceived by both Christian and secular thinkers; it is arrogant in its attitude toward God's Word and sin (as evidenced by its unwillingness to submit to biblical truth); and it is apathetic to the dangers it faces from the enemies of the gospel and of biblical morality.

The biblical mandates found in Ephesians 5 and 1 Corinthians 5–6 demand from the church four responses to homosexuality.

The Church Must Confront Homosexuality as Sin

Homosexuality is more than a mere sexual preference, a social choice, or a genetic predisposition as some say; it is a sin against God.

It is a willful assault on His person and His work. Homosexuality is against God in at least four ways. First, it is in violation of God's creative order. The Bible is clear about mankind's sexuality, about its purpose and its nature. Consider these references:

> God created man in His own image, in the image of God He created him; male and female He created them. God blessed them; and God said to them, "Be fruitful and multiply, and fill the earth, and subdue it; and rule over the fish of the sea and over the birds of the sky and over every living thing that moves on the earth" (Genesis 1:27-28).

> The LORD God fashioned into a woman the rib which He had taken from the man, and brought her to the man. The man said, "This is now bone of my bones, and flesh of my flesh; she shall be called Woman, because she was taken out of Man." For this reason a man shall leave his father and his mother, and be joined to his wife; and they shall become one flesh (Genesis 2:22-24).

> He answered and said, "Have you not read that He who created them from the beginning made them male and female, and said, 'For this reason a man shall leave his father and mother and be joined to his wife, and the two shall become one flesh'? So they are no longer two, but one flesh. What therefore God has joined together, let no man separate" (Matthew 19:4-6).

> Marriage is to be held in honor among all, and the marriage bed is to be undefiled; for fornicators and adulterers God will judge (Hebrews 13:4).

From creation, God's purpose was that marriage (and the sexual relations associated with that union) would be limited to one man (the husband) and one woman (the wife). Any violation of the creative purposes of God is a sin against Him; and homosexuality constitutes a perversion of the created order. The apostle Paul was clear when he wrote:

God gave them over in the lusts of their hearts to impurity, so that their bodies would be dishonored among them...For this reason God gave them over to degrading passions; for their women exchanged the natural function for that which is unnatural, and in the same way also the men abandoned the natural function of the woman and burned in their desire toward one another, men with men committing indecent acts and receiving in their own persons the due penalty of their error (Romans 1:24-27).

A second way that homosexuality is against God is that it is a violation of God's law (1 Timothy 1:8-11). The Scriptures identify homosexuality as a sin which violates the express law of God. In Paul's discussion of God's law, he states,

Realizing the fact that law is not made for a righteous person, but for those who are lawless and rebellious, for the ungodly and sinners, for the unholy and profane, for those who kill their fathers and mothers, for murderers and immoral men and homosexuals and kidnappers and liars and perjurers, and whatever else is contrary to sound teaching, according to the glorious gospel of the blessed God, with which I have been entrusted (verses 9-11).

The apostle clearly makes homosexuality a sin which cannot be reconciled with the gospel of Jesus Christ.

The third way that homosexuality is against God is that it constitutes a sin against God's kingdom (1 Corinthians 6:9-10). Paul unambiguously explained that unrepentant homosexuality excludes one from inheriting the kingdom of God. A homosexual who does not repent will not inherit eternal life; instead, he will be guilty of sin and subject to eternal punishment in hell. Note what Paul said:

Do you not know that the unrighteous will not inherit the kingdom of God? Do not be deceived; neither fornicators, nor idolaters, nor adulterers, nor effeminate, nor homosexuals, nor thieves, nor the covetous, nor drunkards, nor revilers, nor swindlers, will inherit the kingdom of God (verses 9-10).

Finally, the fourth way that homosexuality is against God is that it violates God's holiness. The Bible is clear on God's expectation for His people. The apostle Peter wrote, "Like the Holy One who called you, be holy yourselves also in all your behavior; because it is written, 'You shall be holy, for I am holy'" (1 Peter 1:15-16). First Thessalonians 4:3-8 makes it clear that this holiness pertains to the area of sexuality:

> This is the will of God, your sanctification; that is, that you abstain from sexual immorality; that each of you know how to possess his own vessel in sanctification and honor, not in lustful passion, like the Gentiles who do not know God... For God has not called us for the purpose of impurity, but in sanctification. So, he who rejects this is not rejecting man but the God who gives His Holy Spirit to you.

Hence, Christians are under obligation to confront the sinfulness of homosexuality. They cannot be swept away by the tide of public opinion or political decrees; nor can they stay silent about the terrible consequences that await those who practice homosexuality. They must warn people about the temporal wrath associated with homosexuality—that as a temporal judgment of God, it degrades human nature and destroys the body (Romans 1:18, 26-27). They must also make known the eternal wrath to be faced by those who practice this sin (Romans 1:32; 1 Corinthians 6:10). They must be told that "the Lord is the avenger in all these things" (1 Thessalonians 4:6), and that "fornicators and adulterers God will judge" (Hebrews 13:4). As the watchman of Israel was warned not to be silent about the judgment coming upon the nation, so too Christians dare not remain quiet about the dangers homosexuals face (cf. Ezekiel 3:17-19).

The Church Must Extend God's Grace to Homosexuals

Indeed, homosexuality is a sin against God, but it is also one of many sins against God, and it is a sin for which Christ died. This is a truth that the church must never forget. Believers are called upon by Christ to extend the grace of the cross to homosexuals, to assure them that God's forgiveness, peace, and the hope of eternal life is available to them as well.

If believers seek to reach those in the homosexual community with the gospel, they must first learn to show compassion to sinners. Tim Wilkins said, "Over time I've discovered that when it comes to homosexuality, Christians show great passion in one of two areas. Either they are passionate about extinguishing the pro-gay movement or about expanding God's movement by introducing them to His Son." [2] Obviously, our desire to see the gospel advance should transcend any political agenda we might have.

Sadly, the church can be guilty of the attitude exhibited by the Pharisees toward the sinners of their day. The Pharisees utterly lacked concern and compassion for those who were lost (cf. Luke 15:1-32). By contrast, Christ taught compassion for lost people, as demonstrated by the following incident:

> Then it happened that as Jesus was reclining at the table in the house, behold, many tax collectors and sinners came and were dining with Jesus and His disciples. When the Pharisees saw this, they said to His disciples, "Why is your Teacher eating with tax collectors and sinners?" But when Jesus heard this, He said, "It is not those who are healthy who need a physician, but those who are sick. But go and learn what this means: 'I desire compassion, and not sacrifice,' for I did not come to call the righteous, but sinners" (Matthew 9:10-13).

Commenting on the need for Christian compassion, Albert Mohler writes, "Homosexuals are waiting to see if the Christian church has anything more to say after we declare that homosexuality is a sin." [3] Like all unbelievers, homosexuals are people in desperate need of the Savior. Thus, they need more than condemnation; they also need compassion.

Second, Christians must be willing to interact with people who are part of the homosexual community, for the sake of telling them the gospel. The church can sometimes misunderstand what it means to be in the world but not of it. We may think that it means believers should have absolutely nothing to do with homosexuals. But the Bible shows us that it is necessary to interact with lost people, including homosexuals, if we are to present the gospel to them. Paul corrected the Corinthians when he said,

> I wrote you in my letter not to associate with immoral people; I did not at all mean with the immoral people of this world, or with the covetous and swindlers, or with idolaters, for then you would have to go out of the world (1 Corinthians 5:9-10).

Clearly we must dispel the label of being "homophobic." By showing homosexuals the love of Christ, we have nothing to fear and everything to gain for the gospel's sake.

Third, the church must maintain its confidence in the power of the gospel to convert homosexuals to faith in Christ. Modern society and mainstream psychology insist that homosexuals cannot (and should not) be changed.[4] But the power of the Holy Spirit is such that any sinner, including the homosexual, can be transformed into a new creature in Christ (2 Corinthians 5:17). The church has always believed that the gospel "is the power of God for salvation to everyone who believes, to the Jew first and also to the Greek" (Romans 1:16). The power of the gospel is the force which counteracts the power of sin to enslave and to condemn.

After the condemnation of homosexuality in Romans 1, Paul wrote, "All have sinned and fall short of the glory of God, being justified as a gift by His grace through the redemption which is in Christ Jesus" (Romans 3:23-24). After the condemnation of homosexuality in 1 Corinthians 6:9, the apostle added, "Such were some of you; but you were washed, but you were sanctified, but you were justified in the name of our Lord Jesus Christ and in the Spirit of our God" (verse 11).

Like any sinner, the homosexual can experience regeneration through the Holy Spirit, the power to triumph over indwelling sin as described in Romans 6, and the full assurance offered to all believers in the justifying work of Christ (cf. Romans 8).

Mark Christopher gives the church a great admonition when he states,

> Homosexuality is not a greater sin than other sins and does not require a different plan on God's part to save and redeem. What the above passage [1 Cor. 6:9-11] teaches us is that there is more grace in God than there is sin in your past! As someone once said, "He is a better Savior than you are a sinner"! The message of amazing grace is exactly what the Church needs to promote and practice.[5]

After the condemnation of homosexuality in 1 Timothy 1:10, Paul magnified his own sin above all sins and said, "It is a trustworthy statement, deserving full acceptance, that Christ Jesus came into the world to save sinners, among whom I am foremost of all" (1 Timothy 1:15). If God can save the worst, then He can obviously save those trapped in homosexuality.

Wherever man's depravity and sinfulness are magnified, so also is the grace of God magnified so as to more than make up for man's fallen nature. Consider the testimony of Ephesians 2:1-10 and Titus 3:3-7. These gospel promises apply to homosexuals as well, if they will embrace the Lord Jesus in repentant faith.

A fourth way the church can extend the grace of God to homosexuals is by providing special discipleship for former homosexuals. The New Testament testifies to the possibility and frequency of a believer's relapse into their former way of life (cf. Romans 7:14-25). The convert from a homosexual lifestyle is no exception. Christians should not be surprised by the difficulties encountered by some in overcoming their former lusts, nor should they give up in their efforts to disciple them as they mature in their new life in Christ (cf. Galatians 6:1-2).

Finally, if the church is to extend God's grace to homosexuals, it must effectively minister to former homosexuals who are now believers by fully incorporating them into the body of Christ. At times the church has allowed the stigma of homosexuality to follow former homosexuals into their new life in Christ. Having been saved out of a homosexual lifestyle, they may not be welcomed nor easily assimilated into the fellowship of believers. But that is not how it should be.

The Corinthian church serves as a model in the way it was composed of people from all sorts of sinful backgrounds. Note how Paul addressed the church: "Such were some of you; but you were washed" (1 Corinthians 6:11). The "some" refers to the fact that the church contained some ex-fornicators, ex-idolaters, ex-adulterers, ex-effeminates, ex-homosexuals, ex-thieves, and so on. The past tense of the verb "were" indicates that these former slaves to sin were liberated by the gospel, being converted from a life of iniquity to a new relationship with Christ. As a result, they were welcomed into the fellowship of believers in Corinth. The church today must not adopt an arrogant attitude toward those who were saved by God's grace from a life of homosexual sin. Instead, the church ought to rejoice that God has redeemed them, and welcome them accordingly.

The Church Must Discipline Unrepentant Sin

Since the sexual revolution of the 1960s, a tidal wave of immorality has invaded the church, and the church has done little to stop it. Sexual sin in all of its forms can be found in the church, ranging from divorce to fornication to lewdness to homosexuality. As in Corinth, the church today needs to deal with the corruption within.

The church in Corinth was tolerating a man living in an incestuous relationship with his father's wife. Instead of mourning over this sinful situation, the Corinthians responded with arrogance and allowed the offender to stay in the church (1 Corinthians 5:2). But Paul instructed them to exercise church discipline and remove the wicked man from their midst (verse 13).

The church today is in a similarly sad state of affairs—tolerating all kinds of moral compromise. In some denominations, the debate is not about removing those who engage in sexual sin, but about whether or not they should appoint a homosexual priest, pastor, or bishop in the church. Consider the statement made by Horace L. Griffin, an Episcopalian priest and teacher at an Episcopalian seminary. He wrote:

> Knowing that sexuality can be mysterious even when it is revealing, and recognizing that scientific and social research informs us about our bodies and sexual expressions in ways that were hidden from those who lived twenty centuries ago, it is reasonable that Paul could not have known about homosexuality as we know about it today. To accept this reality as responsible reasonable Christians, we can conclude that the apostle makes an uninformed judgment limited by his time and space.[6]

In an effort to make room for homosexuals in the church, Griffin claims that the apostle Paul was uninformed and, therefore, wrong. But to openly defy the teaching of Scripture represents the epitome of human arrogance. It was this type of arrogance that characterized those in the Corinthian church who defied Paul's apostolic authority (cf. 1 Corinthians 4:18-21). The contemporary theological landscape is littered with such revisionists who continue to pass off their arrogant speculations as novel theological insights. The church should cry, "Enough!" and refuse to listen to them anymore.

At the local church level, congregations must have the conviction to practice church discipline on their own membership (cf. Matthew 18:15-18). This was part of the solution to the immorality that had crept into the church at Corinth. The church's initial response was one of arrogance and tolerance. God's solution was the biblical practice of church discipline and removal of unrepentant sinners from the life of the church. Excommunication was necessary to preserve the purity of the church (1 Corinthians 5:6-8). The sad truth is that most churches do not deal biblically with the sin within their walls, including the sin of homosexuality.

The danger of deception is always present in the church. Paul's appeal to the Corinthians in 1 Corinthians 6:9 not only clarifies who will (or will not) inherit the kingdom of heaven; it also serves a warning to the so-called brother of 5:11. (Note that all the sins committed by the so-called brother of 5:11 are mentioned in 6:9-10.) Paul's point was that a professing believer who lives in unrepentant sin is not an actual believer, and thus will not go to heaven. That stern reminder is needed for the multitudes of "tares" who fill the pews of the church. They may not possess eternal life, and thus are greatly deceived (cf. Matthew 7:21-23).

The Church Must Resist the Homosexual Agenda

In 1 Corinthians, Paul did not address a danger that exists today in our democratic society. The apostle could only tell the Corinthians that they had a responsibility to judge those within the church; those outside the church, God would judge (1 Corinthians 5:12-13). The Christians in Corinth had little, if any, influence in the civil affairs of the city. Today, Christians in a democratic society play a significant role in determining the legal and moral trajectory of their communities.

What Christians in America need to know is that the homosexual community has an organized agenda to change the moral fabric of American society. As one author explains, "The homosexual agenda is an all-out assault on everything we believe in and an attack on everything our Founding Fathers hoped to give us when they fought to establish this great nation." [7] Thus, the church should be aware of the purposeful effort to sell the homosexual lifestyle to America.

Author David Kupelian shows the sophisticated strategy gay activists have employed to change the way Americans think about homosexuality. He writes of three phases called "desensitization," "jamming," and "conversion." "Desensitization" consists of inundating the public in a continuous flood of gay-related advertising presented in the least offensive manner possible. "Jamming" is psychological terrorism meant to silence support for any dissenting opinion. "Conversion" is the changing of the average American's emotions, mind, and will, through a planned psychological attack, in the form of propaganda fed to the nation via the media.[8]

To accomplish their agenda, these activists offer a number of strategies:

- Talk about gays and gayness as loudly and as often as possible.

- Portray gays as victims, not as aggressive challengers.

- Give protectors a just cause.

- Make gays look good.

- Make the victimizers look bad.[9]

The effect this effort has had in the minds of the American public is already obvious. Though the homosexual community represents only a small percentage of the total population, it has been able to gain popular approval and support across the country. The reason behind this is their ability to organize themselves into an effective force for change and influence.

A major focus of the homosexual agenda has been to get laws passed that will secure their status and normalize their behavior. Their greatest success to date came in June 2015, when the US Supreme Court legalized same-sex marriage across the nation. Spurred on by such legal victories, gay activists will continue to promote their homosexual agenda through a sympathetic judicial system, even though the lifestyle they embrace poses a physical, social, and moral threat to America.[10]

Clearly, it is important for Christians to be aware of what is happening around them. We are to be the conscience of our culture (Matthew 5:13), which means we must boldly declare what God has said about sin and its consequences. Now is not the time for the church to cower in the face of political correctness; now is the time to stand for the truth by exposing the deeds of darkness and proclaiming the light of the gospel (Ephesians 5:11-13), even if doing so is unpopular.

Responding with Love and Truth

What is to be the church's response to homosexuality? This chapter has offered a fourfold response that seeks to be both biblical and balanced. We as Christians must exercise both love and truth. On the one hand, we must demonstrate the love of Christ, as articulated in the gospel. We have been called to proclaim the good news of salvation and forgiveness from sin—including homosexual sin—which is offered to all who will repent and believe in the Lord Jesus. To proclaim the gospel to those who are lost is the most loving thing we can do for them.

On the other hand, the church must also be a bulwark for the truth. We cannot bow to the whims of secular culture, because to do so would cause us to compromise our commitment to the Word of God. Thus, we cannot simply tolerate sin, or pretend that homosexual behavior is somehow acceptable in God's sight. Rather, we must lovingly speak the truth (Ephesians 4:15). Believers are to be the light in the midst of a perverse generation (Matthew 5:14-16); and as society grows darker, our light ought to shine all the more brighter.

CHAPTER 5

Is This Jesus Calling?

Evaluating a Bestselling Book in Light of Biblical Truth

JESSE JOHNSON

When someone claims to speak for God, the New Testament urges believers to exercise spiritual discernment. The apostle Paul instructed his readers to investigate such messages with diligence: "Examine everything carefully; hold fast to that which is good; abstain from every form of evil" (1 Thessalonians 5:21-22). The book *Jesus Calling* by Sarah Young claims to be filled with messages from God. But how do those claims hold up under examination? This chapter addresses that question by reviewing Young's popular work in the light of biblical truth.

Prayerlessness. It's a contemporary evangelical epidemic.

When I read biographies of Christian leaders from a century ago, I'm stunned by how central prayer was in their lives. From leaders to lay people, extended time in prayer was considered a normal spiritual discipline. Churches used to have prayer meetings. Christians used to have prayer partners. Prayer was a primary component of family devotions, as well as church services. People knew how their pastors prayed, and churches knew who their "prayer warriors" were.

I hope it is still that way for you and your church, and if so, praise God. But the anecdotal evidence is strong that evangelicals are becoming increasingly prayerless. In many churches, prayer meetings are gone—a victim to our consumeristic approach to church. Prayer partners are replaced with "accountability partners," while family devotionals strike many as an antiquated form of puritanism. Prayer in worship services is viewed as a time-thief, and is approached almost flippantly, if at all. The prayer warriors are dying off, and one wonders if they will ever be replaced.

Even when believers read Scripture for their private devotions, there are so many potential distractions and tools at their disposal that prayer often gets left behind. If a passage is difficult to understand, believers can check their study Bible, their favorite pastor online, or any one of the countless commentaries accessible on their computer. All that to say: Praying for the gift of illumination, that the Spirit would enlighten the hearts of His people to understand and embrace the truths of His Word, also seems to be the habit of a bygone era.

This decline in prayer is essential to understanding the popularity of *Jesus Calling*, by Sarah Young. Arguably, *Jesus Calling* is the most widely read book on prayer ever, having sold more than ten million copies since it was first published in 2004. It is a collection of daily devotionals designed to springboard from a Bible verse into practical application through meditation.

I was prepared to like *Jesus Calling*, because I see the need for a return to a sense of prayerful dependence on God in our daily devotional lives. This book seems to want that too, and in fact it is even structured around the idea of beginning your day with your Bible and prayer. What could go wrong?

As it turns out, a lot went wrong. In spite of the goal of driving people to prayer, the book actually causes spiritual harm to those who read it and follow its model. Instead of helping evangelicals develop deeper patterns of prayerfulness, *Jesus Calling* actually retards the biblical example of the praying life.

Background

Sarah Young is a disciple of L'Abri, the European ministry founded by Francis and Edith Schaeffer. She has several master's degrees, including a master of arts in biblical studies from Covenant Theological Seminary. After seminary she married and moved to Australia as a pastor's wife (her husband pastored a Japanese-language church there). It was while in Australia that she wrote *Jesus Calling*. She and her husband eventually returned to the United States, where she receives treatment for Lyme Disease and leads a relatively secluded life.

But it was back in France with L'Abri ministries where Young discovered what would become the foundation of her future book. There she "first experienced the Presence of God." [1] What she means by "the Presence of God" is that she became aware of God's nearness to her, a nearness that manifested itself in brilliant light shining around her. She experienced this by becoming "aware of a lovely Presence with me." [2]

It is critical to understand what she is *not* saying. Young is not saying that she came to faith in Christ there. She is not saying that she *did* anything to merit or achieve this special experience of God's Presence (throughout the book, she capitalizes *Presence*, which I will do in this chapter). In fact, she even writes, "I had not sought this powerful experience of God's Presence." [3] Rather, it was something that just happened to her.

It was an experience that would be repeated years later when she was in Australia. There, she was counseling women who were coming from backgrounds of spiritual warfare, some of whom were even recovering from "satanic ritual abuse" and "spiritual bondage." [4] In the midst of those experiences she was praying for God's protection on her family, when "I was suddenly enveloped in brilliant light and profound peace." She later described it as God "bathing me in His glorious light." [5] Again, this was not something she sought; rather, it was something that *happened* to her.

A year later, Young started to consider the implications of her two experiences. She had read A.J. Russell's book *God Calling*, which gave her a framework through which to interpret her two encounters with God's Presence. *God Calling* is a mystical, doctrinally questionable devotional that claims to be a series of messages received through experiential communion with the Spirit of God.

Young began to look at her experiences with God's Presence through Russell's description of receiving messages from God, and she began to wonder if God had messages for her too. If He did, these messages were most likely to be received during times of experiencing His Presence, which Young set out to do by changing her prayer life. She described this as setting out to "change my prayer times from monologue to dialogue." [6]

Practically, this kind of "prayer time" consisted of Young reading a passage of Scripture, then seeking to empty her mind of everything except the desire to "seek His Presence."[7] She alleges that this kind of prayer is modeled in Psalm 46:10—"Be still, and know that I am God" (ESV). Young says that "be still" can be understood as "relax" or "let go," which is what she sought to do.

While letting go of everything in this world, she would "'listen' with pen in hand, writing down whatever I 'heard' in my mind."[8] With this approach, she recorded what she felt Jesus was telling her about the verses she had read. It was a way of pursuing God's Presence that also brought with it the application of Scripture to her daily life, and "this new way of communicating with God became the high point of my day."[9]

She then assembled her writings into a series of daily devotionals, which were later published as *Jesus Calling*. They are given as a series of messages from Jesus to Sarah, which she then edits to give the impression that they are given from Jesus directly to the reader. Hence the book's choice of pronouns: "I am with you and for you," and "when you decide on a course of action that is in line with My will, nothing in heaven or on earth can stop you."[10] The messages from Jesus to Sarah are presented as if they apply to every reader personally.

What is the goal of this approach? That the reader would take *Jesus Calling* and a Bible, go to a "quiet place," where he or she can "enjoy His Presence and His Peace in ever increasing measure."[11]

Strengths

There are some positive elements in *Jesus Calling*. It is clear that Young wants her readers to develop a daily habit of praying. The repeated theme of her daily devotions is that God is sovereign, even if the world is chaotic. Peace is found when people trust God's plan for their lives, and His plans are always perfect. For this reason, *Jesus Calling* contains many reminders of the fact that God rules every inch of this world, and He is in control. "As you make plans for the day, remember that it is I who orchestrates the events of your life."[12]

With that in mind, Young encourages us to train our minds to trust in God's providence. The more we think about His rule in times of peace, the more we will be ready to believe it in times of trial. For example, "Practice trusting Me during quiet days, when nothing much seems to be happening" so that "when storms come," we will be ready to trust God even then.[13] This is good advice, and a truth every pastor knows. When trials come, it is often too late to teach people to trust God's sovereignty. That is a foundation that has to be built ahead of time.

In her own life, Young has obviously experienced profound suffering. She writes as someone who knows pain, and yet she does not make excuses for God. She does not attempt to get God off the hook for pain and suffering in the world, but clearly proclaims that He is sovereign even over trials. "Give up on the illusion that you deserve a problem-free life," the book warns. "It is possible to enjoy Me and glorify Me in the midst of adverse circumstances." [14] *Jesus Calling* articulates a better theodicy than most evangelicals actually believe.

Another strength of *Jesus Calling* is that Young encourages readers to not be so adverse to change that they refuse to take steps of faith. In the United States—as in Australia too, I imagine—Christians can be so addicted to the comforts of our culture that we lose our dependence on God. We have food, so we don't pray, "Give us this day our daily bread." Young rightly refers to this as "idolatry" and challenges her readers to resist "finding security within the boundaries you build around your life." [15] "Anything that you desire more than Me [that is, the Lord] becomes an idol," Young warns.[16]

Young also implores her readers to put off the sin of worry. She notes that worry comes when we foolishly think our plans are the best way forward, and then some obstacle arises. Rather than seeing the obstacle as God's way of changing our plans to something better, we immediately grow anxious. Young warns against the sin of worry because it "wraps you up in yourself, trapping you in your own thoughts." Instead, "Don't take yourself too seriously…You have Me on the other side, so what are you worried about?" [17] That is timely counsel in our me-first culture of worry.

Troubling Aspects

Nonetheless, these strengths do not take away from the overall spiritual damage *Jesus Calling* can do to the person who reads it and attempts to practice it. There are at least two reasons *Jesus Calling* should be avoided: first, it purports to be revelation from God; and second, it promotes a quietist model of sanctification.

Revelation from God?

Throughout *Jesus Calling*, Young's fanciful way of doing devotions is presented as an improvement to simply reading her Bible, and this has the effect of raising the Jesus who speaks in her imagination *above* the Jesus who is revealed in Scripture. When Young writes that her practice of projecting her thoughts of Jesus onto paper has "increased my intimacy with Him more than any other spiritual discipline,"[18] she elevates the power of her own imagination above God's actual revelation. Thus the entire premise of *Jesus Calling* is a flagrant violation of the Lord's warning in Isaiah 55:8-9: "My thoughts are not your thoughts, neither are my ways your ways...For as the heavens are higher than the earth, so are my ways higher than your ways and my thoughts than your thoughts." Young fails to heed this warning by elevating her projected thoughts about God communicating with her above the actual words of God Himself.

Again, I lament the lack of prayer in much of evangelicalism. I long for prayer's return as a spiritual discipline, and obviously the dearth of prayer has given many Christians an appetite for *Jesus Calling*. But to be clear, what Young does in *Jesus Calling* is not praying for God to help her understand the Bible. If it were, she could not describe her own words as more efficacious than simply reading her Bible. Even the language she uses in describing her Bible reading ("monologue" vs. "dialogue"[19]) shows a condescending attitude toward Scripture. As she acknowledges in the women's edition of *Jesus Calling*, "I knew that God communicated with me through the Bible, but I yearned for more. Increasingly I wanted to hear what God had to say to me personally on a given day."[20] In other words, reading the Bible was not enough. She wanted something more.

But Young's approach to devotions did not end with Jesus talking to her every morning. Rather, she took what she perceived to be happening to the next logical step. If these messages were indeed from Jesus, then surely they should not be reserved only for her. So she formatted them into devotional form, edited them, added some italics to show references to Scripture, and the result is a book for others to use in their own devotions—right alongside the Bible!

Now, Young does grant that her devotionals are not Scripture; but she never explains *how* they are different from Scripture. She does write that the content of *Jesus Calling* should be measured against Scripture[21]—but that is true of Scripture as well. In the end, there is no substantial difference in how Young expects us to view Jesus' words to her, than how we are to view the Bible; they are literally packaged in such a way that the reader is instructed to derive his or her devotions from them every day.

That is bad enough, but when one considers that Young's stated inspiration for this kind of devotional practice was Russell's *God Calling*, it becomes impossible to escape the impression that Young is actively promoting either charismatic ongoing revelation, or mystical channeling. Russell often claimed that he did not even write the content of *God Calling*, but instead employed two "listeners" who channeled God's thoughts, and they became the source for his devotional. Young obviously chose the title *Jesus Calling* for her book as a "nod" to Russell's influence ("nod" is how the publisher describes it).

But *Jesus Calling* is more than a nod to *God Calling*. It encourages people to empty their minds so that they can take hold of what God's Presence wants them to write down. It personalizes the sense of "bright light" that Young experienced, giving it words and thoughts, and then records those thoughts as if they were from God. Finally, it presents those words to others so that through her words they can experience "a close relationship with the Lord."[22]

Yet the stubborn fact remains that what Young records are not words from Jesus. They are not inspired. They are not anything more than Young's own words, with pronouns confusingly moved around to give the impression of an authority her words simply do not have on their own.

Given Young's experience as a pastor's wife and missionary, she probably has much to say that would be helpful and edifying for those in ministry. Her own life experience gives her a platform to speak to others who are going through trials, and encourage them to trust the Lord through those trials. But she does not avail herself of that opportunity. Instead, she presents these words as if they are from Jesus instead of from herself. The result is confusion about revelation, confusion about prayer, and confusion about the voice of God.

Simply put, the Jesus of *Jesus Calling* is not the Jesus of the Bible. By projecting her thoughts of what Jesus would say to her onto paper, Young has invented a form of Jesus in her own image. As a result, her version of Jesus does not sound anything like the Jesus revealed in Scripture.

In the Gospels, the words of Christ are characterized by a profound depth. They can be mined for content, cross references, and prophetic implications. There is a richness to His words that makes them unlike anything ever spoken before. He has an economy with language unmatched in human history. Jesus' ability to use stories to simultaneously reveal and conceal demonstrates that He is the Master communicator. His words have a way of convicting the heart and showing God to the world.

They are not merely human words.

But Young's presentation of Jesus falls far short of the biblical Jesus. Nor does it measure up to the awe-filled description of the glorified Christ described in the first chapter of Revelation. Instead, in *Jesus Calling*, the glorious King of kings—whose word is like a two-edged sword (Revelation 1:16; 19:15, 21)—sounds more like a sappy motivational speaker, always wanting to hold us close in His wonderfully radiant Presence. That sentimental tone may sell millions of books, but it does not match the way Jesus speaks in the Bible.

Quietism

A second troubling aspect of *Jesus Calling* is its promotion of quietism as a spiritual model. Quietism—also called "higher living"—is an approach to the spiritual life that emphasizes "letting go and letting God." It often borders on a strange dualism, where the physical world is considered frail and transient, while the spiritual world is the home of truth and joy. In quietism, prayer is stressed as the emptying of the mind to just "rest" in the Presence of God. It presents the clear mind as the opposite of worry, and the spiritual mind is the one that is still, almost disconnected from the physical world around it.

If quietism has a distorted view of prayer, it has an even more dangerous view of sanctification—insisting on the passivity of the Christian while holding out a sort of "secret" to the higher life. In other words, Christians are most sanctified when they cease from striving, and instead have a mystical experience with God that elevates them to a spiritual plateau where they experience true sanctification.

Young's whole method in *Jesus Calling* bears all the trademarks of quietism: She had a spiritual experience that elevated her into the Presence of God. That experience is repeatable, mystical, and results in spiritual growth that is far superior to anything the Bible offers on its own. She stresses an inner stillness in which the person is consumed by the knowledge of the Presence of God, and a form of obedience that consists entirely of inward passivity.

Quietism has always been a threat to the church. There are traces of it in early-church Gnosticism, it is latent in much of Roman Catholic monasticism, and it is a trademark of Christian mystics. It refuses to recognize the Christian's active involvement in progressive sanctification (cf. Philippians 2:12; 1 Timothy 4:7), and instead claims that true sanctification is found in *not* doing, rather than doing.

In contrast, the Bible models prayer as an effort where believers plead with God (Exodus 8:9; 10:18; Job 8:5; Psalms 30:8; 119:154; 142:1). We cry out to Him with supplications and requests (Philippians 4:6; 1 Timothy 2:1; 5:5; Hebrews 5:7). The book of Acts describes how the early church was devoted to prayer, and the example is always one of effort, seeking the Lord with earnest hearts. In fact, every New Testament example of prayer is categorically different than what one finds in *Jesus Calling*.

Nowhere does the Bible model the quietist's approach to prayer. Notwithstanding Young's appeal to Psalm 46:10 (which in context is a rebuke against the striving of the pagan nations, not a call for greater levels of relaxation), prayer in the Bible is never passive. Young quotes J.I. Packer as a model of this kind of passive prayer; Packer writes, "God guides our minds as we think things out in his presence."[23] But in the original context, Packer is not arguing for a quietistic kind of prayer. Rather, he is making a statement about *obedience*. In fact, in that same context Packer writes, "He guides us, rather, to obey his Word and to choose between options by the exercise of the Christlike, God-honoring farseeing wisdom that is modeled for us in the Bible."[24] If anything, Packer is arguing against quietism.

The charge of quietism is not incidental to *Jesus Calling*. Much of the book is built on the premise that as Christians empty their minds they will encounter the Presence of God in a transforming way. By my count, of the 365 devotions in *Jesus Calling*, "Presence" is in 228 of them. It is also in the subtitle of the book. It is not an exaggeration to say that pursuing a mystical experience of the Presence of God through meditation is *the* theme of the book.

But the Presence of God is not something mystical that should be pursued through mindless meditation as a post-conversion experience. After all, God already *is* everywhere vis-à-vis His omniscience (Hebrews 4:13). In addition, the Holy Spirit indwells believers at salvation, and He never leaves us (Ephesians 1:13; 4:30; Hebrews 13:5). Clearly there are times when we are less aware of God's indwelling presence—particularly in times of sin—but this is not what Young is describing.

Instead, she is presenting a Christian life in which there are the *haves* and the *have nots*. The *haves* are those who have figured out the secret to experiencing God's Presence, much like she did in the mountains of France many years ago. The *have nots* include all those who have yet to enjoy this higher-life experience, and are left trying to lead the Christian life on their own (with nothing more than the Scriptures). This disjunction is not biblical.

Quietism presents the secret to the higher life as drawing near to the inner life of stillness. In reality, the "secret" to spiritual life is simply drawing upon the revealed truth in Scripture (1 Peter 2:2-3). Quietism presents sanctification as "letting go and letting God," whereas the Bible presents sanctification as waging war against the flesh, putting off and putting on (Romans 13:12; 2 Corinthians 10:3; 1 Peter 2:11).

Drinking Deeply from God's Word

Jesus Calling is troubling because it steers readers away from the sufficiency of Scripture. It teaches them that Bible reading is dry, but a personal word from the Lord is available. Young even writes, "The more difficult my life circumstances, the more I need these encouraging directives from my Creator."[25]

Recently I preached verse by verse through Psalm 119, and that psalm makes the point that the more difficult the circumstance, the more believers need to rely on the truth of Scripture. It is evident that the attitude about Scripture as exhibited in Psalm 119 is exactly contrary to Young's.

In light of this, I find *Jesus Calling* troublesome, and would not recommend it. I grant that a person could read it without giving much thought to the introduction, and just take the devotionals as a novel way to talk about God. But Young is selling these words as if they *were* God's words. And that (as I've heard R.C. Sproul rightly quip) is a serious theological no-no.

There are people who, because of the drought of prayer in churches today, might be tempted to drink deeply at the well of *Jesus Calling.* But the water is tainted. Scripture invites you to drink deeply of the pure milk of the Word of God (1 Peter 2:2-3). Spiritual maturity results from imbibing biblical truth; not by drinking from an empty cistern of human imagination.

I understand Young's desire to hear Jesus talking to His church today. But there is a section of the Bible which contains Jesus' words to His church: Revelation 2–3. There, Jesus calls for His church to repent from sin and hold on to her testimony of faith, or eternally perish. And His words in those chapters sound nothing like the imaginary Jesus of *Jesus Calling.*

SECTION II:

THE **CHURCH** AND **SOUND** DOCTRINE

CHAPTER 6

Who's in Charge of Your Church?

Submitting to the Headship of Christ in Everything

MICHAEL MAHONEY

The truth that Jesus Christ is the head of the church is an essential doctrine. Though most in the modern church would pay lip service to the absolute authority of Christ, many fail to reflect that truth consistently in the way they approach life and ministry. This chapter serves as a call to the church to reclaim its commitment to this vital doctrine.

The New Testament uses a myriad of titles to describe Jesus Christ. He is our advocate (1 John 2:1); the Alpha and Omega (Revelation 21:6); the Author of Life (Acts 3:15); the Bread of Life (John 6:35); the Bridegroom (Mark 2:19-20); the Chief Cornerstone (Ephesians 2:20); the Chief Shepherd (1 Peter 5:4); the Light of the World (John 9:5); the Lamb of God (John 1:29); the Lord of Glory (1 Corinthians 2:8); and the Perfector of Faith (Hebrew 12:2). He is also described as Teacher, the Vine, the Way, and the Word of God. "He is the radiance of His glory and the exact representation of His nature, and upholds all things by the word of His power" (Hebrews 1:3). As the preeminent One, He is the precious cornerstone (1 Peter 2:6); the cornerstone of the church (Acts 4:11; Ephesians 2:20; 1 Peter 2:7); the Bridegroom of the church (Matthew 9:15; Revelation 21:2); and the husband of the church (2 Corinthians 11:2; Revelation 21:9).

Yet the glorious preeminence of Christ over the church is perhaps most clearly expressed in His title, *the head of the church*. Colossians 1:18 declares the Lord Jesus to be "the head of the body, the church." Ephesians 1:22 explains that God the Father "gave Him as head over all things to the church" (cf. Ephesians 4:15). As those passages demonstrate, Christ's leadership is unrivaled and His authority supremely established. The church is His church, and it will prevail because, as Jesus Himself promised, the "gates of Hades will not overpower it" (Matthew 16:18).

The reality that Christ is the head of the church ought to inject vigor into the life of His people. When believers understand and embrace this doctrine, they gladly submit to His lordship in everything. But when they disregard or dismiss this doctrine, choosing to shirk His authority by ignoring the directives revealed in His Word, serious problems inevitably arise.

A Matter of Authority

The Scriptures are clear: As the head of the church, Jesus Christ exercises sovereign lordship and absolute authority over His body. Yet in spite of the Bible's clarity, some in the academic community have leveled their challenges against Christ's authority. One such charge alleges that the concept of "head" does not refer to leadership and authority, but only to source.[1] Those who make this argument primarily target Ephesians 5:23, where the apostle Paul wrote: "The husband is the head of the wife, as Christ also is the head of the church." These critics are primarily motivated by a desire to undermine the God-given authority given to husbands. Yet in order to do so, they simultaneously undermine the authority of Christ—arguing that in Ephesians 5:23 the word "head" (*kephalē* in Greek) means nothing more than "source."

But such a view is entirely unwarranted. After an extensive investigation of both biblical and nonbiblical Greek literature in which the term *kephalē* occurs, Wayne Grudem concludes, "There is no linguistic basis for proposing that the New Testament texts which speak of Christ as the head of the church or the husband as the head of the wife can rightly be read apart from the attribution of authority to the one designed as 'head.'"[2]

Grudem helps us see past what might be called the hermeneutics of ambiguity—an approach to interpreting Scripture that seeks to obscure the clear and obvious meaning of the text. Sadly, there are many today who adopt this kind of approach to God's Word, twisting and turning the words to mean whatever they want them to mean. But the meaning of Ephesians 5:23 and the rest of the New Testament is unmistakably clear.[3] The Lord Jesus Christ is the head of the church not just in the sense of source, but in the sense of authority. He is her Master and King.

The Headship of Christ in Church History

Throughout the centuries, faithful Christians have defended the doctrine of Christ's headship with their very lives. At a time when popes and bishops usurped the headship of Christ in the church, courageous preachers like John Huss were burned at the stake for defending this truth. Huss, in his monumental work entitled *The Church,* wrote:

> Christ is the outward head of every particular church and of the universal church by virtue of his divinity, and he is the inward head of the universal church by virtue of his humanity; and these two natures, divinity and humanity, are one Christ, who is the only head of his bride, the universal church, and this is the totality of the predestinate.[4]

Huss stressed the truth that "the church always has had and now has Christ as its head, from whom it cannot fall away, for she is the bride knit to him, her head, by a love that never ends."[5] Fueled by his commitment to this doctrine, Huss boldly defied the Pope. In fact, he said, "The head of the church is not a pope who through ignorance and love of money is corrupt."[6] He denied that any man is head of the church, stating that the title belonged to Christ alone. For taking such a stand, Huss was arrested, falsely accused, and then burned at the stake.

A century later, Martin Luther was so moved by Huss's works that he engaged in the same fight for the headship of Christ over His church. Alongside Luther were other Reformers like John Calvin and John Knox, and later preachers like C.H. Spurgeon and Martyn Lloyd-Jones. As we follow in their footsteps, we too ought to have an undaunted zeal for reclaiming the truth that Christ is the head of the church. Let us say with Luther: "Let good and kindred go; this mortal life also."[7] Let us join Spurgeon in his profound declaration:

> Let us not be slow with unshaken courage to declare yet again that kings and princes and parliaments have no lawful jurisdiction over the church of Jesus Christ, and that the best of monarchs have no right to claim those royal prerogatives which God has given to his only-begotten Son. Jesus alone is the Head of his spiritual kingdom, the church; and all others who come within her pale to exercise power are but usurpers and Antichrist, and not for one moment to be respected in their usurped authority by the true church of the living God.[8]

We must join the ranks of those who have faithfully and sacrificially gone before us. History gives us the weighty testimony of the vital importance this truth should hold within our own lives and ministry.

Consider the seventeenth-century Scottish Covenanters, who boldly affirmed that they would not submit themselves to the crown or the Pope. Instead, they produced a national covenant stating that Jesus Christ alone is the head of the church. William Blaikie wrote of this time in history,

> The attempt by the State party [the English Crown] to force a new liturgy on the Church, the use of which should be binding under the highest penalties, showed a determination to set aside Christ's authority, and tyrannise over His heritage even in the most sacred region of worship.[9]

The battle raged, but the Scottish people would not recognize anyone but Christ as the head of the church. Blaikie wrote, "By force of reaction the Church was thrown upon the more full assertion of Christ's claims as Head of the Church, and the glorious privilege of the Church to follow her divine Head. The more this truth was thought of, the more glorious did it seem."[10] The more it was defended, the more magnificent the reality of this truth became to those faithful Scottish believers.

In light of this history, how could it be that many modern evangelicals, at least in practice, have allowed the church to lose sight of this precious doctrine? This glorious reality must be defended, guarded, and maintained. Not to do so constitutes a serious dereliction of duty. It is nothing short of mutiny for those in the body of Christ to deny or ignore the authority of the head, the Lord Jesus Himself.

The Right Response

We must come to understand that the church is in need of an intensive and rigorous battle to recapture the glorious truth of the headship of Christ. We expect the culture to reject His authority, but not the church. Yet sadly, modern evangelicalism has largely abandoned this doctrine—an abandonment seen, first and foremost, in how many churches treat the Word of God. Rather than looking to Scripture to define their approach to ministry, they rely on demographic surveys and market-driven strategies. Instead of boldly exposing biblical truth, they seek to entertain and amuse in order to draw a crowd. Rather than resting in the sufficiency of Scripture, they look for words from God outside of His written Word. Whenever and wherever the Word of Christ is diminished or disregarded, it evidences a lack of submission to Christ Himself. In other words, Christ's headship and authority are usurped when His Word is silenced or ignored in His church.

To undermine or undervalue Scripture is to undermine and undervalue the divine Author of Scripture. Yet there are many pulpits where the Word of Christ is not preached faithfully. Such an approach removes protection from error and sin. It cripples worship by robbing Christ of His glory, and fosters compromise by eliminating biblical clarity. Moreover, in its neglect of the sword of the Spirit (Ephesians 6:17), it severely cripples the effectiveness of the church. When the voice of the head is silenced, the testimony of His body is extinguished.

Clearly, the headship of Christ over His church is of extreme magnitude. It matters because Jesus Himself said, "I will build My church"

(Matthew 16:18). The church belongs solely to Him. Who dares to say otherwise? Only Christ sustains His church. If it were sustained by men, it would have disintegrated long ago. The church is being built by Christ for His glory and for His honor. Pastors and church leaders are merely undershepherds, called to submit wholly to the authority of the Chief Shepherd. It is His voice that is to be heard—determining the direction, teaching, and practice of the church (cf. John 10:3, 18).

Christ is the head of the church, and His rule and authority are established from beginning to end. The New Testament closes with this vivid picture of Christ standing in the midst of His church in complete control:

> In the middle of the lampstands I saw one like a son of man...
> In His right hand He held seven stars...When I saw Him, I
> fell at His feet like a dead man. And He placed His right
> hand on me, saying, "Do not be afraid; I am the first and
> the last, and the living One; and I was dead, and behold,
> I am alive forevermore, and I have the keys of death and
> of Hades...As for the mystery of the seven stars which you
> saw in My right hand, and the seven golden lampstands:
> the seven stars are the angels of the seven churches, and the
> seven lampstands are the seven churches" (Revelation 1:12,
> 16-18, 20).

As those verses indicate, the Lord Jesus is the ruler of all the churches. He holds them in His hand like one holds a lampstand. John Stott explains, "That the seven lampstands are the seven churches...links the vision of Christ with His authority to rule and judge His churches." [11]

In the first chapter of Ephesians we are presented with another vivid description of the majestic, exalted Christ. Verses 21-23 declare that God the Father has exalted Christ "far above all rule and authority and power and dominion, and every name that is named, not only in this age but also in the one to come. And He put all things in subjection under His feet, and gave Him as head over all things to the church, which is His body, the fullness of Him who fills all in all."

Commenting on those verses, John MacArthur writes,

> Since He has such a unique and intimate relationship with
> the redeemed whom He loves, all His power will be used
> in their behalf to fulfill His loving purpose for them. He is
> completely over us and completely in us, our supreme Lord
> and supreme power.[12]

Christ is far above all things. His authority is greater than any other
authority. He is infinitely above all beings, rulers, and authorities. He
exceeds all human power and magnitude. Jesus Christ alone is the
primary one. He and He alone has complete dominion. He is over
everything not only in this age, but in the age to come.

Now and forevermore Jesus is Lord and the head of His church.
Every conceivable power is encompassed within the mighty reign of
the Lord Jesus Christ. As Colossians 2:10 declares, "He is the head over
all rule and authority." Colossians 2:19 similarly admonishes believers
to be "holding fast to the head, from whom the entire body, being
supplied and held together by the joints and ligaments, grows with
a growth which is from God." Earlier in Colossians, the apostle Paul
similarly proclaimed of Christ, "He is also the head of the body, the
church; and He is the beginning, the firstborn from the dead, so that
He Himself will come to have first place in everything" (1:18).

These verses resound with glorious language given by the Holy
Spirit to describe the headship of Christ. What a beautiful picture of
the love of Christ for His church. Martyn Lloyd-Jones highlighted this
truth with these words: "There is a sense in which we as the church are
his fullness...A head alone is not complete. A head needs a body, and
you cannot think of a head without a body. So the body and the head
are one in this mystical sense. As such we Christian people are part of
'the fullness' of the Lord Jesus Christ." [13]

Jesus Christ is the high and exalted sovereign King of the universe.
Writing on the theme of Christ's headship, the renowned Puritan John
Owen responded to the dazzling glories of Christ's authority:

He is gloriously exalted above *angels* in this his authority...
They are all under his feet, at his command and absolute
disposal. He is at the right hand of God, in the highest exaltation possible, and in full possession of a kingdom over the
whole creation; having received a "*name* above every name."
Thus is he glorious in his *throne*, which is at "the right hand
of the Majesty on high," glorious in his *commission*, which
is "all power in heaven and earth;" glorious in his *name*, a
name above every name—"Lord of lords, and King of
kings;" glorious in his *scepter*—"a sceptre of righteousness
is the sceptre of his kingdom;" glorious in his *attendants*—
"his chariots are twenty thousand, even thousands of angels,"
among them he rideth on the heavens, and sendeth out the
voice of his strength, attended with ten thousand times ten
thousand of his holy ones; glorious in his *subjects*—all creatures in heaven and in earth, nothing is left that is not put
in subjection to him; glorious in his *way of rule*, and the
administration of his kingdom—full of sweetness, efficacy,
power, serenity, holiness, righteousness, and grace, in and
towards his elect—of terror, vengeance, and certain destruction towards the rebellious angels and men; glorious in the
issue of his kingdom, when every knee shall bow before him,
and all shall stand before his judgment seat. And what a little
portion of his glory is it that we have pointed to! This is the
Beloved of the church—its head, its husband; this is he with
whom we have communion.[14]

The contemporary church would do well to respond in a similar
vein—with overflowing adoration and praise for our Savior and Lord.
We have been given the King of the universe to be our head and our
Bridegroom and our Shepherd!

The supreme authority of Christ over His church, and over every
believer, is a truth grounded in Scripture. It has been celebrated and
defended by believers throughout church history. And it is incumbent
upon pastors and church leaders in this generation to do the same. Let

us be those who submit to Christ as head and defend His headship with our very lives.

The Headship of Christ and the Local Church

The headship of Christ over His church demands that believers submit to His rule in every area of life and ministry. As Abraham Kuyper rightly noted, "There is not a square inch in the whole domain of our human existence over which Christ, who is sovereign over all, does not cry, Mine!" [15] Such certainly extends to the way things operate within the church. Kuyper continued, "Christians are mandated to affirm Christ's Lordship in every sphere. The result is a vision that emphasizes the uniqueness of the church." [16]

In light of that mandate, pastors and church leaders need to make sure that every area of the local church is in submission to Christ's authority. That focus starts with the pulpit, but necessarily extends to every other local church ministry. The primacy of preaching, and the exaltation of the head of the church from the pulpit, should reverberate throughout every area of church life.

The question that must be asked is this: How does the headship of Christ over the church reflect itself in the ministry of my church? David Prince comments on the need to reflect the glory of God in all areas of ministry:

> If a pastor cannot explain how the church's commitment to the Word and the gospel impacts how the church handles parking, greets visitors, does announcements, and so on, then that reflects a reductionistic and diminished view of the primacy of the Word...When our commitment to the primacy of the Word and gospel does not trickle down to every aspect of congregational life, we are like the obese person lecturing on the primacy of personal fitness or someone living an opulent lifestyle lecturing about frugality. The Bible tells us that God is at work in the world summing up all things in Christ (Eph. 1:10), so please do not try to co-opt Jesus to

endorse ministry minimalism and laziness that refuses to sum everything up in Him.[17]

The headship of Christ in His church ought to be reflected in everything the church does. It is especially seen in the commitment to Word-centered preaching that makes it possible for the Word of Christ to permeate the minds and hearts of His people (cf. Colossians 3:16). It is also seen in a commitment to excellence in how ministry is accomplished, for the Lord's glory (cf. 1 Corinthians 10:31; 2 Corinthians 5:9). Furthermore, it reminds church leaders that they are stewards who serve the Chief Shepherd. They are not to abuse their positions of influence over God's people, but are to submit to Christ's authority as they shepherd the flock with genuine care (cf. 1 Peter 5:1-4).

The Bible is clear. We have been called to celebrate and submit to the glorious headship of Jesus Christ. May the testimony of that commitment shine forth to the world as we seek to give all glory, honor, and praise to our exalted head. With that truth firmly established in our hearts, our lips can resound with words of praise. As the well-known hymn writer, Charles Wesley, so eloquently wrote:

> Head of Thy Church triumphant,
> We joyfully adore Thee;
> Till Thou appear, Thy members here
> Shall sing like those in glory:
> We lift our hearts and voices
> With blest anticipation,
> And cry aloud, and give to God
> The praise of our salvation.

CHAPTER 7

Nothing But the Truth

Why We Cannot Compromise Our Commitment to Scripture

ABNER CHOU

The divine Author of Scripture describes Himself as one "who cannot lie" (Titus 1:2) and whose "word is truth" (John 17:17). Because God cannot err, it follows that His Word is without error. Most evangelicals affirm the doctrine of inerrancy, but they rarely consider the implications it should have on how they think and act. This chapter considers the effect that the reality of Scripture's absolute truthfulness ought to have on the minds and hearts of believers—from pastors to lay people.

We live in a culture driven by feelings. Emotions determine the viability of relationships, purchasing decisions, political agendas, identity, and morality. Our culture regulates everything by sentiment. In sum, if it feels right, then believe and do it even if it doesn't make sense. This mentality has infected the church.

If we take a broad look at the American church, we can observe how the church has switched out truth for emotion. Christian bookstores are filled with "feel good" books. Emotional singing increases but sermon time decreases. In addition, congregations prefer having "conversations" instead of listening to sermons. They don't want to be preached at but want a say on any given topic. These examples evidence how the church is more interested in feelings than the truth. People don't want the truth of Scripture to define them; they want their desires to define the truth.

The shift from truth to sentiment has allowed a flood of false teaching and worldly philosophy to enter the church. Ideologies like psychology, sociology, and pragmatism now claim an equal place with

Scripture if not more. The church at large doesn't care if these faulty ideas stand for something completely different than what the Bible says. Since there is no standard of truth—just your emotions—anything goes. The church has jettisoned Scripture for worldly thinking and, as a result, it has become shallow. It offers nothing different than the sentiment of the world because it, in fact, is no different than the world. The church, disconnected from biblical truth, inevitably assimilates into the world and disappears.[1]

How do we stop this downward spiral? We need to reclaim the truth. Truth is what distinguishes us from the world and allows us to speak definitively to the world. This is why the doctrine of inerrancy is vital. Inerrancy declares Scripture alone is our authoritative standard because it is the truth. However, we cannot merely say we believe in inerrancy; we need to show it starting with how we think. If we not only want our churches to survive but to be the bastion of the gospel, we need to learn how inerrancy drives our thinking. We need to recover how to think the truth, the whole truth, and nothing but the truth.

Recovering Christian Thinking

Before we talk about how inerrancy shapes our thinking, we must establish the necessity of thinking. This is particularly important since our culture and church have prized emotion to the point where they reject careful thought. However, the doctrine of inerrancy presupposes we must think. Inerrancy is a thinking man's doctrine. It requires one to understand the nature of truth, discern claims, make distinctions, and grasp the relationships of ideas. In addition, truth and thinking go hand in hand in Scripture. The Bible talks about how we are to speak truth in love (Ephesian 4:15), believe the truth (John 19:35), know the truth (John 8:32), meditate upon truth (Psalm 119:15), and learn the truth (Psalm 119:17). For inerrancy to function, we need to be thinkers. Even more, the Bible speaks of renewing our mind and how we are to love God with our mind (Matthew 22:37; Romans 12:2; Ephesians 4:23). Thinking is not just essential for inerrancy but for the Christian life.

Yet Christians can really struggle with the idea that we need to think, learn, and discern. They might not believe thinking is a priority since everything in our culture is about emotions. They might also feel learning theology and truth is the job of the pastor. Pastors, however, can struggle with the need to think as well. With all that is on their plate, they may suppose careful study should be up to the professor and commentator. To some pastors, being well-versed in theology and Scripture is simply not necessary. They have no interest in becoming a "pastor theologian." Theology may be good in seminary, but is irrelevant for the church.

To deal with these objections, we need to remember we didn't make up this responsibility. While terms like *Christian thinking* or *pastor theologian* might be new, the job is not.[2] This is a legacy handed down from generations past to us. The Old Testament prophets were deep biblical thinkers. They meditated on Scripture day and night (Psalm 1:2), knew how to use truth to confront their culture (Isaiah 1:2-20), expounded upon biblical doctrines (Psalm 67:1-7; 136:1-26), and defended against false prophets (1 Kings 18:20-40; Jeremiah 28:1-17; Ezekiel 13:1-23). They were theologians in their own right who prepared the way for Christ, the ultimate prophet (Hebrews 1:1-2). As such, Christ also takes up the mantle of championing truth. From a young age, He knew the Scriptures (Luke 2:40-52) and upheld the truth against the false teachers of His era (Matthew 22:1-46). His insights into Scripture were so compelling even His enemies said, "Never has a man spoken the way this man speaks" (John 7:46). Jesus is the most profound thinker of truth and He bestows the stewardship of truth to the church (cf. Acts 1:8).

Accordingly, throughout the New Testament, the apostles defended against false teachers (Galatians 1:1-8), engaged false philosophies (Acts 17:16-34), expounded upon doctrine (Romans 1:17–3:31), and contemplated how to live out truth (Ephesians 4:1–6:20). The apostles were theologians like the prophets and Christ before them, and they bestow this responsibility to us. In his final letter, Paul handed off his Scripture-centered ministry (2 Timothy 1:13) to Timothy (2 Timothy 2:2), who handed it down to faithful men who have now given it to us.

Being deep thinkers of Scripture is not novel. Throughout every generation, the prophets, Christ, and the apostles upheld this task. They have handed that sacred trust to us. So now it is our turn. If we are to be faithful in our redemptive history, we need to follow in the footsteps of those who have gone before us and take hold of our role as Christian thinkers and pastor theologians.

Thinking the Truth

So how do we do that? Fundamentally, we need to ensure that Scripture is the sole authority in our thinking. The very nature of inerrancy demands this. The doctrine asserts the Bible is the truth, the very definition of reality. Thus, every claim of the Bible is final in the way we think, for that is the way the world really is.

That challenges the church's current mentality. In many churches, various human ideologies are held equal to Scripture. Some even believe Scripture is outdated and irrelevant and their philosophies are better. For quite a few believers, the attitude is "the Bible *and...*" However, inerrancy asserts the opposite is true. Only God's Word can explain the totality of reality, and if we are to think the truth, then our thoughts must be fixated upon what the Bible says.

The book of Job explains why this is the case. Job is the first book of the Bible chronologically and introduces us to why we need Scripture. It demonstrates man by himself cannot fully understand this life. We recall how unhelpful Job's friends were. They never comforted Job or discerned why he was suffering. This isn't because they were dumb. Actually, they were experts in history (Job 5:27), science (8:11), and philosophy (11:7-8). Nevertheless, they never came close to understanding what was really going on.

Job concluded from this that even though man can accomplish so much (28:1-11), he can never fully understand how this life works. Man does not know wisdom because he doesn't have the whole picture of this life (28:12-14). Man cannot buy wisdom because that is not how wisdom works (28:15-19). Man cannot discern wisdom because he is far too limited. Even the birds have better senses than him (28:21).

Job shows man's knowledge, resources, and abilities can never obtain wisdom. With that, he proves people categorically cannot figure life out. We are too finite. Instead, only God knows the truth because He understands the entire cosmos, ordains how it works, and has thought through everything (28:23-27). Job realized we need to stop trusting our finite understanding and listen to the One who really knows what He is talking about. For this reason, the fear of the Lord is the beginning of wisdom (28:28).

Job laid out the issue plainly. Should we trust ourselves, who really don't know much, or the God who knows everything? Although current ideas may sound hip, cutting edge, and sophisticated, the Bible reminds us they are still elementary and primitive (Colossians 2:8). If we are going to think correctly, we should not become caught up in the allure of worldly thinking. The first step in knowing how to think rightly is to always anchor our thinking only in what is right and true: the inerrant Word of God.

Thinking the Whole Truth

Inerrancy not only demands *that* we think on the Bible, but also determines *how* we think through that sacred text. Inerrancy reminds us every part of Scripture is true. The Bible then is consistent, compounding, and sophisticated in its theology. This demands our thinking to be equally compelling, comprehensive, and complex— mature thinking that has deliberated the whole truth of God's Word in all of its immensity.

We should admit that at times we can be pretty shallow thinkers. We tend to give cliché answers to defend what we believe and do, perhaps appealing to a few proof texts for support. To be sure, Scripture is authoritative and its claims should settle any debate. Nevertheless, we sell the Bible short when we respond to complex issues in a trite or overly simplistic way. In fact, pat answers can be dangerous in our skeptical culture because they might convey to people that Scripture has no deep or convincing answers for their questions; the very opposite of what the whole truth of Scripture offers.

So what does thinking the whole truth look like? We can go back to the original biblical thinkers—the prophets, Christ, and the apostles—to observe this. The biblical writers at times used a single word from Scripture to proclaim profound theology. Consider Jesus' use of the term "gods" to defend His divinity (John 10:35), or the tense of a verb to prove the resurrection (Matthew 22:32). Paul utilized the word "seed" to connect the Abrahamic Covenant with Christ (Galatians 3:16). Mark even used a color to prove Jesus is God. He talked of the "green" grass during the feeding of the 5000. Why did he describe the grass as "green"? The word points back to Psalm 23:2, where God caused David to lie down in green pastures. By connecting Jesus with Psalm 23, Mark showed Jesus is the good Shepherd; He is God Himself. The biblical writers understood Scripture was inerrant down to each word, knew the individual words of Scripture, and used them to prove their point.

In addition, the biblical writers knew the breadth of Scripture and could also pull it all together to answer the issues of their day. For instance, Daniel and Nehemiah recounted all that God had done in Israel's past to understand how one should pray (Daniel 9:1-19) and act (Nehemiah 9:1-38). The author of Hebrews wove a series of texts together from the Psalms to show Christ's supremacy (Hebrews 1:3-14). In Galatians, Paul thought through texts in Genesis, Exodus, Leviticus, Deuteronomy, and Isaiah to explain how faith and promise work so that we would know how to be sanctified (Galatians 3:1-29). The biblical authors firmly believed the Scripture is true in every part and recalled the whole of the Bible to deal with certain situations.

The biblical writers teach us how the Bible works and how we should think through it. They do not give some pat answer or cliché. They knew Scripture is inerrant in breadth and depth and all of it is profitable. We need to be able to articulate how Scripture gives insight into issues passage by passage, from beginning to end and down to the very word. That's what it means to be a biblical thinker.

Thinking thoroughly through Scripture provides deep answers that can address the skeptics and encourage believers. Marriage is a great example. Our culture wonders why Christians are so defensive about marriage. Society believes if people love each other, we should let them do whatever they want. From the world's perspective, the church's insistence about the nature of marriage makes Christians seem bigoted and unable to understand love. So how are people in the church to share their concerns about why marriage is so important?

We might be tempted to give pat answers, but the Bible does not. Marriage is a reflection of the Trinity by design at creation (cf. Genesis 1:26; 2:24). Husband-wife relationships mirror the way the Son submits to the Father for salvation (1 Corinthians 11:3). In addition, marriage encompasses the love Christ has in redeeming the church by being one with His people (Ephesians 5:21-33). Marriage, by God's design, displays the full spectrum of His love from within the Trinity to His people. We care about marriage not because we are clueless about love but because we actually have the highest view of love.

Furthermore, even though marriage may not seem as spectacular as other ways to serve the Lord, it is one of the most amazing acts in all creation. It is a masterful portrayal of the gospel, displaying not only how God saved two sinners but also brought them together to mirror the very love that He showed them in salvation. Marriage is indeed beautiful, but we can only see that beauty if we take the time, studying through the Scriptures, to think through the whole truth.

The example of marriage illustrates everything we believe and do has a reason. The Bible provides deep and compelling answers to our questions. Our answers need to match the complexity of God's Word. We need to search the breadth and depth of Scriptures to provide captivating reasons for what we believe and do. Inerrancy demands us not to give shallow responses but profound insights based upon the whole truth.

Thinking Nothing But the Truth

Inerrancy shapes our thinking in one more way. Inerrancy states the Bible is without error. It is nothing but the truth. This demands us to distinguish between truth and error. Accordingly, we not only need to be astute thinkers of all of Scripture. We must also devote our think-ing to engage false ideologies, exploit error, and defend sound doctrine. We need to take our stand against falsehood in order to ensure our churches have only the pure truth found in God's Word.

The biblical writers exhibited this mentality. They exerted great effort to combat false teaching. The prophets preached against false prophets (Jeremiah 28:1-17) and Israel's faulty ideas (Jeremiah 7:1-12). Jesus opposed the false teaching of the religious leaders of His day (Matthew 23:1-39). In addition, nearly every New Testament book defends truth against error. Paul fought against the Judaizers (Galatians 4:9-31), those who claimed the resurrection had already happened (2 Timothy 2:18), diminished the supremacy of Christ (Colossians 2:1-23), and had faulty eschatology (2 Thessalonians 2:1-17). Peter warned against false teachers who infiltrate the flock (2 Peter 2:1). Jude contended for the faith against erroneous teaching (Jude 3). John fought against the Gnostics (1 John 2:18-26) and delivered messages against those who tolerate heresy (Revelation 2:12-17) and false practice (Revelation 2:18-29).

Repeatedly, the biblical authors used their thinking in order to debunk error and to preserve life-giving truth. They then handed this responsibility down to us. Paul commanded Timothy to correct false teachers and to spurn those who rebelled against the truth (2 Timothy 2:24-25; 3:5). Paul tells Titus the elders' job is to rebuke those who contradict sound instruction (Titus 1:9). Paul reminded the Galatian church to stand against false teachers (Galatians 6:16). Fighting against error for the sake of truth is the task of every Christian thinker and pastor theologian.

Why is confronting error so important? What is at stake? In a word: the gospel. Failing to engage against false teaching will lead to the dissolution of the gospel itself. The New Testament reminds us of this. The apostle John stood his ground against a form of Gnosti-cism that threatened the deity of Christ and the gospel itself (1 John 4:1-3). Paul attacked the Judaizers' perverted understanding of sanc-tification because that led to a different gospel (Galatians 1:6; 2:14).

Paul also discussed Christology at length because the gospel was at risk (Colossians 1:23). Even bad eschatology can destroy gospel hope (1 Corinthians 15:1-58). The apostles did not talk about Greek philosophy or Judaism to score academic points, but to protect the gospel. They understood that if you allow error to creep in, it will eventually corrupt that which is central to us. That is how error works.

The errors we face today operate the same way. For instance, creation is a hot topic of debate in Christian circles. We cannot shy away from this debate. If we do not have a sound understanding about the reality and theology of Genesis 1–3, we will lose the gospel. How can you have a second Adam without a first (Romans 5:12)? How is the gospel effective if death happened before the Fall and sin was not the cause of death (Roman 5:16-21)? If we do not stand firm on these matters, the very foundation of the gospel will erode.

Likewise, incorrect thinking on the issue of homosexuality can result in the corruption of the gospel. In 1 Corinthians 6:10-11, Paul stated that God sanctified us from sins like homosexuality. However, if homosexuality was never wrong, then the gospel sanctified us from something it should have sanctioned. Error in this matter will eventually force us to conclude the gospel made a mistake.

Finally, even faulty thinking on inerrancy can put the gospel at risk. Although the doctrine seems theoretical, losing inerrancy forfeits the gospel. If the Bible is not inerrant and does not provide the definition of the gospel, then something else will. Consequently, something will either be added to (e.g., works) or subtracted from (e.g., sin, hell) the gospel.[3] A faulty view of Scripture allows for an alternate authority to Scripture and thereby an alternative gospel.

We cannot be apathetic on the issue of engaging error and defending the truth. The gospel is always at stake. There are some who say that calling out people's error is mean or unloving. However, Scripture paints an entirely different picture. The Bible demands we instruct those who are wrong, and we are to do so with kindness and gentleness (2 Timothy 2:24-25). Preaching should occur with all patience (2 Timothy 4:2). We should even endure suffering in this process (2 Timothy

2:24b). The Bible demonstrates how confronting error can be filled with love.

Society claims if we point out someone's error, then we don't love them. Scripture proclaims we never have to sacrifice love to speak the truth (cf. 2 John 5-11). Even more, it also reminds us we never have to sacrifice truth to be loving. After all, the Scripture says the goal of loving those in error is that "God may grant them repentance leading to the knowledge of the truth" (2 Timothy 2:25). We need to relearn how to speak the truth in love (Ephesians 4:15) as we deal with error.

Paul is the model of how to defend the truth in love. In Galatians 2:5 he said, "We did not yield in subjection to them for even an hour, so that the truth of the gospel would remain with you." Paul did not shy away from confronting error. He challenged the Judaizers and unleashed dense theological argumentation to tear apart their ideas (Galatians 2–4). At the same time, he loved the Galatians with an intense love, like that which a mother has for her children (Galatians 4:19). Ultimately, the reason Paul engaged these false teachers was to ensure "the truth of the gospel" would remain. The apostle knew that if he allowed even a little error to infiltrate the church, the truth and purity of the gospel would be contaminated.

We must have the same attitude. We must engage error in order to preserve the gospel for our generation and for generations to come.

Becoming the Pillar and Support of the Truth

In 1 Timothy 3:15, Paul called the church the "pillar and support of the truth." That sums up all we've been discussing in this chapter. One of the church's major functions in God's plan is to uphold the truth to this world, and we should never underestimate the significance of that calling. Truth is not just information. Truth saves souls (Ephesians 1:13), gives hope (Colossians 1:5), sets the captive free (John 8:32), and makes the eternal difference between heaven and hell (John 3:32-36; Roman 1:18).

Truth also makes history. At the beginning of history, truth was violated as man obtained knowledge in rebellion (Genesis 3:6). At the end of history, truth will be victorious and "the earth will be full of the knowledge of the LORD as the waters cover the sea" (Isaiah 11:9). Truth then is the extension of God's omnipotent activity, and the church has been entrusted with such powerful truth in His Word. Thus, in a culture set adrift by emotion, the doctrine of inerrancy reminds us that the church has what culture needs. Everyone has emotions, but only the church has the truth. We need to fulfill our role as the mainstay of the truth.

But there is a warning in Paul's words in 1 Timothy 3:15. Because we are the pillar and support of the truth, protecting and proclaiming the truth stands or falls with us. Generation after generation has fulfilled the calling of being theologians who declared the truth. They have now handed that sacred task to us. If we fail to be thinkers, proclaimers, and theologians, then our witness to the truth will disappear from our communities.

So we need to restore the primacy of truth and thinking in our churches. We must be those who are eager to learn about God, man, sin, salvation, and the entire plan of God. We need to be dedicated to knowing the Scriptures book by book, passage by passage, and word by word. We need to stamp out biblical illiteracy within our congregations and in our homes. And as we learn Scripture, we need to have the conviction that what the Bible says is the way things are, and that is the way we must think about the world. Its categories become our own, for it is our final authority.

For pastors, we must reclaim the role of being the chief theologians for our churches and stop outsourcing this to the academies. This does not mean we have to earn a PhD or stop learning from other gifted men. This does mean we need to have immense facility with Scripture and doctrine, and voraciously read faithful theologians who have gone before us. We need to be those who are relentless in making sure our thinking factors in all that Scripture has to say, that we are thoroughly ready to give an overwhelming defense for the hope within us (1 Peter 3:15). Based upon this, we must be ready to engage the matters of our day, discerning through the issues we face and subjecting every false idea to the lordship of Christ (2 Corinthians 10:5). We do this in love and with determination so that our people are not confused by error but have the truth.

This is the way we preserve the gospel. This is the way we fulfill the responsibility the prophets, Christ, and apostles have given to us. This is the way we become Christian thinkers and pastor theologians. May it be that in this generation we love God with our mind (Mark 12:30) and lay hold of what has been entrusted to us: to be the pillar and support of the truth.

CHAPTER 8

The Hallmarks of Heresy

*Discerning the Difference Between Doctrinal
Confusion and False Teaching*

MICHAEL RICCARDI

Scripture repeatedly warns its readers about the threat of false teachers.
Proponents of heresy are roundly denounced as spiritual frauds who are
headed for eternal judgment. But the New Testament also contains examples
of true believers who were confused on certain issues and, rather than being
condemned, merely needed to be corrected. So how can Christians today
delineate between those errors that constitute "damnable heresy" and those
that might be simply described as "doctrinal confusion"?

S ome years ago, Al Mohler wrote a seminal blog post outlining
what he called "theological triage."[1] Borrowing the term from
the emergency room, Mohler discussed the need for Christians to prioritize certain doctrinal issues over others. In what can be the chaos of
an emergency room, medical professionals must know how to weigh
the urgency of various patients' needs against one another. That is, a
gunshot wound should be prioritized over chest pain. Similarly, in the
theological world, Christians must understand the difference between
(a) first-order doctrines—where to hold an errant position actually
precludes one from being a true brother in Christ—and (b) second-
and third-order doctrines—issues on which two genuine Christians
can disagree and nevertheless be truly saved. In other words, a right-
thinking church needs to be able to discern the difference between
erroneous teaching (on nonfundamental issues) and *heresy*.

All biblical doctrine is important. I would even go so far as to say
that all biblical doctrine is *essential*. It is difficult to put any doctrine

into a second or third tier, because it somehow feels as if to do so is to say that those doctrines are not important. But employing theological triage does not mean that only first-order doctrines matter while second-order doctrines are unimportant; the doctor who prioritizes a gunshot wound doesn't necessarily think chest pain is unimportant. The fact remains, though, that Christians can disagree on doctrines like the mode and recipients of baptism, the proper form of church government, or the timing of the rapture and still have fellowship with one another as genuine brothers and sisters in Christ. At the same time, if one man disagrees with another on the Tri-unity of God, then genuine fellowship is not possible, for one of those men is not a Christian at all.

The Reality of Damning Error

Some people reject the very notion that disagreements about doctrine *could* preclude someone from salvation. "After all," it is often argued, "no one has perfect theology, and we're saved by believing in *Christ*, not by believing in *doctrine*!" Indeed, the influence of Western secularism's dogmatic antidogmatism, its absolute disdain for moral absolutes, and its penchant for celebrating spiritual failure and moral weakness as "authenticity," leaves little room for tolerating biblical Christianity's insistence upon sound doctrine. Now, it's true that regeneration does not guarantee protection from all error; true Christians do still get things wrong. But regeneration does provide protection from *some* error—that is, the kind of errors which, if believed, indicate one is not a child of God at all. We know that kind of theological error exists because the apostle Paul wrote this in Galatians 1:6-9:

> I am amazed that you are so quickly deserting Him who called you by the grace of Christ, for a different gospel; which is really not another; only there are some who are disturbing you and want to distort the gospel of Christ. But even if we, or an angel from heaven, should preach to you a gospel contrary to what we have preached to you, he is to be accursed! As we have said before, so I say again now, if

any man is preaching to you a gospel contrary to what you
received, he is to be accursed!

Paul wrote those verses about the error of the Judaizers, who taught
that keeping the customs of the Mosaic Law was necessary for salvation in addition to trusting in Jesus. And if you think about it, by some
evaluations, the Judaizers' error was quite a fine point of doctrinal disagreement. Consider everything the Judaizers shared *in common* with
the faith once-for-all delivered to the saints. They believed in one God,
who exists eternally in three Persons: the Father, Son, and Holy Spirit.
They believed in the full deity and full humanity of Christ—that He
was the God-Man. They believed that Jesus was Israel's Messiah in fulfillment of the Old Testament prophecies and promises. They believed
in penal substitutionary atonement—that on the cross Christ bore the
punishment of God's wrath in the place of His people so that they
might be free from sin's penalty and power (and one day its presence).
They believed that He was buried, and that He rose from the dead on
the third day. And they believed that repentance and faith in Christ
was absolutely necessary for forgiveness of sins and fellowship with
God in heaven. That is a lot of really important doctrine to get right!

Their one problem boiled down to whether good works were the *cause*
or the *result* of salvation. Was law-keeping the *ground* or *merely the evidence* of saving faith? Are we saved by faith *alone*, or by faith in Christ
plus our religious observance? Some would call that quite a fine doctrinal
distinction. And yet Paul nevertheless employed the harshest language of
condemnation for their error. He called it "a different gospel" (Galatians
1:6), which is no true gospel at all (verse 7). He anathematized the purvey-
ors of this error, saying, "He is to be accursed!" That is, condemned to hell
(verses 8-9). Such a teacher is "severed from Christ" (Galatians 5:4), and
unless he repents, he "will bear his judgment" (verse 10). Paul went so far
as to say, "I wish those who unsettle you would emasculate themselves!"
(verse 12 ESV). Those are strong words for a disagreement on the *ordo
salutis* (order of salvation)!

Paul's comments in Galatians teach us that there are certain doctrines which, if believed, preclude someone from salvation, because to believe those things is to believe a different gospel, which is really no true gospel at all, and therefore is a gospel that cannot save.

What Are the Fundamental Doctrines?

The natural question, then, is this: Which teachings can one get wrong and still be a true child of God? Or said another way: What are those false doctrines which, if believed, by definition indicate that someone is not truly saved?

We get a clue by understanding why Paul so severely condemned the Judaizers' doctrine. It's because there was something fundamental to that teaching that denied—and was mutually exclusive to—the gospel of grace. That is how we answer the question of what is bad doctrine versus what breaches the bounds into heresy. The wrong beliefs that indicate someone is not saved are those teachings which, if believed, necessarily undermine or deny the gospel of salvation by grace alone through faith alone in Christ alone according to Scripture alone for the glory of God alone.

But what are those wrong beliefs? We can answer that by asking a number of questions that span several categories of Christian doctrine.

Soteriology

It is proper to start with the Bible's doctrine of salvation, because the question "What false doctrines preclude salvation?" is a fundamentally soteriological question. When considering whether a particular teaching is a soteriological heresy, we should ask: Does this teaching instruct us to trust in ourselves to contribute to our righteousness before God, even in part? Does this teaching encourage us to trust in anything else other than Christ alone for righteousness? Does this teaching tell us that salvation is something other than our redemption and deliverance from sin through the work of God in Christ?

The Roman Catholic Church's denial of *sola fide* is a false doctrine that requires an affirmative answer to those questions. By denying that sinners are declared righteous through the instrumentation of faith alone, Roman Catholicism actually makes the very same error as the Judaizers; it simply advocates adding different human works to Christ's righteousness for salvation. But in salvation, Christ will do everything, or He will do nothing. Why? Because if salvation "is by grace, it is no longer on the basis of works, otherwise grace is no longer grace" (Romans 11:6). To introduce works as any part of the ground of our righteousness is to corrupt the gospel of grace, which is the only gospel that saves.

However, the Wesleyan Arminian's doctrine of synergism, though unbiblical and rightly labeled as bad theology, is not a damning error. Synergism is the doctrine that man must cooperate with God to receive salvation. It is based upon a doctrine called prevenient grace, which teaches that, due to Christ's work on the cross, all people have received a kind of grace that neutralizes the effects of original sin, depravity, and corruption, bringing them into a state of spiritual neutrality in which they can freely choose to accept or reject Christ for salvation. This doctrine is unbiblical because Scripture simply does not speak of unbelievers as if they have been restored to spiritual neutrality. On the contrary, unsaved man is blind (2 Corinthians 4:4), dead (Ephesians 2:1), a slave to sin (John 8:34; Romans 6:17), hostile to God (Romans 8:7), and unable to please Him (verse 8). Further, the synergist cannot account for why one man believes in Christ while another doesn't without fatally undermining the doctrine of salvation by grace alone. If every human being has received the same *kind* of grace and the same *amount* of grace, the difference-maker in salvation must be man's decision.

Yet while the logical implications of synergism seem to necessarily entail a heretical denial of *sola gratia*, Wesleyan Arminians deny that logical conclusion and explicitly affirm that the source of their faith is God's grace alone and not at all in themselves. Their doctrine of prevenient grace is not to be found anywhere in Scripture, and they cannot consistently account for why one believes in Christ while another doesn't without undermining salvation by grace, but they are in a manner saved by their inconsistency, as they nevertheless look to

Christ alone through faith alone for salvation. The logical conclusion of synergism may be heresy, but if these teachers explicitly deny that heretical conclusion, we ought not to consider them heretics.

Theology Proper

Because God Himself is the author of salvation, we cannot be truly saved if we are trusting in anyone but the true God. Many people—even those who would call themselves Christians—profess faith in the God of the Bible but have transgressed so far that they have recast the true God into a god made in their own image. There is something about their god that is fundamentally different from the true God. When considering whether one's doctrine of God is heretical, we should ask: Does this teaching affirm something about God that is so false—so antithetical to His nature—that to believe it is to truly believe in a different god, and not the God of Scripture?

We are constrained to answer yes to that question in consideration of the god of Open Theism. Open Theists suggest that God is "in process," is continually learning, and does not know the future. This is an outright denial of the omniscience of God—the One who insists that He declares the end from the beginning, and brings to pass all the plans of His heart (Isaiah 46:9-10; Psalm 33:11; cf. Psalm 139:16; Hebrews 4:13). Denying God's sovereignty, immutability, and omniscience is not a case of having several misunderstandings about the God who truly exists. Instead, it's a case of conceiving of a fundamentally different god. A so-called god who is handcuffed by the thoughts and schemes of man, who is driven here and there in response to his creatures, and who is ignorant of the future is an altogether different being than the God who has revealed Himself in Scripture.

However, we would answer no to the above question with respect to the differing positions concerning the order of the divine decrees. Infralapsarians believe that God's pre-temporal decrees to create the world and ordain the fall of man logically (note: not chronologically) preceded God's decree to elect some unto salvation. On the other hand, supralapsarians believe that God's decree to elect and save was logically prior even to the decrees to create and ordain the fall. Neither of these positions so distort the person and character of God as to make Him a different god than what Scripture reveals; nor does either position undermine the gospel of salvation in any way. While infralapsarians might conclude that supralapsarians are in error, this is not a first-order issue.

Christology

In 2 Corinthians 11, Paul told the Corinthians that the false apostles were proclaiming to them "another Jesus" (verse 4). That is to say, the false apostles were teaching something about Jesus that was so fundamentally unlike the true Christ that their "Jesus" was different from the only Jesus who actually exists. Paul also paired that designation with the concept of teaching "a different gospel" (verse 4). Since salvation comes only through the work of Jesus Christ, we must trust in the Christ who exists, and not in "another Jesus" whom we have concocted according to our own understanding. When considering whether a particular teaching is a Christological heresy, we ought to ask: Does this teaching affirm something about the person or work of Christ that is so false—so antithetical to His nature and ministry—that to believe it is to truly believe in a different Jesus?

Arianism is such a teaching. Named for the fourth-century heretic Arius but propagated by the contemporary cult called Jehovah's Witnesses, Arianism teaches that Jesus is not of precisely the same substance (or essence) as the Father, but that He is of *similar* substance. According to them, Jesus is not truly divine, but neither is He merely human. He is god-*like*, but He is not God. Of course, the Christ of Scripture *is* God Himself; He is not the Father, but He is God the Son, the second person of the Trinity (John 1:1-3; 8:58; 10:30; Romans 9:5; Titus 2:13; Hebrews 1:8; 2 Peter 1:1). Now, there cannot be a more fundamental difference than the difference between one who is God and one who is not. A Jesus who is *not* God could never be said to be the same Jesus who *is* God, albeit understood just a bit differently. Therefore, Arians believe in another Jesus, a Jesus who is fundamentally different than the Christ of Scripture. Such a Jesus does not exist, and therefore cannot save. Those who put their trust in this fictitious savior cannot hope for a true salvation.

On the other hand, the doctrine of incarnational sonship is an example of a Christological error that is not heretical. Those who hold to this doctrine teach that Christ did not relate to the Father *as Son* from all eternity, but rather that He entered into the role of sonship at His birth (still others say only at His resurrection). Yet God *sent* His only *Son* (John 3:16); He did not send one who would only *become* His Son. The Father has always been the Father, and yet He cannot have eternally been the Father without having an eternal Son. Incarnational sonship ought to be abandoned in favor of the doctrine of the eternal sonship of Christ.

Nevertheless, those who hold to incarnational sonship do not intend to undermine Christ's deity, His eternality, or His distinction from the Father and the Spirit. They eagerly, although inconsistently, confess that He is very God of very God, of the same substance of the Father, coequal and coeternal with the Father and Holy Spirit yet distinct from them. Their inconsistency stems from misunderstanding the Second Person's subsistence as *Son* as a merely *functional* property, and therefore they do not intend to undermine anything essential to the divine nature of Christ. As with others, they are in a manner saved by their inconsistency. To believe incarnational sonship while also confessing the full deity of Christ is not to believe in another Jesus.

Pneumatology

We cannot forget about the third person of the Trinity. The Holy Spirit is God just as the Father is God and the Son is God. Therefore, to believe error concerning the Holy Spirit is to have a false view of God, and warrants the same concern as the doctrines of theology proper and Christology. When evaluating pneumatological error, we must ask ourselves: Does this teaching affirm something about the person or work of the Holy Spirit that is so false—so antithetical to His nature—that to believe it is to truly believe in a different God?

We ought to answer yes with respect to the cultic doctrine that the Spirit is not a Person but merely a force, a teaching shared by Jehovah's Witnesses (Arians) and others who deny the Trinity. Yet Scripture declares that the Holy Spirit can be lied to (Acts 5:3-4), that He speaks (Acts 13:2), that He sends missionaries (Acts 13:4), that He prophesies (Acts 21:11), that He knows the thoughts of God (1 Corinthians 2:11), and that He can be grieved (Ephesians 4:30). A force can do none of these things; these are properties and characteristics of persons. Put simply, the Holy Spirit is a "He," not an "it" (John 16:8).[2] To deny the personhood of the Holy Spirit, then, is to deny something that is fundamentally true about the Spirit's nature. It is to deny that the Spirit is God, and that God eternally exists in three coequal, coeternal, and consubstantial persons. Thus, this is an error that crosses the line into heresy.

But we would have to answer no to this question if it were asked about the continuation of the miraculous gifts of the Spirit. The present author is a convinced cessationist, and so regards the redefinition of the gifts of prophecy, tongues, and healing (as is done even in the conservative continuationist movement) as a prime example of errant theology. Yet continuationism is not heretical, because the case cannot be made that it makes a different god out of the Holy Spirit. Continuationism simply asserts that the gifts the Spirit once gave He is still giving today. This is not to say that there is no such thing as Charismatics who *are* heretics; even a brief perusal of TBN programming will show, sadly, that is far from the truth. But those teachers cross the line into heresy by virtue of their mysticism, their faith in so-called positive confession, and their idolatry of health, wealth, and prosperity.

Trinitarian

We've spoken about theology proper, Christology, and pneumatology—discussing doctrinal errors related to each person of the Godhead. But we also need to speak about doctrine that relates to the three-in-oneness of God. The God who is one in His essence (or being) eternally exists in three coequal, coeternal, consubstantial persons: Father, Son, and Holy Spirit. To deny any aspect of this is to deny something so intrinsic to the very nature of God Himself that it would result in conceiving of a fundamentally different god. Therefore, with respect to Trinitarian errors, we must ask: Does this teaching so distort the doctrines of either the threeness or the oneness of the Godhead that to believe it is to undermine God's Triunity, and thus to cause us to believe in a different god than the Triune God of Scripture?

Modalism is an example of a Trinitarian heresy. Contemporary modalists like Oneness Pentecostals deny the essential threeness of the persons of the Godhead, teaching that there is one God who can be designated by three different names ("Father," "Son," and "Holy Spirit") at different times, but that these three are not distinct persons. As mentioned above, this issue of personhood cuts to the very heart of what it means for God to be God. To say He is something other than one God eternally existing in three persons is to speak of an entirely different being. Thus, modalism is heresy.

But a Trinitarian issue on which there can be disagreement between true believers is the *filioque* controversy—the issue of whether the Spirit proceeds eternally from the Father alone or from the Father *and* the Son (note: *filioque* means "and the Son"). While this issue was important enough to split the Eastern and Western churches, it does not undermine the unity or identity of the God who is three-in-one.

Bibliology

The sole authoritative basis for all theological discussion is Scripture. Therefore, to believe something about the Bible that undermines its authority in any sense is to surrender a truly Christian epistemology and worldview and to exalt one's own reasoning above God's revelation. Concerning bibliological error, then, we have to ask: Does this teaching so distort the doctrine of Scripture that it truly undermines biblical authority? Does this teaching deny biblical authority in such a way as to invest ultimate authority in oneself, another person, or a tribunal of people?

A denial of the inspiration of Scripture would clearly place one outside the bounds of orthodoxy. "All Scripture is inspired by God" (2 Timothy 3:16), said the apostle. To claim that any portion of Scripture is not the Word of God, or to treat it in such a way as to impugn the character of the God whose Word it is, is to exalt one's own reasoning above God's revelation. It is to extricate oneself from the authority of God and make one's own understanding the measuring line of truth. This is no longer truly Christian, but humanistic, and as such it crosses the line into heretical doctrine.

But there are some bibliological debates upon which true believers may disagree. One example would be the debate over the manner of inspiration. Some Christians rather naively believe that inspiration implies *dictation only*—that is, that God dictated revelation to the human authors and they simply transcribed what they heard. Now, there were certainly times where that *was* the manner of revelation (for example, Exodus 34:27), but it was not the only one. In general, Scripture is said to have been inspired by the superintending work of the Holy Spirit (2 Peter 1:20-21). The Spirit did not override the thoughts, intentions, and personalities of the authors of Scripture, but He so sovereignly superintended them and worked *with* and *through* their thoughts, intentions, and personalities such that they wrote precisely what He intended. Nevertheless, the dictation-only model of inspiration does not so undermine the character or authority of Scripture so as to preclude one from genuine Christianity.

Saving Faith Is Doctrinally Sound

The charge of heresy is a serious one. We cannot be frivolous in throwing around the term, accusing as heretics everyone with whom we disagree on every minor point of doctrine. But Paul's response to the Judaizers teaches us that there *are* times when we must draw clear lines of separation, even among those who would call themselves Christians. The stakes are high, for, as the apostle John said, "Anyone who goes too far and does not abide in the doctrine of Christ, does not have God; the one who abides in the doctrine, this one has both the Father and the Son" (2 John 1:9, author's translation). For this reason, the elders of

Christ's church have been charged "both to exhort in sound doctrine and to refute those who contradict" (Titus 1:9), and her members have been charged to "contend earnestly for the faith which was once for all handed down to the saints" (Jude 3). Faithfulness to Christ requires His followers to discern between error and heresy. The questions stated in this chapter will aid you in that weighty task.

It is true that we are not saved by believing in sound doctrine *per se*, but by believing in *Christ* for the forgiveness of our sins. It is true that we are saved by faith alone, not merely by confessing the doctrine of *sola fide*. Nevertheless, the very moment we ask, "Saved by faith alone *in what? Who is this Christ in whom I must believe?*" the response will necessarily be a *doctrinal* answer. No, we are not saved by confessing sound doctrine, but the faith by which we *are* saved must of necessity be doctrinally sound. In a time in which the visible church has gone astray, may Christ's true bride be found faithful stewards of the pattern of sound words which have been entrusted to us as a treasure (2 Timothy 1:13-14)—for the purity of the gospel, and for the glory of Christ.

CHAPTER 9

The Charismatic Question

Are the Miraculous Gifts Still in Operation Today?[1]

NATHAN BUSENITZ

With more than 500 million adherents worldwide, the contemporary charismatic movement represents a significant theological force within broader Christendom. But is its basic premise—that the miraculous sign gifts described in the New Testament are still available to believers today—a valid assumption? Answering that question correctly is critical, since it affects both a person's doctrine (with regard to the work of the Holy Spirit) and practice (with regard to church worship and private devotion).

When addressing a theological topic, it is important to begin by defining key terms. *Cessationism* is the belief that the revelatory gifts (like prophecy and tongues) and the miraculous sign gifts (like the healings performed by the apostles) passed away, or ceased, shortly after the apostolic age ended and the canon of Scripture closed. Cessationists assert that those gifts are no longer in operation, and thus should not be sought by believers in the church today. Conversely, *continuationism* is the view that all of the spiritual gifts delineated in the New Testament—including prophecy, tongues, and healing—have continued throughout church history. Continuationists contend that those gifts are available to the contemporary church and should be eagerly sought by Christians.[2] Within conservative evangelical circles, cessationism and continuationism represent opposite perspectives regarding how to answer the charismatic question of whether or not the miraculous gifts of the Spirit are still in operation today.

Throughout church history, the majority of evangelical Christians (including individuals like Martin Luther, Matthew Henry, Jonathan

Edwards, and Charles Spurgeon) have articulated a cessationist position.[3] They believed the revelatory and miraculous sign gifts of the New Testament era ceased shortly after the apostolic age ended. With the birth of Pentecostalism in 1901, followed by the Charismatic Renewal in the 1960s and especially the Third Wave in the 1980s, evangelicalism found itself divided in its view regarding charismatic gifts. Toward the end of the twentieth century, a number of widely read evangelical pastors and theologians became vocal proponents of continuationism. As a result, an issue that was not controversial for most of post-Reformation church history (that is, evangelicalism's position on the cessation of the sign gifts) has become a flashpoint of controversy in recent decades.

The charismatic movement is admittedly complex, making it impossible to address every theological nuance associated with it in a short essay. The goal of this chapter is simply to provide a framework, from a cessationist perspective, for navigating the discussion surrounding the charismatic question. In order to do so, we will posit three fundamental questions: *What? When?* and *Why?*

The *What* Question

This question might be stated as follows: *What were the gifts in the New Testament, and how does that biblical description compare to what is happening in contemporary charismatic circles?* If contemporary charismatic experiences of prophecy, tongues, and healing match the New Testament description of those extraordinary gifts, then the continuationist position would obviously be strengthened. On the other hand, if the modern phenomena do not line up with the biblical data, then the continuationist position is severely weakened.

Many continuationists affirm that the apostolic age ended when John, the last of the apostles, died around AD 100. By acknowledging that apostleship did not continue beyond the first century, they agree with cessationists that there are no apostles in the church today.[4] This acknowledgment is significant, because it demonstrates that even continuationists recognize that at least one major gift/office of the New

Testament period (listed in both 1 Corinthians 12:28-30 and Ephesians 4:11) has ceased.[5]

Moving beyond apostleship, continuationists generally espouse a two-tier approach to the biblical gifts of prophecy, tongues, and healing. Thus, they assert that there are two kinds of New Testament prophecy. The first kind (Tier 1) was inerrant, authoritative, and on par with Old Testament prophecy. The second type (Tier 2) consisted of a congregational prophecy that was fallible, prone to error, and nonbinding. Of these two tiers, continuationists admit that the first ended when the canon of Scripture was closed (and the apostolic era ended); only the second continues today.[6] That is why continuationists do not hold modern prophets to the biblical standards of absolute accuracy and doctrinal orthodoxy.[7]

Continuationists similarly suggest that there are two categories of New Testament tongues. The first type (Tier 1) consisted of the supernatural ability to speak in authentic foreign languages and was seen on the Day of Pentecost in Acts 2. The second type (Tier 2) is a "private prayer language" made up of seemingly random strings of syllables.[8] Continuationists acknowledge that it is the second category of tongues that is practiced in charismatic churches today.[9]

Regarding the gift of healing, continuationists assert that there are at least two different classes of New Testament healings. The first kind (Tier 1) resulted in immediate, complete, and undeniable healings. These were the kind of healings performed by Christ in the gospels, and the apostles in the book of Acts. But continuationists insist that there is a second type of healing (Tier 2), in which believers pray for the sick and then wait to see how God might heal. Many continuationists acknowledge that the healing ministries of Jesus and the apostles were unique, meaning that the miraculous healings they performed should not be expected today.[10] Instead, when continuationists suggest that the gift of healing is still operational today, they often limit it to prayer requests offered to God in faith.[11]

In summary, continuationists generally acknowledge, whether explicitly or implicitly, that the Tier 1 versions of these gifts passed away when the apostolic age ended, and only the Tier 2 versions have continued throughout church history. That point is significant, because it is a tacit acknowledgment of the cessationist position. If that which was truly extraordinary about the New Testament gifts of prophecy, tongues, and healing has indeed passed away, then all that has continued is errant "prophecy," nonsensical "tongues," and questionable "healings."

Cessationists are convinced that the true gifts, as described in the New Testament, consisted only of the Tier 1 versions described above. Thus, they are unwilling to accept the two-tier definition of the gifts proposed by continuationists. Not only does such a distinction lack biblical support, cessationists are convinced that it is a paradigm being imposed on Scripture in order to legitimize contemporary charismatic practices.

The argument for a fallible form of congregational prophecy (that would parallel the error-filled prophecies of modern charismatics) does not hold up under scrutiny. The New Testament nowhere suggests that there were two classes of prophets in the early church who were held to two different standards. Rather, when New Testament prophets spoke for God, they were required to be both theologically sound (meaning that their teaching must be in line with what had been previously revealed), and free from error (meaning that the words of their prophecy were totally true). All prophets were to be tested (1 Corinthians 14:29; 1 Thessalonians 5:21). Those who taught what was good were to be embraced (1 Thessalonians 5:21). But those who taught what was evil were to be rejected (verse 21). Those who failed the biblical tests of doctrinal orthodoxy and revelatory accuracy were regarded as false prophets (cf. Deuteronomy 13:1-5; 18:20-22; Isaiah 44:26; Jeremiah 28:9; Ezekiel 12:25; Matthew 7:15-16; Romans 12:6; 2 Peter 2:1-2; Jude 3-4).[12]

Similarly, cessationists assert that there was only one category of the gift of tongues—namely, the miraculous ability to speak fluently in foreign languages that the speaker had not previously learned. This gift is most clearly depicted in Acts 2, when the apostles spoke in tongues on the Day of Pentecost. The same gift was given to Cornelius in Acts

10:46 (cf. Acts 11:15). The clear data from the book of Acts helps us interpret 1 Corinthians 12–14, where the gift of tongues again refers to real foreign languages (1 Corinthians 14:10-12)—a point underscored by the fact that they ought to be translated (verses 13, 27-28).[13]

Finally, a survey of the ministries of Jesus and the apostles demonstrates that the healing miracles they performed were complete, immediate, unfailing, and undeniable (cf. Matthew 14:36; Mark 1:42; John 11:47-48; Acts 4:16-17; etc.).[14] While cessationists affirm that believers should pray for God to heal those who are sick, doing so according to His perfect timing and providential purposes, they do not regard such prayers as constituting the New Testament gift of healing.[15]

When cessationists compare the biblical evidence to modern charismatic and continuationist experience, they are convinced the two are not the same. The New Testament does not set forward two types of prophecy—one of which can be full of errors. It does not affirm two classes of tongues—one of which consists of strings of unintelligible syllables. And it does not portray two categories of miraculous healing gifts—one of which fails to produce immediate and undeniable results. In sum, the Tier 2 "gifts" that continuationists claim have continued simply do not measure up to the Tier 1 realities described in Scripture.[16]

When we approach the continuationist/cessationist debate by first defining the gifts biblically, it becomes apparent that modern charismatic practice does not match the New Testament precedent. Though continuationists use New Testament terminology to describe their contemporary experience, the reality is that such experiences are far different than what was actually happening in the first-century church.

The *When* Question

The *when* question might be stated as follows: *If the revelatory gifts and extraordinary sign gifts described in the New Testament are not occurring in the church today, then does the Bible indicate when those gifts would pass away?* In interacting with the *when* question, at least five passages of Scripture must be considered.[17] Some of these biblical texts are used by continuationists to argue for the ongoing nature of the miraculous gifts, while others anticipate their cessation. It is therefore necessary to interact with each of these passages, though we will do so only briefly because of limited space.

Acts 2:16-21

Acts 2 records the birth of the church on the Day of Pentecost, with Peter's powerful evangelistic sermon beginning in verse 14. Based on Peter's reference to Joel 2:28-32 (in Acts 2:16-21), some continuationists argue that the miraculous gifts should be expected to continue throughout the entire church age.[18] The problem with this interpretation, however, is that it cannot account for the cosmic signs that are also part of Joel's prophecy (such as the sun being darkened and the moon turned to blood—cf. Acts 2:19-20). If the charismatic signs of Acts 2:17-18 were intended to characterize the entire church age (as charismatics assert), then why haven't the cosmic signs (of verses 19-20) also characterized the entire church age?

Even if Acts 2 is regarded as the complete fulfillment of Joel 2, it does not demonstrate the continuation of spiritual gifts throughout the entire church age. Rather, it suggests that the church age is book-ended by supernatural phenomena—marked by charismatic signs at the beginning and cosmic signs at the end. Moreover, the prophecy predicted in Joel 2 (cf. Acts 2:18) is the Old Testament form of prophecy (Tier 1 prophecy)—which poses a problem for continuationists, since they acknowledge that the Tier 1 form of prophecy has passed away. For dispensationalists who see a partial fulfillment of Joel 2 in Acts 2, this passage does not present a problem, since the full fulfillment of Joel 2 will take place during the Tribulation period, after the church age has ended.

1 Corinthians 13:8-12

In this passage, Paul clearly states that prophecy will "pass away" and tongues "will cease" (1 Corinthians 13:8). However, the timing of that cessation is hotly debated. The controversy primarily centers on the meaning of the "perfect" in verse 10. The Greek word translated "perfect" can also be rendered "mature," or "complete." It is important to note that the cessationist position does not stand or fall with one's interpretation of the "perfect." There are several cessationist interpretations of the "perfect" in this passage, including (a) the mature church,[19] (b) the completed canon,[20] (c) the Parousia,[21] and (d) the glorified state of the believer.[22] Ironically, both cessationists and continuationists often appeal to 1 Corinthians 13:8-12 to make their case—usually without persuading those in the other camp. As Anthony Thiselton notes in his commentary on 1 Corinthians, "The one important point to make here is that few or none of the serious 'cessationist' arguments depends on a specific exegesis of 1 Corinthians 13:8-11...*These verses should not be used as a polemic for either side in this debate.*"[23]

Ephesians 2:20

In this verse, Paul explains that the church has "been built on the foundation of the apostles and prophets, Christ Jesus Himself being the corner stone." This statement is significant because it indicates that the "apostles and prophets" played a fundamental role in laying the doctrinal foundation for the church. In light of Paul's later discussion in Ephesians 3:5 and 4:11, the prophets in 2:20 must refer to New Testament prophets.[24]

Based on this text, cessationists conclude that both apostles and prophets passed off the scene once the doctrinal foundation for the church was laid. In the same way that apostleship passed off the scene (a point acknowledged by many continuationists), so prophecy also came to an end. Following Paul's metaphor, the foundation of a building is laid only once, at the beginning of construction. So once the doctrinal foundation of the church was established through the ministry of the apostles and prophets, those offices (and the gifts associated with them) passed away because they were no longer necessary. The cessation of those gifts sets a precedent for the cessation of other miraculous and revelatory gifts (like miraculous healings and tongues).[25]

Ephesians 4:11-13

This passage articulates the effect that apostles, prophets, evangelists, pastors, and teachers have in equipping God's people for the building up of the church. Some continuationists suggest that this text indicates that all five of the ministries listed (including apostles and prophets) should be expected to continue throughout the church age. But the grammar of the passage does not support that assertion. Rather, it is the "building up" process of verse 12 (and not the "giving" of apostles and prophets in verse 11) that is said to continue until the church reaches a state of maturity (verse 13). Though the apostles and prophets were limited to the foundation stage of church history (a point already established by Paul in Ephesians 2:20), the "building up" of the church has continued throughout the centuries. In other words, the edifying effects of their ministry in the first century (particularly through the writing of Scripture) continue to reverberate throughout the subsequent epochs of church history.

Hebrews 2:3-5

Although this passage describes the miraculous gifts in the past tense, it is not conclusive about the duration of the gifts in church history. However, it may suggest that the gifts had largely begun to subside by the time the book of Hebrews was written. Consequently, some cessationists appeal to this passage in making a case for when the gifts began to pass away in church history.[26]

Summary Observations

With regard to answering the *when* question, many cessationist scholars find Ephesians 2:20 to be the most conclusive of the texts surveyed above. The gifts of apostleship and prophecy were for the foundational age of the church. Therefore they ought not to be expected after the foundational age ends and the canon of Scripture is closed. The cessation of the apostolate, in particular, limits that foundational period to the first century.

Because gifts of miracle-working and healing were signs associated with the apostles and the initial advancement of the gospel (Acts 3:1-11; 5:15-16; 6:8; 8:1-7; 9:32-43; 14:3; 14:8-10; 16:16-18; 19:11-12; 20:9-12; 28:8-9; Hebrews 2:3-4), and because the gift of tongues was also a sign gift (1 Corinthians 14:21-22) which was closely associated with the gift of prophecy (note the connection between tongues and prophecy in Acts 2:17 and in 1 Corinthians 14), cessationists conclude that those gifts were likewise limited to the foundational age of the church.

Thus, they assert that the miraculous sign gifts that authenticated the advancement of the gospel through the apostles and early evangelists (like Stephen and Philip), along with the revelatory gifts (through which the doctrinal foundation of the church was established), passed away after the foundational age of the church came to an end.

The *Why* Question

So far, we have briefly considered the *what* question and the *when* question. Regarding the *what* question, cessationists conclude that what took place in the New Testament (with regard to the miraculous gifts) is not happening in the church today—even if charismatics are using biblical terminology to refer to nonbiblical practices. Regarding the *when* question, cessationists conclude (on the basis of passages like Ephesians 2:20) that the miraculous and revelatory gifts were intended only for the foundational (apostolic) age of the church. Thus, they should not be expected to continue after the time of the apostles.

But this raises a third question, which might be stated as follows: *Why were these gifts given, such that they are no longer necessary after the foundation age ended?* At least three purposes can be derived from Scripture:

To Authenticate God's Messengers

This purpose might be stated in this way: *The miraculous gifts were given as a sign by which God authenticated His messengers during a time of transition from Israel to the church. That purpose was no longer necessary once the transition was complete and the church was firmly established.*

A primary purpose of the miracles and healings that Jesus performed was as a sign to authenticate His claims (cf. John 2:11, 23; 3:2;

4:54; 6:2, 14; 7:31; 10:37-38; 12:37; 20:30). As Peter told the Jews at Pentecost: "Men of Israel, listen to these words: Jesus the Nazarene, a man attested to you by God with miracles and wonders and signs which God performed through Him in your midst, just as you yourselves know…" (Acts 2:22).

The disciples were given power by Christ to perform similar signs (cf. Matthew 10:1, 7; Mark 6:12-13; 16:20). The record of Acts depicts the apostles performing miracles and healings as signs that authenticated their message (cf. Acts 2:43; 4:30; 5:12; 6:8; 8:6, 13; 14:3; 15:12). Extraordinary experiences were shared by ordinary Gentile converts (like Cornelius in Acts 10). This was also a sign that God was working through the church (cf. Acts 11:17-18). Thus, Paul could tell the Corinthians that their ability to speak in tongues was a sign to the unbelieving world (1 Corinthians 14:22). He then quoted from Isaiah 28:11, indicating that it was specifically a sign of God's judgment against unbelieving Israel.

Paul described his evangelistic ministry to the Gentiles as being authenticated by "signs and wonders" (Romans 15:19). In 2 Corinthians 12:12, Paul defended his apostleship by noting that his ministry was characterized by the signs of an apostle. He told the Corinthians, "The signs of a true apostle were performed among you with all perseverance, by signs and wonders and miracles."

Finally, in Hebrews 2:3-4, the link between the sign gifts and God's authentication is made overtly clear. The author wrote, "How will we escape if we neglect so great a salvation? After it was at the first spoken through the Lord, it was confirmed to us by those who heard, God also testifying with them, both by signs and wonders and by various miracles and by gifts of the Holy Spirit according to His own will."

At other select times in redemptive history, God used miraculous gifts (such as miracle-working and healing) to authenticate His messengers (for example, the Exodus from Egypt and the lifetimes of Elijah and Elisha). This was also true during the apostolic age. But it has not continued to be true throughout church history.

To Reveal Divine Truth

A second purpose is this: *The revelatory gifts were given in order to give additional revelation to the church. That purpose ceased to be necessary once the canon of Scripture was complete.* By definition, the written Word of God consists of that which God has revealed through the inspiration of the Holy Spirit. As Peter wrote in 2 Peter 1:20-21, "Know this first of all, that no prophecy of Scripture is a matter of one's own interpretation [*creation* or *origination*], for no prophecy was ever made by an act of human will, but men moved by the Holy Spirit spoke from God."

In the Old Testament, God's Word was revealed through His prophets. In the New Testament, God's Word was revealed through His Son (Jesus Christ). The author of Hebrews explained it this way: "God, after He spoke long ago to the fathers in the prophets in many portions and in many ways, in these last days has spoken to us in His Son, whom He appointed heir of all things, through whom also He made the world" (Hebrews 1:1-2).

The Lord Jesus promised that He would give additional revelation to His church through His authorized representatives—namely, the apostles (John 14:23-26; 16:12-15). By extension, additional revelation would also come to the church through New Testament prophets who operated under the authority of the apostles.

The apostles, therefore, rightly recognized their own inspired writings as being part of the biblical canon, on par with the books of the Old Testament (1 Thessalonians 2:13; 2 Peter 3:15-16). New Testament prophecy had to be measured against both Old Testament Scripture apostolic teaching (cf. Romans 12:6, where it is best translated "*the* faith"; 1 Thessalonians 5:20-22; Jude 3; compare 1 Corinthians 14:29 with Acts 17:11), because the danger of false prophets was a constant reality in the first century church. Once the New Testament canon was complete (and the apostles passed off the scene), there was no longer a need for additional prophetic revelation—either in church history or in the church today. To claim otherwise is to undermine the sufficiency of Scripture. As Richard Gaffin observes:

A dilemma confronts noncessationists. If prophecy and tongues (as they function in the New Testament) continue today, then the noncessationist is faced with the quite practical and troublesome implication that Scripture alone is *not* a sufficient verbal revelation from God. At best, the canon is *relatively* closed. Alternatively, if—as most noncessationists insist—'prophecy' and 'tongues' today are not revelatory or are less than fully revelatory, then these contemporary phenomena are misnamed. They are something *other* than the gifts of prophecy and tongues that we find in the New Testament.[27]

To Edify the Saints

A secondary purpose of both the miraculous sign gifts and the revelatory gifts was that they provided a means by which believers could edify others in the church. This is still a purpose of the nonmiraculous and nonrevelatory gifts, but it does not necessitate the continuation of the foundational gifts (like apostleship, prophecy, tongues, and healing).

The exercise of sign gifts (like healing) and revelatory gifts (like prophecy) naturally brought benefits to other people, even if that was not the only purpose of the gift. For example, when Jesus healed a man born blind, the primary purpose of that miracle was that God would be glorified (John 9:3) and Christ's claims would be validated (John 10:21, 37-38). But the blind man was certainly edified, because he was now able to see. Moreover, he later came to saving faith (John 9:38). Thus, the primary purpose of that miracle (to glorify God and authenticate His Son) simultaneously accomplished a secondary purpose (to edify a blind man by giving him physical and spiritual sight). The apostle Paul similarly stated that the primary purpose of the gift of tongues was to serve as a sign to unbelievers (1 Corinthians 14:21-22), yet it can (and should) also be used for edification within the context of the local church (cf. verse 5).

As Paul made clear in that passage, the gifts were not to be used selfishly. They were to contribute to the mutual edification of the body of Christ. In 1 Corinthians 12:7, Paul stated that "to each one is given the manifestation of the Spirit for the common good." This is consistent with Ephesians 4:11-12, in which the gifts of apostles, prophets, evangelists, pastors, and teachers are given by Christ so that the body might be edified.

Thus, in an age when all the gifts were active, all the gifts were to be used for the edification of others. Today, at a time when only some of the gifts remain, those remaining gifts are to be used for building up one another in the body of Christ. Of course, the church today is still edified through the miraculous and revelatory gifts that characterized the apostolic age (even though the operation of those gifts has passed away). Every time we pick up a Bible, we are benefiting from the prophetic gifts that characterized their apostolic ministries (cf. 2 Peter 1:19-21). The fact that God authenticated their message with signs and wonders only increases our confidence in their message.

Thus, continuing edification in the church is *not* dependent on the continuation of the miraculous sign gifts or the revelatory gifts. The apostolic age has ended and the canon is complete. Yet through the apostolic witness of Scripture and the empowering work of the Holy Spirit, believers continue to edify one another in the church—building on the foundation laid by the apostles and prophets—as they seek to glorify the head, Jesus Christ.

Finally, when continuationists argue that self-edification is a valid purpose of the gifts (for example, using devotional tongues merely to edify oneself), they do so contrary to Paul's instruction in 1 Corinthians 12–14.[28] Cessationist author Thomas Edgar makes this important observation:

> The entire New Testament describes spiritual gifts as being used to minister to others. In no instance does it state that gifts were to be used for personal benefit. The nature of the gifts themselves indicates that they are given to enable the recipient to minister to others. For example, the gift of teacher is given to teach others, and the gift of helps is given to help others. Spiritual gifts are given by God in order to enable the one who has the gift to minister to others. Some

gifts focus on ministry to unbelievers, while other gifts focus on ministry to believers. God did not give any gift merely to benefit the recipient of the gift.[29]

God's Purposes Accomplished

In this chapter, we have attempted to simplify the contemporary controversy regarding charismatic gifts by reducing it down to three basic questions. The *what* question asks: What were the gifts in the New Testament, and are those same phenomena actually occurring in the church today? If one answers *no* to that question, he is a *de facto* cessationist.

The *when* question follows by asking: If New Testament-quality gifts are not happening today, when did they pass away? Passages like Ephesians 2:20 help us see that the miraculous and revelatory gifts were given specifically for the foundational, apostolic age of the church. Once that era ended those gifts were no longer needed.

Finally, the *why* question asks: If the miraculous gifts ceased shortly after the apostolic age, why did they cease? When one considers the primary reason the miraculous sign gifts and revelatory gifts were given, it becomes evident that those purposes were fulfilled during the foundational age of the church. Once the apostolic age passed, and the canon of Scripture was completed, the primary purpose for those gifts was fulfilled and they ceased.

CHAPTER 10

Things That Should Not Be Forgotten

Why Church Leaders Should Care about Church History[1]

NATHAN BUSENITZ

It has famously been said that those who do not know history are doomed to repeat it. While history may not always repeat itself exactly, it is certainly true that history teaches its students valuable lessons that apply to both the present and the future. Sadly, modern evangelicals are not known for being well-grounded in the history of the church, which is to their detriment. This chapter considers ten reasons contemporary Christians, and especially church leaders, should become better acquainted with church history.

I am writing this at the beginning of a new semester.

As another school year dawns, I will make my way to a classroom full of (mostly) first-year seminary students. I can imagine it already.

When I open the door, there will be the inevitable and slightly uncomfortable pause in the hubbub of pre-class conversation. It is the awkward moment every teacher experiences at the start of a new semester—when you enter a room full of unfamiliar faces and everyone stops talking to turn and watch you.

But there is no turning back.

Under the watchful gaze of my students, with first impressions already forming, I will walk to the front of the room and set down my bag on the lecture table. Without looking up, I'll get out my laptop, turn it on, and make sure it's connected to the projector. Then I'll arrange whatever books or notes I've brought with me.

Soon, everything will be ready to go. I'll give a nonchalant glance to the clock on the back wall, which will remind me that it's time to start. Without further delay, I'll take a deep breath, smile, and hear the following words come out of my mouth.

"Good afternoon, class. Welcome to Historical Theology."

There. The ice has been broken. Now we can get to work.

In the hour-and-a-half that follows, I will muster all of my pro-fessorial enthusiasm to persuade these students that church history is important. But this is more than a just a blatant attempt to sell them on the class. (I really am trying to do more than just get them excited about homework assignments.) This expansive subject is important to me. Vitally so. And it should be important to them (and you) too.

Despite the misconceptions they arrived with, church history is not trivial, or boring, or irrelevant. It is so much more than just names, dates, timelines, and charts. Some of the students came in thinking, *I hate history.* Maybe so, but this class is not so much about *history.* It's about *the church*, the bride of Christ, the most precious institution on earth. It's about what God has been doing in the church for the last 2000 years. And that means it should matter—especially to men who are training to serve in ministry.

Others will probably wonder why they have to take a *history* class when they are supposed to be studying *the Bible.* What they don't realize is that the study of church history, properly framed, actually increases one's love for the Scriptures. I have experienced that reality firsthand. The deeper I have investigated the history of the church, the more I have grown to appreciate the power and authority of the Word of God—because I have seen that power vividly illustrated in the tes-timonies of generations of believers. Scripture alone is the authority for all we believe and do; but history provides wonderful affirmation of the truthfulness of those foundational biblical truths.

Over the course of the lecture, I will give my students ten reasons why the study of church history matters. They are as follows:

1. Studying church history is important because most contempo-rary Christians are clueless about it. And they shouldn't be. The sad reality is that most American evangelicals know very little about the history of Christianity. Even in Reformed circles, an understanding of church history often goes back only to the Reformation. But the history of the gospel spans all the way back to the New Testament.

If your knowledge of church history jumps from the apostle John (on Patmos) to Martin Luther (at Wittenberg), with little to nothing in between, you ought to seriously consider filling in the gaps. The 1500 years between Pentecost and the Reformation include many significant people—fellow believers and faithful leaders—whom God used in strategic ways to advance His kingdom purposes.

One of the great blind spots in contemporary American evangelicalism is its lack of historical awareness. With his characteristic wit, Carl Trueman explained the problem like this:

> I was asked last week why some evangelicals convert to Eastern Orthodoxy and Roman Catholicism. Reasons vary, I am sure, but I commented that one theme I have noticed over the years is the fact that evangelicalism lacks historical roots. That is not to say that it has no history; rather it is to say that a consciousness of history is not part of the package. Rock band worship, Beautiful People everywhere (miserable middle-aged plain people need not apply), and history nowhere in sight unless it is a reference in the sermon to an early Coldplay album. On that level, I can understand why people looking for something serious, something with a sense of theological and historical gravitas, simply give up on evangelicalism and start looking elsewhere. Some adults want a faith that is similarly adult, after all.[2]

Evangelical church history—all 2000 years of it—is a rich gold mine of theological treasure. In their attempts to juvenilize the church, many evangelical congregations spurn history as if it were outdated and unimportant. But, as Trueman points out, we do ourselves a great disservice if we choose to remain ignorant.

Does God consider history to be important? Certainly He does. Though it is not church history, God used Israel's history to teach them spiritual truths throughout the Old Testament (cf. Deuteronomy

6:21-25). And in the New Testament, the Holy Spirit saw fit to inspire a book of church history, starting from the Day of Pentecost and running through Paul's first Roman imprisonment.

While any inspired account of church history ends with the book of Acts, Christians are blessed to have wonderful resources that detail the history of the church from the first century to the present. Those who ignore the profound riches of their own spiritual heritage don't know what they are missing—namely, the life-changing opportunity to be challenged, instructed, and encouraged in the faith by those who've gone before us.

2. Because God is at work in history. Conversely, history is a testimony to God's sovereign providence. Pardon the cliché, but it really is *His story*. Everything is working according to His plans, and He is orchestrating all of it for His eternal glory (cf. 1 Corinthians 15:20-28). God declares Himself to be the Lord of history:

> Remember the former things long past, for I am God, and there is no other; I am God, and there is no one like Me, declaring the end from the beginning, and from ancient times things which have not been done, saying, "My purpose will be established, and I will accomplish all My good pleasure" (Isaiah 46:9-10).

Studying church history reminds us that our God is on His throne. He reigns. He is perfectly accomplishing His purposes and providentially preserving His people and His truth in every generation. No matter how bad society becomes—no matter how antagonistic or immoral—we already know how history ends. What comfort there is in remembering that the Lord of history is working all things together for His glory and our good.

One of the greatest theological lessons any believer can learn is to rest in the sovereignty of God. The Scriptures are filled with examples of men and women who trusted God and acted upon their faith in Him (cf. Hebrews 11). Church history, likewise, consists of wonderful examples of faithful Christians whose lives are testimonies to the providential care of their heavenly Father.

3. Because the Lord Jesus said He would build His church. To study church history is to watch His promise unfold. In Matthew 16:15-18, we read:

> [Jesus] said to them, "But who do you say that I am?" Simon Peter answered, "You are the Christ, the Son of the living God." And Jesus said to him, "Blessed are you, Simon Barjona, because flesh and blood did not reveal this to you, but My Father who is in heaven. I also say to you that you are Peter, and upon this rock I will build My church; and the gates of Hades will not overpower it."

The church is established on the gospel truth that Jesus is the Christ, the Son of the Living God. The church's unconquerable history is evidence that He is indeed who He claimed to be. Commenting on that passage, John MacArthur says it well:

> No matter how liberal, fanatical, ritualistic, apathetic, or apostate its outward adherents may be, and no matter how decadent the rest of the world may become, Christ will build His church. Therefore, no matter how oppressive and hopeless their outward circumstances may appear from a human perspective, God's people belong to a cause that cannot fail.[3]

The church is an institution established by Jesus Himself. That alone is reason enough to study church history. Moreover, His promise—that the gates of hell will never overpower the church—gives us reason to hope even when the church appears to be weak and infirm. At times, the contemporary evangelical landscape gives us reason to grow pessimistic and discouraged. But Christ's promise keeps us optimistic, because our hope is in Him and not in the things of this world.

When we study church history we are reminded of those times when the gates of hell appeared ominous and threatening, and yet the

church survived and prevailed through God's power. When courageous Christians were severely persecuted to the point of death for
the sake of the truth; or when Arianism threatened to overrun the
Roman Empire and Athanasius stood, nearly alone against the world;
or when the sacramental system of the late-medieval church threatened to eclipse the gospel of grace; or when liberal theology infiltrated
the universities of nineteenth- and twentieth-century Western society.
These and countless other examples embolden us to face today's challenges and persecutions with the confidence of knowing that we belong
to a cause that cannot fail.

4. Because church history is our history as members of His body.
When we study the history of the church, we are not merely studying
people, places, and events; we are studying the history of the bride of
Christ. If we belong to Christ, then we too are part of that bride. As
Paul explained to the Ephesians:

> Husbands, love your wives, just as Christ also loved the
> church and gave Himself up for her, so that He might sanc-
> tify her, having cleansed her by the washing of water with
> the word, that He might present to Himself the church in all
> her glory, having no spot or wrinkle or any such thing; but
> that she would be holy and blameless (Ephesians 5:25-27).

So when we study church history, we come to see who we are,
where we've come from, and how we fit into the flow of God's kingdom work in the world. We are studying our spiritual family tree. The
Lord Jesus Himself cares deeply about His bride (cf. Revelation 1–3),
and we should too.

On a practical note, one of the great ways to remind ourselves that
we are part of a body of believers that spans the centuries is through singing hymns. Along those lines, Carl Trueman's suggestion is a good one:

> Deliberately mine the historic tradition of psalmody and
> hymnody for worship. Not that anything written by anyone
> still alive is to be excluded. Far from it. But try to make

sure the songs of worship reflect the chronological sweep of the church's life, from the Book of Psalms onwards. Make people aware that praise did not begin six months ago.[4]

When we sing hymns like "Be Thou My Vision" (a sixth-century Irish hymn) or "O Sacred Head, Now Wounded" (penned by either Bernard of Clairvaux in the twelfth century or Arnulf of Louvain in the thirteenth) or "A Mighty Fortress Is Our God" (written by Martin Luther in the sixteenth century), we connect ourselves to the history of the church.

Knowing the history behind the hymns reminds us that we belong to the corporate body of believers, the universal church. And just as we have brothers and sisters across the world, we also have brothers and sisters from generations past who are now in heaven rejoicing around Christ's throne. The study of church history allows us to meet them, as it were, as we read their testimonies and learn about their lives. It also reminds us that one day soon we will go to join with them in eternal praise, when we see our Savior face to face.

Studying the history of the church reminds us that we are part of something bigger than ourselves, or our own local congregations, or even the century in which we live. We are part of the bride of Christ—and His bride consists of all the redeemed from every generation.

5. Because sound doctrine has been guarded and passed down by faithful generations throughout history. In 2 Timothy 2:2, Paul told his son in the faith, "The things which you have heard from me in the presence of many witnesses, entrust these to faithful men who will be able to teach others also." To study church history is to meet the generations of Christians who loved biblical truth and faithfully passed it on to those who came after. Moreover, it is encouraging to know that the truths we hold dear have been cherished by believers all the way back to the time of the apostles.

The study of church history reminds us that we are standing on the shoulders of those who have come before us. The halls of history are filled with accounts of those who loved the truth and fought valiantly to preserve it. Thus, while we recognize that church history is not authoritative (only Scripture is), we are wise to glean from the wisdom of past church leaders, theologians, and pastors. Their creeds, commentaries, and sermons represent lifetimes of meditating on the text and walking with God. We would be unwise to ignore their voices and their insights as we similarly seek to rightly divide the Word.

Furthermore, when we study church history we are reminded that some truths are worth fighting for (and dying for). We remember that we are part of something bigger than ourselves. And like those who have come before us, we too have a responsibility to faithfully guard the treasure of biblical truth and sound doctrine that has been entrusted to us, being careful to pass it on to those who will follow us.

6. Because, just as we are encouraged by the history of truth, we are also warned by the history of error. This enables us to be equipped as apologists. The New Testament is full of warnings about false teaching, both refuting it in the first century and warning that it would come in the centuries that followed (Acts 20:28-30; 1 Timothy 4:1). When we study church history, we not only learn the history of the truth but also the history of error. We see where the cults originated; and we have the benefit of seeing orthodoxy defended and the truth being preserved.

The New Testament calls all Christians to be able to defend the faith. In the words of 1 Peter 3:15: "Sanctify Christ as Lord in your hearts, always being ready to make a defense to everyone who asks you to give an account for the hope that is in you, yet with gentleness and reverence." Titus 1:8-10 similarly requires that an elder must be one who holds "fast the faithful word which is in accordance with the teaching, so that he will be able both to exhort in sound doctrine and to refute those who contradict." That is a quality all believers should desire to emulate.

Any defense of the Christian faith must be founded on the Scriptures. But church history also serves as a valuable (albeit secondary) apologetic tool.

For example, knowing a little church history quickly silences silly allegations against Christianity (like those made by Dan Brown's *The Da Vinci Code*). Knowing a little church history is especially helpful in witnessing to Muslims, Mormons, Jehovah's Witnesses, and members of other pseudo-Christian cults. Understanding church history is even helpful in defending key areas of doctrine—showing that a contemporary evangelical understanding of Scripture has not deviated from the teachings of the apostolic church.

As believers, we are commanded to be ready to give a defense for our hope. The study of church history is an ally in that cause.

7. Because we have much to learn from those who walked with God. In Hebrews 12:1, we read of "a great cloud of witnesses"—believers in generations past whose lives give testimony to the faithfulness of God. While the author of Hebrews was specifically referring to Old Testament saints (cf. Hebrews 11), the testimonies of all who have come before us provide a powerful encouragement to remain faithful ourselves.

Faithfulness to the Lord, to His Word, and to His people is what defines a hero of the faith. And church history offers us many such faithful men and women to choose from. Their lives should inspire, motivate, and encourage us as we run the race with endurance. Their heaven-focused perspective reminds us to keep our eyes on Christ, the Author and Perfecter of the faith. As C.S. Lewis famously said, "If you read history you will find out that the Christians who did most for the present world were precisely those who thought most of the next."[5] Gleaning those kinds of devotional gems begins with reading church history.

Seasoned pastors often talk about identifying "mentors" from church history, faithful Christians from the past whose lives they have studied and desire to emulate. That is a practice all believers should seriously consider. In the opinion of this writer, Christian biography ought to be a staple part of any believer's regular reading diet. I highly recommend reading at least one church history biography every year. You will be greatly encouraged and inspired to continued faithfulness by that simple practice alone.

8. Because just as we can learn from the good examples of faithful Christians, we likewise have much to learn from those who failed at various points. As we observed at the beginning of this chapter, those who don't know history are often destined to repeat the mistakes of the past.

In church history, we see examples of all kinds of spiritual failure. There are those who fell into heresy, those who gave way to corruption, those who denied the faith, and those who fell morally. The lives of such individuals serve as a warning for us.

In 1 Corinthians 10:1-12, the apostle Paul used the negative illustration of the Israelites in the wilderness to teach his readers an important spiritual lesson. Paul's example sets a precedent for the way we think about both biblical history and church history.

We can learn powerful lessons about what to avoid from things like the influx of paganism into Roman Christianity, the corruption of the papacy, the Crusades, the development of liberalism, and so on. Learning from past failures helps guard us from repeating those same errors.

Church history is proof that spiritual failure can come rapidly with devastating results, a point illustrated in the New Testament by the Galatians—who were quickly tempted to abandon the true gospel (Galatians 1:6-9). It reminds us of the need to be vigilant—to watch our lives and our doctrine closely so as not to fall into similar snares and pitfalls.

On a practical note, not all the historical biographies you read have to be positive. Sometimes it is helpful to read a book that critically engages with some form of error or failure. Iain Murray's *Revival and Revivalism*, George Marsden's *Reforming Fundamentalism*, and Eric Chamberlain's *The Bad Popes* are examples of these types of resources.

9. Because studying the past helps us understand the resources, opportunities, and freedoms that we enjoy in the present. Often we take for granted the blessings that we enjoy living in the modern age. The study of church history reminds us of the great sacrifices made and challenges faced by previous generations of believers. It increases our thankfulness for what we have, and it motivates us to be good stewards of the incredible opportunities that God has afforded us.

The history of the English Bible, for example, reminds us to be thankful that we have a personal copy of God's Word in our own language. The history of persecution emboldens us in our evangelism as we witness the faithfulness of the martyrs and recognize how unique the freedoms we enjoy really are. The history of missions makes us grateful for advancements in travel and technology, while simultaneously inspiring us to do more in our effort to reach the world for Christ.

It is also interesting, on a tangential note, to realize that our generation represents the first to really wrestle with the implications of the information age for the church. In many ways, modern technology affords us with opportunities that those of previous generations could never have imagined. But such advancements also put the onus on us to think carefully and biblically about the way we use them. We are setting the precedent for the way future generations will think about the church's interaction with technology and media.

10. Because history helps twenty-first-century pastors have a right perspective about their own place in the church age. It is important to realize that we are part of church history. We are part of the current generation of believers, and we have a responsibility to faithfully guard the truth and pass it on to those who come after us.

Studying church history helps us recognize that we are part of something much bigger than ourselves, our local congregation, or even the evangelical movement as it exists today. The history of Christianity spans two millennia, of which we are but a momentary blip.

Studying church history also opens our eyes to the fact that every generation of believers is greatly affected by the time and culture in which they live, such that they themselves do not even realize the effects. We can then, in turn, ask ourselves what impact our culture has on our own application of biblical truth.

Finally, and most importantly, studying church history helps us remember that Christ is the Lord of the church in every age, and reminds us of what a great privilege it is to minister in His service. It also motivates us to look forward to the day when He returns and church history officially comes to its end.[6]

SECTION III:

THE **CHURCH** AND THE **GREAT** **COMMISSION**

CHAPTER 11

To the Ends of the Earth

God's Global Agenda to Reach the Lost[1]

IRV BUSENITZ

In Matthew 28:19, the Lord Jesus instructed His followers to "go therefore and make disciples of all the nations." That charge remains the church's Great Commission, to preach the good news of the gospel throughout the world so that lost souls might be reconciled to God through faith in His Son. When churches lose sight of that evangelistic priority, they stray from the primary mission God has called them to accomplish on this earth.

Cover to cover, the Bible is a missionary story. From Genesis to Revelation (Genesis 3:15; Revelation 21–22), God is about the business of "reconciling the world to Himself" (2 Corinthians 5:19). Remarkably, God has ordained His people—those who were once His enemies but now have been redeemed—to herald His incredible offer of forgiveness to the lost. Christ's closing charge, to go and make disciples (Matthew 28:18-20), is a mandate from the greatest missionary of all time—One sent by His Father to open the door of reconciliation to all who "will call on the name of the Lord" (Romans 10:13).

In some respects, never in the history of mankind has this commission been easier to carry out. The world has become small and continues to shrink at an incredible rate. High-speed travel, electronic communications, and computers have dramatically neutralized the impact of the Tower of Babel.

At the same time, there has been a growing apathy in the West. The Western church, it seems, has fallen prey to a seduction of prosperity (Deuteronomy 31:20; Revelation 2:4) and a cultural syncretism that afflicted the ancient nation of Israel (Amos 5:25-26; Acts 7:42-43).

Although we disdain the health-and-wealth gospel, many in the West have intentionally or unintentionally bought into it. A health-and-wealth mentality does not send missionaries. Instead, it creates "a deep mission-forgetfulness within the church." [2]

But there is much for which to be thankful. New centers of Christianity are rising out of the ash heap of darkness, extending the influence of the gospel to places previously unreached. And yet, while the wealthy West invests financially in the work of these new major centers of Christianity (and thus soothes its conscience for no longer investing with manpower), monetary backing alone does not abrogate or alleviate the divine exhortations for a more personal investment.

God's Eternal Purpose

Discerning God's global agenda in Scripture commences with an understanding of God Himself. From the opening chapters of Genesis, the reality of Romans 3:11—"there is none who seeks for God"—stands in stark contrast to God's insatiable pursuit of man.[3] While mankind throughout history has been bent on self-destruction (cf. Genesis 4:8, 23-24; 6:5, 11), God repeatedly declares His intent to redeem.

Glimpses of God's redemptive plan are first revealed in the *protoevangelium* (Genesis 3:15), in the sacrificial provision of clothing to cover the first sin and sinners (Genesis 3:21), and in the saving of Noah and his family in the ark (Genesis 6–9). But it is the divine promise to Abram (Genesis 12:1-3) that unveils something more than a scant keyhole perspective. "In you all the families of the earth will be blessed" (12:3), thereby including both Jews and Gentiles (Genesis 26:2-4; 28:13; Acts 10:34-36; Romans 4:11-12, 16-17; 11:11ff).

God's redemptive plan is sprinkled throughout the Psalms (86:9; 22:27; 66:4; 67:1-2) and the prophets (Isaiah 49:6b; 60:3; 45:22; 52:10; Jeremiah 1:5, 10; 3:17; Jonah 3:10–4:2). Nebuchadnezzar responded to the testimony of Daniel and his three friends (Daniel 4:34-37). Thus, while the Old Testament gives significant focus to God's creation of a covenant-bearing, covenant-witnessing people through whom He would announce and prepare His plan of redemption, one should not lose sight of the fact that His plan of redemption from the beginning includes an invitation to "all the families of the earth" (Genesis 12:3)—that is, people from "every tribe and tongue and people and nation" (Revelation 5:9-10). As one Old Testament scholar explains, "The fact remains that the goal of the Old Testament was to see both Jews and Gentiles come to a saving knowledge of the Messiah who was to come...God's eternal plan was to provide salvation for all peoples."[4]

This divine intention is accentuated in the major events of Christ's earthly life. The incarnation was a *missionary* event (Matthew 1:21; Luke 2:10). The Messiah's death and resurrection is about extending His kingdom to all nations (Luke 24:47; 2 Corinthians 5:19-21). His final instruction to His disciples was to take this good news to the ends of the earth (Matthew 28:16-20; Acts 1:8). The life of Christ reflects the emphasis of the Scriptures—from cover to cover, it is consumed with God's global missionary agenda.

God's Ethnic Priority

God's redemptive plan is intended for all people (2 Peter 3:9). To implement this sovereign design, God charted a plan that would astound the world (1 Corinthians 1:18-31). The offer to all would come through the family of one; the family of Abraham would be given priority.[5]

Priority of Birthright

In ancient times, the firstborn child was dedicated to God (Exodus 22:29) and entitled to a double share of the family inheritance (Deuteronomy 21:17). That Israel as a nation was to be the recipient of this birthright is unveiled in God's covenant with Abram,[6] specifically that it would be through Abram's seed—"*in you* will all the families of the earth be blessed" (Genesis 12:3). God's chosen people would be the channel of His blessing to the world.[7]

Priority of Privilege

Israel was given a unique place of honor in all of history. She was the only one "chosen among all the families of the earth" (Amos 3:2) and given phenomenal blessings (see Psalm 105:18; 147:19-20a; Romans 9:4-5; Ezekiel 16:6, 8, 10-14; 40:34-35; Zechariah 2:8). The leaders of Israel were very cognizant of the privileges given to them (Deuteronomy 4:8; Psalm 147:19-20).

Priority of Responsibility

Responsibilities are always concomitant with privilege and status. And Israel realized that. But they also knew that their standing among the nations was not without obligations; it came with significant spiritual duties. Scripture reveals two of these responsibilities most prominently.

A priest to the nations—representing the nations before God. The Mosaic Covenant not only reaffirmed God's redemptive initiative made with Abram, but it also spelled out the priority His chosen people would have in its implementation. The preamble to this theocratic constitution (Exodus 19:4-6) specified that Israel was to be "a kingdom of priests." As a nation, Israel was to fulfill a mediatorial function, representing other nations to God.[8] She would be "a people that will occupy among humanity the place fulfilled by the priests within each nation."[9]

From the very outset, both the Abrahamic and Mosaic Covenants reveal that God's eternal design was not restricted to the house of Israel; rather, it was international in scope. How else would the nation of Israel be able to perform her role as a priest to the nations unless God's redemptive grace would extend to other, non-Israelite families of the earth? (Isaiah 2:1-4; 55:5; 60:6; 66:16; Jeremiah 12:15-16; Zechariah 8:20-23; 14:16).

A light to the nations—representing God before the nations. Israel was also created to declare God's greatness and lovingkindness to the nations—something other nations could not do. "Other nations can give no witness for their own impotent deities, but Israel has so much to declare; for the Lord's wonderful works have been done before her and on her behalf."[10] As a result, Abraham (Genesis 12:8; 21:33),

David (Psalm 57:9; 108:3), Jonah (Jonah 1:2; 3:10–4:2), and Solomon exhort their people to live righteously "in order that all the peoples of the earth may know Your name, to fear You" (1 Kings 8:43).

Like a city set on a hill (Matthew 5:14-16), every Jew viewed himself as "a light to those who are in darkness" (Roman 2:19). Furthermore, Israel was to be a forerunner of the Coming One, the One who would be "a light of revelation to the Gentiles, and the glory of Your people Israel" (Luke 2:32). Isaiah prophesied seven centuries earlier that the nations would come to behold the light of His glorious presence (Isaiah 9:2; cf. Isaiah 42:6; 49:6; cf. 60:1, 3). Paul reiterated this in his defense before Agrippa, noting that the Christ "would be the first to proclaim light both to the Jewish people and to the Gentiles" (Acts 26:23; cf. Acts 13:47; 26:18; Philippians 2:15; Colossians 1:12-13; 1 Peter 2:9).

Priority of Chronology/Methodology

The apostle Paul exclaimed that the gospel of Christ "is the power of God for salvation to everyone who believes, *to the Jew first* and also to the Greek" (Romans 1:16; cf. 2:9-10). While the gospel is for all, on the same terms without distinction, yet there is a stated prerogative— "to the Jew first." Historically, Jesus instructed the 12 disciples to go to their fellow Israelites (Matthew 10:6), focusing His evangelistic efforts on "the lost sheep of the house of Israel" (Matthew 15:24). Even after being rejected by His own people, He nevertheless instructed His followers to begin their missionary endeavors in Jerusalem and Judea before launching out into Samaria and the remote parts of the world (Luke 24:47; Acts 1:8).

When the apostle Paul employed the phrase "to the Jew first," he seemed to have something more than mere historical chronology in view. The apostle's use of "first" (*prōton*) requires an essential "priority rather than a sequential order of events." [11] As Wayne Brindle observes: "The promise of the gospel has a special applicability to Israel. Romans 9–11 is sufficient to show this." [12] Douglas Moo concurs:

> [T]he promises of God realized in the gospel are "first of all" for the Jew. To Israel the promises were first given, and

to the Jews they still particularly apply. Without in any way subtracting from the equal access that all people now have to the gospel, then, Paul insists that the gospel, "promised beforehand...in the holy Scriptures" (1:2), has a special relevance to the Jew.[13]

That priority must not be lost in our endeavor to reach the world. Paul's mention of "to the Jew first" was given not only to reflect Christ's instructions to His disciples or to explain Paul's own chronological practice. Nor was he demanding that the gospel be given to the Jew first as a principle of methodology. Rather, "to the Jew first" must be understood from a theological perspective. "Christ's mission to fulfill God's covenants with Israel has theological priority." [14] It is a perspective that ought to pervade our missions perspective.[15]

God's Effectual Plan

From the very beginning, human instrumentality was a central feature of God's plan for reaching the world. The Scriptures exhort God's redeemed people to declare His mercy and grace (cf. Psalms 96:3; 107:1-2; 146:10-12). His redeemed are given the privileged position of being His emissaries (2 Corinthians 5:18, 20). Along with evidences from general revelation, believers are able to be a light to the world both by example and through evangelistic outreach.

Evidences

General revelation is limited in its role, but it does have a place in reaching the world. God planted witnesses of His divine character and being into the physical creation of the universe (Psalm 19; Romans 1:20). The powerful force of this nonverbal communication must not be undersold. God's divine attributes, power, and nature are "clearly seen" and even "understood."

Paul told the Lystrans that God's divine attributes can be seen in the "rains from heaven and fruitful seasons, satisfying your hearts with food and gladness" (Acts 14:17). John Murray adds: "A clear apprehension of God's perfections may be gained from his observable handiwork.

Phenomena disclose the noumena [or, reality] of God's transcendent perfection and specific divinity." [16]

Furthermore, the innermost being of the human heart testifies to that as well (Ecclesiastes 3:11; Romans 2:15). The same was true during Jesus' earthly ministry, where His miracles were designed to attest to His deity (John 5:36; 14:11; 20:31).

Evidences possess evangelistic value and purpose. Though inadequate in and of themselves to generate saving faith, they are instruments used by the Spirit of God to evoke faith.

Example

Closely related to the role of evidences, the life of the believer is to reflect the reality of Christ's redemptive work (Matthew 5:16). Elders are instructed to "have a good reputation with those outside the church" (1 Timothy 3:7). Peter admonished wives to live in such a way before unbelieving husbands so that "they may be won without a word" (1 Peter 3:1-2).

Godly living provides powerful ammunition in every missionary's arsenal. A life of holiness makes the gospel visible, not just audible.[17] Thus Paul exhorts the Philippians to "prove yourselves to be blameless and innocent, children of God above reproach in the midst of a crooked and perverse generation, among whom you appear as lights in the world" (2:15).[18]

That is the essence of Paul's exhortation to the Corinthians: "You are our letter, written in our hearts, known and read by all men; being manifested that you are a letter of Christ...written not with ink but with the Spirit of the living God, not on tablets of stone but on tablets of human hearts" (2 Corinthians 3:2-3). These words were on the heart of Annie Johnson Flint when she penned this poem:

> We are the only Bibles
> The careless world will read
> We are the sinner's gospel,
> We are the scoffer's creed.

We are the Lord's last message
Given in deed and word;
What if the type is crooked?
What if the print is blurred?[19]

Evangelism

A third, and most obvious, element of reaching the world is evangelism (*euangelion*)—"to announce good news." The spectacle of God's creation, the incredible miracles of Jesus' earthly ministry, the holy life of a believer all testify to the character and power of God. But they do not generate redemption or produce reconciliation between God and man. Rather, it is the Word that is the divine catalyst in the regenerative work of the Spirit (1 Corinthians 1:18; John 16:13; 2 Peter 1:16-21).

Effective evangelists not only proclaim the truth of the gospel, they are also characterized by both a passion for reaching the lost and an attitude of prayerfulness.

Passion. Remarkably, evangelism does not begin with preaching; it begins with a heart of passion, as the nature and character of God reveals. As noted earlier, the unredeemed heart does not seek God. Yet God has an unending desire for all people to be saved (1 Timothy 2:4) and passionately pursues them (2 Peter 3:9).[20] This is unique to Christianity. God's passion was so strong that He was pleased to crush His own Son at Calvary (Isaiah 53:10). It was this same passion that motivated Christ to die for us—while we were "sinners" and "enemies" (Romans 5:8, 10; 9:1-3).

Following one of the greatest passages on the sovereignty of God in salvation (Romans 9:6-33), Paul reiterated his strong desire for Israel's salvation (Romans 10:1). His understanding of the sovereignty of God in bringing people to salvation did not undermine his immense yearning and passionate pleading for his kinsmen.

Prayer. In all missionary endeavors, prayer follows closely on the heels of passion. In John 15:16, Jesus connected prayer with missionary endeavors. In Ephesians 6:17-18, the "sword of the Spirit, which is the word of God" is wielded by prayer. Knowing this, Paul added intercessory prayer to his treatise on proclaiming the gospel (Romans 10:1). Because of his intense passion and desire, he was driven to his knees in prayer for the salvation of his kinsmen.[21]

Prayer is not missions; rather, it is a prerequisite to it. Prayer wraps the passion and desire of the missionary's heart within the full acknowledgment that God is sovereign in salvation.

Proclamation. Any missionary endeavor requires preaching the Word. That was Paul's point in Romans 10. In a series of rhetorical questions, he laid out the essence of biblical missions: "How then will they call upon Him in whom they have not believed? How will they believe in Him whom they have not heard? And how will they hear without a preacher? How will they preach unless they are sent?" (Romans 10:14-15).

Proclamation begins with a herald, someone sent on a mission to deliver a message. Sending someone to proclaim the good news of salvation is an essential element of biblical missions and the lifeblood of every healthy church. The apostle John, writing to Gaius regarding missionaries who had visited his church, admonished him: "You will do well *to send them on their way* in a manner worthy of God…Therefore we *ought* to support such men, so that we may be fellow workers with the truth" (3 John 6, 8). Steller observes, "This phrase, 'to send on one's way,' occurs nine times in the New Testament,[22] and each one occurs in a missionary context." [23]

God's Exclusive Power

The Scriptures. The source of power for salvation is centered in the Word of the cross (1 Corinthians 1:18). Being God's emissary requires knowing His Word. Carl Henry explains: "No Christian movement can impact society if its leaders are ignorant of or continually undermining the veracity of and applicability of its charter documents." [24] Any attempt to accomplish the Great Commission without an unequivocal commitment to announce God's instructions is to violate the divine trust and responsibility given to the messenger. It is destined to fail.[25]

The words of the psalmist reinforce the divine power for salvation inherent in the Scriptures. David noted: "The law of the LORD is perfect, restoring the soul" (Psalm 19:7). Only the Word is capable of transforming the soul; it is the only means through which conversion can take place. And remarkably, it comes with a guarantee—it will not return empty (Isaiah 55:10-11).

The Spirit. The Holy Spirit is the catalyst, infusing the preached Word with divine power. Nowhere is that truth more evident than in Ephesians 6:17, where the "sword of the Spirit" is identified as "the word of God."[26] Furthermore, Paul's use of the Greek word *rhema* instead of his usual *logos* suggests that this power of the Spirit extends not just to the written Word but also to the proclamation of the Word as well. Biblical commentator Peter O'Brien explains:

> This sword of the Spirit is identified with "the word of God," a term which in Paul often signifies the gospel. However, he normally uses *logos* ("word") instead of *rhema*, which appears here. The two terms are often interchangeable, but the latter tends to emphasize the word as spoken or proclaimed (as in 5:26). If this distinction holds here, then Paul is referring to the gospel (cf. Rom. 10:17), but stressing the actual speaking forth of the message, which is given its penetration and power by the Spirit.[27]

The Word of God and the Spirit of God go hand in hand; they are inextricably linked (John 16:13; also cf. Galatians 3:3; Titus 3:5; John 3:5; 6:63; 16:8). The Word of God without the Spirit of God is powerless, and the Spirit of God without the Word of God is speechless!

With the Word of God and the Holy Spirit, the missionary's arsenal is fully supplied. Empowered with the Word and the Spirit, the believer is granted "everything pertaining to life and godliness, through the true knowledge of Him" (2 Peter 1:3). Like an arrow launched from a strong hand bears within itself the strength of the archer long after it has left the bow, the Word of God, empowered by the Spirit, will never fail to hit its mark; it is promised perpetual vitality.[28] It cannot be defeated (Isaiah 40:8).

God's End Product

Worship is the epitome of missions, the capstone of God's global agenda. Proclaiming the good news and making disciples reach their ultimate triumph in bringing God glory and worshiping Him. Redemption's inaugural purpose and final achievement is that we should be "to the praise of His glory" (Ephesians 1:12, 14).

God's Every-Person Plea

The central element of Christianity is the proclamation of the gospel. It is the critical component of the Great Commission and sits at the very core of every believer's responsibility. Unless the gospel is shared verbally, it is impossible "to proclaim liberty to the captives and freedom to prisoners" (Isaiah 61:1). Serving as an ambassador of reconciliation (2 Corinthians 5:18-19) in God's kingdom requires proclaiming the good news to those who reside in the kingdom of darkness.

But the freedom to carry out this mandate is not always granted. Fearing terrorist retaliation, governments around the world are increasingly restricting this central feature and obligation of the Christian faith. In numerous countries, even those outside the Islamic world, public evangelism is strictly forbidden. In Greece, for example, any attempt to proselytize is met with arrest and imprisonment. Being instrumental in someone's conversion is a crime. Jordan trumpets its freedom of worship, but does not permit Muslim-background believers, including those from any other country, to attend the local evangelical seminary. Russia's parliament has made attempts recently to pass legislation that would restrict evangelism outside the walls of the church.[29]

And the United States may not be far behind! A growing chorus of individuals in American government has begun substituting the phrase "freedom of worship" for "freedom of religion." At first blush, this change of terminology may seem innocuous. It is not! "Freedom of worship" restricts one's religious activities to the church building, whereas the "freedom of religion" allows for the public proclamation and evangelism. According to the US Commission on International

Religious Freedom, "the new language signals concrete policy implications for religious freedom because *freedom of worship* is 'a much
narrower view' of religious liberties." [30] Public preaching and open-air
evangelism is protected by the principles of the First Amendment. But
this is much more than a First Amendment, freedom of speech issue.
It is a biblical issue. Freedom to publicly declare God's Word is at stake.

> It is vital if we are to understand Paul's gospel and his urgency
> in preaching it to realize that natural revelation leads not to
> salvation but to the demonstration that God's condemna-
> tion is just: people are "without excuse." That verdict stands
> over the people we meet every day just as much as over the
> people Paul rubbed shoulders with in the first century, and
> our urgency in communicating the gospel should be as great
> as Paul's. [31]

The public proclamation of the gospel is an intrinsic part of Christ's
mandate to every believer. Reaching the world is dependent on it. The
Great Commission cannot be obeyed without it.

CHAPTER 12

Compassion Without Compromise

Thinking about Social Justice in Light of the Great Commission

JESSE JOHNSON

How should the church view issues related to social justice? Should believers simply turn a blind eye to cultural ills and injustices? Or should they make social activism a primary focus of their ministry efforts, expending physical and financial resources to support certain causes? This chapter seeks to find a biblical balance—one that encourages Christians to confront injustice with biblical truth without losing sight of their evangelistic responsibility to fulfill the Great Commission.

One obvious effect of sin in a fallen world is the existence of physical poverty. Human suffering caused by poverty is real, ubiquitous, and heart-wrenching. Contributing factors include government corruption, drought, bodily injury, negligence, and even sinful laziness.

The faces of the poor are diverse; there is the image of refugees in war-torn nations, and the picture of the suffering orphan in suburban cities. Some are obviously born into their situation through no fault of their own, and with no real hope of escaping the cycle of poverty. Others—especially in developed nations—have made foolish choices that have catapulted their lives out of control, out of hope, and out of the reach of sympathy.

Ultimately, while suffering is profound, it is also the result of the fact that sin reigns in this world system. Because poverty is ultimately caused by sin, this issue demands a coherent response from those who follow Christ. Yet for various reasons, many Christians often fail to understand their Lord's commands regarding poverty, and by extension the concept of social justice. In general, there has been a failure to implement relief and speak on behalf of the oppressed in a way that is based on biblical principles.

Churches have too often viewed *social justice* as an umbrella term that mandates believers to combat not only poverty, but all manner of systemic wrongs. But in so doing, Christian leaders demonstrate an acute lack of awareness regarding what our Lord teaches about both poverty and sin. By seeing a gospel mandate to wage an unwinnable war, the church commits its resources to battle against flesh and blood (Ephesians 6:12). When Jesus said, "You will always have the poor with you" He was implying that physical poverty cannot be eradicated in the church age (Matthew 26:11). What a contrast with His words in Matthew 16:18: "I will build my church; and the gates of Hades will not overpower it."

There are two primary errors committed when it comes to issues of social justice in the church. The first error is to fail to have compassion on the victims of injustice. The second is to think it is the church's job to eliminate injustice in society. The first error makes too much of sin, the second too little of it. One shows a lack of understanding of the comprehensive nature of the gospel (and the compassion inherent in it), while the other reveals a lack of understanding of the spiritual nature of the gospel (in that it immediately addresses *spiritual problems*, not *social ones*).

In contrast to these errors, the Bible is clear on the issue of how the church is to view the concept of social justice.

Defining *Social Justice*

It is important to note that the very concept of social justice is inherently difficult to define. For some, it is a reference to the lack of justice seen in human slavery, the child-sex trade, and the abortion industry. For others, the concept of social justice is linked to economic patterns, work-force opportunity, income disparity, and even environmental practices.[1]

The result is that too often the term *social justice* simply stands for whatever the cause *du jour* is. Some American politicians view the lack of a national minimum wage as a social justice issue. Others view tax rates, carbon emissions, and reparations to people groups who were historically oppressed as an inherent part of social justice.

This ambiguity is intentional. The modern concept of social justice arose out of a utilitarian philosophy that saw a moral obligation to pursue whatever is generally good for the greatest number of people. Accordingly, utilitarian philosophers argued for forms of wealth redistribution, in which money from the wealthy minority would be used to alleviate the needs of the poor majority. This serves as the foundation for the idea that economic disparity is a form of social injustice.

The very concept of social justice entered modern English through an argument for a form of socialism. But because the issues with which socialism deals vary from generation to generation, the meaning behind *social justice* is necessarily vague. By keeping terms broad enough to include all manner of economic and environmental issues, people can build coalitions around so-called "justice" without ever clarifying what it is, exactly, that they are supporting. The larger the coalition, the more perceived unity there is, but also the less specificity.

Christians should not embrace that kind of ambiguity. The Bible is concerned with justice in the true sense as defined by God, but not with what contemporary culture commonly labels as social justice.

The key difference between the Bible's understanding of justice and the modern concept of social justice is one of perspective. When most people speak of social justice, they use it in reference to *results that are relatively equal*, not to *the process that produces those results*. Thus for the socialist, *outcomes* are the measure of justice. Statistics, like incarceration rates by demographic, or income by nationality, or life expectancy by income, all become markers of so-called social justice. But this is not how God measures justice.

When the Bible speaks about justice in a society, it is never about *outcomes*, but is always about *process*.[2] God declares a society to be just when people have the same access to legal protection, regardless of social class (Leviticus 19:15; Deuteronomy 1:17). Conversely, when a person's income determines their rights or their access to the legal system, a society is unjust (2 Chronicles 19:4-7; Proverbs 24:23; James 2:8-9; 3:17). For example, if the rich can get away with crime because of their power, then there is social injustice. If a person's perceived worth is diminished on the basis of ethnicity or gender, then there is social injustice (cf. Galatians 3:28). But economic inequality itself does not indicate the presence of injustice, because even wealth comes from the Lord (Deuteronomy 8:18; Proverbs 10:22).

Social Justice and Economic Poverty

It is clear that God never intended economic equality in the world outside of Eden. Even Cain and Abel had different abilities, resources, and wealth. God never commands Christians to pursue equal economic outcomes in the world—or for that matter, in the church. That is a good thing, because the church would be ill-equipped if it were called to restructure national economic systems. It's worth noting that many of the fads inspired by social justice advocates in the past, in reality, turned out to harm the societies they intended to help. The sending of used T-shirts to Africa, or cash donations to Haiti, or fair-trade coffee from Central America. All of these initiatives were designed to help, but in hindsight actually hurt the economic development of those nations.[3]

So when defining social injustice, it is essential to focus on *the legal processes* in society, not on *financial outcomes*. But that doesn't mean that economic realities are disconnected from systemic injustice. On the contrary, it is often the poor who are the most victimized by real injustice. It is the poor who are shut out of legal systems (Exodus 23:3; James 2:6). It is the quest for wealth that causes people to exploit others through injustices such as sex trafficking and prostitution (Job 24:10, 14). Jeremiah 5:26-27 connects slave trading to the sinful desire for worldly wealth and power. In the American context, the injustices of segregation and systemic racism are residual evidences of a culture built on the backs of dehumanization engrained through slavery. Tragically, previous generations of American slave owners traded justice for monetary gain, an exchange for which our culture still bears scars.

In contrast, a just culture is one in which people are not stolen for wealth (Jeremiah 5:26-27; 1 Timothy 1:10). A just culture does not exploit the poor (Deuteronomy 24:14; cf. Isaiah 3:5; 58:3). A just culture protects the innocent and values their lives (Deuteronomy 19:10, Proverbs 6:1; Jeremiah 7:6; Joel 3:19). A just culture has both rich and poor, but it does not show favoritism to either group (James 2:9).

Social Justice and the Mission of the Church

Jesus gave His church clear marching orders. Christians are to go into all the world, preaching the gospel, baptizing, and making disciples of all the nations (Matthew 28:19-20). We are to send missionaries who plant churches, and we are to labor among the sheep until Christ is fully formed in us (Titus 1:5; cf. Colossians 4:12; 1 Timothy 3:15). This is *the* mission of the church. God is our general, our master, and our Father. We are His soldiers, His servants, and His children. To be distracted from our evangelistic mission is a dereliction of duty, and brings shame to our Lord (2 Timothy 2:4).

When the church gets sidetracked by social policy, politics, or even simple community functions, it is generally evangelism that suffers. There are a finite number of hours in the day and dollars in the budget; when they get spent on efforts that are not sanctioned by our Lord, they are wasted away (Ephesians 5:16). Make no mistake—appeals to pursue social justice *ends* through ecclesiastical *means* are often in conflict with the Great Commission.

Consider the example of the apostles in Acts 6, who said it was "not desirable" for them to leave the study of God's Word in order to distribute food to widows within the church (Acts 6:1-2). Or, note Paul's instruction to Timothy regarding widows. For a widow to receive aid from the church, she had to meet express criteria so that the church would not be using their resources merely as a social aid (1 Timothy 5:3-16). In both of these examples, the point is not that Christian widows should be ignored. Rather, the point is that they should be helped, *but not as a means of social justice*. Instead, they ought to receive aid as a practical demonstration of the love of Christ for His own body.

This understanding of these passages has informed the church's approach to social justice throughout church history. John Wesley articulated it in a way that still resonates today, asserting that for society to be improved, people need to be saved; so if the church wants to improve society it should do so primarily by advancing the gospel.[4]

Consider how that approach might apply to a historical example. When Christians in eighteenth-century Europe wanted to end the injustice of the slave trade, their best approach was to evangelize both slave owners and slaves. Over time, as the truth of the gospel began to take hold, the evils of slavery were exposed, and those under the influence of Christ (like William Wilberforce) came to positions of authority where they could promote justice and put an end to that wicked enterprise. But the end of slavery was not the ultimate goal—social justice is never the end for the church. The goal was the advancement of the gospel, which works like leaven in a society to advance Christian ethics (Matthew 13:33; 1 Corinthians 5:8).

Such was the example in Paul's letter to Philemon. Philemon was a Christian and a slave owner. The institution of Roman slavery was barbaric and sinful (1 Timothy 1:10). Yet when Philemon's slave, Onesimus, ran away and was later converted, Paul did not command his believing master to release Onesimus. Instead he appealed for Philemon to forgive Onesimus, restore him to fellowship, and then— significantly—"to do even more than what I say" (Philemon 21).

Had Paul viewed the cessation of slavery as his goal, his response to Philemon would have been categorically different. But Paul's agenda was never social or political; it was always spiritual and evangelistic. He preached the gospel, and called those in power to confess faith in Christ. When they did, Paul pressed them to love each other, and to let the influence of the gospel through the power of the Spirit begin to transform their conduct.

We Must Not Be Silent

While social *justice* can be difficult to define, there is clearly such a thing as social *injustice*. In Scripture, that injustice involved the mistreatment and oppression of one's neighbor for the sake of sordid gain.

Modern examples of social injustice would include slavery, sex trafficking, and abortion, all three of which violate the rights and freedoms of their victims for the sake of wealth and power.

As explained above, God has not commissioned the church to end those forms of injustice. Instead, He has sent believers into the world to make disciples of all nations through the proclamation of the gospel. Thus, the church does not have an earthly agenda, but a heavenly one.

At the same time, however, it would be a tragic mistake to conclude that the church should remain *silent* on the issues of the day. While our priority is evangelism, we are also called to be salt in our world (Matthew 5:13). The church ought to function as society's conscience, bringing the truth of God's Word to bear on the culture around us. Hence, Christians ought to use their voice in society to expose the sinfulness of the culture with the light of God's truth (Ephesians 5:11-13).

Because biblical truth transcends culture, Christians are in the unique position to speak to the moral evils in every society. While unbelievers in Greco-Roman culture clung to man-stealing as a political necessity, Paul clearly identified it as a sin (1 Timothy 1:10). When American plantation owners clung to slavery as a cultural way of life, Christians sought to liberate the slaves in both soul and body—by preaching the gospel and by seeking to bring freedom to the South. Today, when U.S. politicians champion the "right" to abortion, the church ought to shine the light of God's Word on the murderous traffic enabled by the government.

The church's primary mission is to evangelize the world. But that does not preclude believers from also being able to confront the sins of the day. We have been given a prophetic voice to declare God's Word. Like the prophets in the Old Testament, our goal is to herald His truth so that sinners might turn from sin and turn to God in worship (1 Thessalonians 1:9).

But worship cannot come about until hearts are broken by the knowledge of sin (Romans 3:9, 20). For evangelism to be effective, we have to bring comfort to the hurting, and we have to shatter the hearts of the proud (Jeremiah 23:29). For lost people to see their sin, the church must call light *light*, and darkness *darkness* (Matthew 4:16; 6:23; Luke 1:79; Acts 26:18; cf. Luke 11:35). Thus, an essential element of the church's evangelistic ministry has to be the public and prophetic denouncement of that which is evil.

Scripture presents an unmistakable hierarchy for what the church is called to do. Our priority is the Great Commission, and we must not compromise in our commitment to the evangelistic responsibility that Christ has given us. But the Great Commission intersects with social justice in two ways: as a *means*, and as a *by-product*. Social justice can be a *means* for gospel proclamation in that as we confront the sin of injustice we are preparing hearts to receive the good news of salvation. It is also a *by-product* of gospel proclamation because as people come to faith in Christ, they repent of their evil motives and practices. Consequently, society is improved when its members desire to practice good deeds that flow from a love for Christ.

An Appeal for Balance

This chapter began by identifying two errors people make regarding social justice and evangelism. One error is to make social justice the primary goal of the church. This error compromises the church's actual mission, evidencing a serious misunderstanding of what God has called the church to do. The second error is to respond without compassion by ignoring the injustices of our day and standing by silently as if those injustices do not matter. Both of these errors fail because they undercut the Great Commission.

If a church were to make social change its objective, it would be committing its resources to an impossible task—a task to which it was never called in the first place. Evangelism would suffer, and so would the people's joy. As they attempted to labor uphill, their disposition would be at the mercy of cultural and political swings, which are out of their control. On the other hand, if the people in a church ignore the issues of sin in their culture, they not only neglect a powerful evangelistic tool, but their silence will inevitably be interpreted as a lack of compassion, courage, and conviction.

Here is a practical example: The social justice issue of our generation is abortion. Nearly one million abortions occur annually in the United States, many of which are performed by unregulated clinics that are funded by tax dollars. The standard of care is so poor that hundreds of mothers, in addition to the hundreds of thousands of babies, die during the procedures.[5] All of this death is legally tolerated because those in our culture—from politicians to members of the media—fuel the lie that for women to be truly powerful they must be able to kill the truly powerless.

Abortion is rooted in economics ("I need more money before I can properly be a parent"), pride ("I have to make something of myself first before I can start a family"), and power ("I don't want to make the commitment to parent"). But the bottom line is that those who are utterly helpless (unborn children) are slaughtered on the altar of self-service. This is certainly the most obvious form of social injustice in our world.

How should churches respond to abortion? The first error would be to make overturning legalized abortion the church's primary objective. That is clearly a noble goal, but it is not the mission of the church; and if the church made it her mission, it would be committing its resources to a political war that it is not commissioned to wage. The joys of the church members would hinge on electoral success, and time would be diverted from the evangelistic responsibility for which God has equipped the church.

The second error would be to ignore the issue of abortion altogether. If a church turns a blind eye to abortion because it is a *social* issue and not a *spiritual* one, that church is also neglecting its God-given mandate. By implication at least, embracing the Great Commission includes embracing the prophetic voice that God has given to the church to shine the light of His Word into the dark shadows of our world. As the church confronts the evils of abortion, along with other forms of sin, it is able to call unbelievers to repentance—offering them the forgiveness made available through the gospel.

This balance is seen in the New Testament. For example, John the Baptist did not advocate for the restructuring of Roman legal institutions, but he openly preached against Herod's illegitimate marriage (Matthew 14:4). The apostle Paul encouraged his readers to submit to governing authorities (Romans 13:1-7), yet when given an audience with political rulers, used his opportunity to call for their repentance and faith in Christ (Acts 26:26-29; Ephesians 6:19-20; 2 Timothy 4:16-17). Similarly, Jesus came as a preacher of the gospel and not a politician advocating social change. Nonetheless, through the preaching of the gospel, He elevated women, shamed those who exploited the poor, and even called the political leaders of His day to repent (Mark 12:41-44; Luke 7:38-39; 10:42; John 19:11).

Jesus called out sin, but labored for faith. He told the woman at the well to believe the gospel and to tell others, and in so doing He freed her from a life of sexual immorality (John 4:16, 29). He did not set out to restructure Israel's taxation system—which was inherently unjust under the Romans—but He preached the gospel to Zacchaeus, who in turn believed and then gave generously to the poor (Luke 19:1-8). When this happened, Jesus did not highlight the advancement of justice, but rather that "today salvation has come to this house" (verse 9).

True social justice is outside of reach this side of heaven. That is not an excuse, but it is the reality of life in a fallen world. One day, the Lord Jesus will return to establish His kingdom. Then the earth will experience true justice. In the meantime, God has not called the church to change the world socially, but rather to turn it upside down with the world-tilting power of the gospel (Acts 17:6).

CHAPTER 13

Fit for the Master's Use

Proclaiming the Gospel from a Platform of Personal Piety

CARL HARGROVE

Nothing does more damage to the church's gospel witness than moral failure in the lives of Christians, and especially Christian leaders. That is why the apostle Paul urged Timothy to pay careful attention to his life and doctrine (1 Timothy 4:16). Paul himself told the Corinthians, "I discipline my body and make it my slave, so that, after I have preached to others, I myself will not be disqualified" (1 Corinthians 9:27). The pursuit of purity and integrity, both in life and in doctrine, is of paramount importance for those who would preach the gospel to others.

The New Testament repeatedly calls believers to pursue holiness, righteousness, and purity. Consider, for example, the apostle Paul's instruction to Timothy: "Have nothing to do with worldly fables fit only for old women. On the other hand, discipline yourself for the purpose of godliness; for bodily discipline is only of little profit, but godliness is profitable for all things, since it holds promise for the present life and also for the life to come" (1 Timothy 4:7-8). Later in that same letter, Paul wrote, "Flee from these things, you man of God, and pursue righteousness, godliness, faith, love, perseverance and gentleness" (6:11).

The apostle Peter similarly called his readers to pursue holiness. He wrote, "As obedient children, do not be conformed to the former lusts which were yours in your ignorance, but like the Holy One who called you, be holy yourselves also in all your behavior; because it is written, 'You shall be holy, for I am holy'" (1 Peter 1:14-16). Speaking of the end of the world, Peter later added, "Since all these things are to be destroyed in this way, what sort of people ought you to be in holy conduct and godliness, looking for and hastening the coming of the day of God, because of which the heavens will be destroyed by burning, and the elements will melt with intense heat!" (2 Peter 3:11-12). A host of other passages could be listed to reiterate this point: The New Testament calls believers to embark on a life of holiness, even as they look forward to the perfection of heavenly glory. To use a term that is not often heard today, they are to be characterized by the pursuit of personal piety.

Properly defined, the word *piety* is a helpful one. It speaks of godliness, devotion, purity, holiness, spiritual discipline, and heavenly mindedness. Though the term can sometimes carry negative connotations (associated with legalism, spiritual pride, isolationism, and even mysticism), that is not the way piety is presented in Scripture, where it denotes a lifestyle of personal holiness and practical righteousness (cf. 1 Timothy 5:4; Hebrews 5:7).

The pursuit of holiness is rightly motivated out of a love for Christ (John 14:15), a desire to please Him in everything (2 Corinthians 5:9), and the anticipation of one day seeing Him face-to-face (1 John 3:2-3). Because this world is not their home, believers are to be a people whose affections, passions, and purposes are not overly invested in this life but the next (Matthew 6:33; Philippians 3:20; Colossians 3:2). But, while seeking to avoid contamination with the world, they are to remain engaged as ambassadors in the marketplace of life, passionately committed to the Savior's commission to reach the lost with the truth of the gospel (Acts 1:8; 1 Corinthians 9:22-23). Piety does not render believers "so heavenly minded as to be no earthly good." Rather, as they "walk by faith, not by sight" (2 Corinthians 5:7), they are able to "run with endurance the race that is set before [them]" (Hebrews 12:1) because their eyes are focused on their Savior (cf. verse 2).

Characteristics of Piety

In order to understand the nature of personal piety, we must first identify some of its distinctive features. First, genuine piety is a work of salvation—godliness is implanted in the believer the moment he comes to faith in Christ (Galatians 2:20; Colossians 1:27). This internal reality is the seed for a life of piety that others may observe (John 17:23; Philippians 2:15; 3:17; 1 Peter 2:12; 3:2).

Second, the pursuit of personal piety begins with private communion with God and the practice of spiritual disciplines (cf. 1 Timothy 4:7-8; 1 Peter 2:1-3). As Robert Murray M'Cheyne rightly observed, "What a man is alone on his knees before God, that he is, and no more."[1] The truth of that statement should resonate with every believer who desires to grow in godliness.

Third, true piety must be observable in the life of the local church and its leadership. Paul's words to Timothy make it abundantly clear: "Let no one look down on your youthfulness, but rather in speech, conduct, love, faith and purity, show yourself an example of those who believe" (1 Timothy 4:12).

Fourth, piety must not be quarantined within the walls of the local church. It must also be evident in public life. Elders and congregants must possess a reputation with those in the world in which they come and go for daily life (Philippians 2:14; 1 Timothy 3:7; 1 Peter 1:15; 2:12). Believers are called to be a light to the world (Matthew 5:14). As they proclaim the words of the gospel, they do so from a platform of personal piety. If their lives do not match with their message, they will have no credibility as heralds of the gospel.

The Need for Piety

Even a quick survey of the contemporary evangelical landscape reveals a church in which the divorce rate is nearly the same as the world's, financial gain defines spiritual success, and leaders at every level live in contradiction to God's moral qualifications. Sadly, pastoral impropriety has become an expected headline instead of a shock. And failures in leadership have had a trickle-down effect: as the shepherd goes, so go the sheep. This reality is painfully true on a daily basis in the church, where members must deal with the consequences of leaders who have lost their way. In some manner, we are like the people of

Judah during the preaching of Jeremiah: "My people have become lost sheep; their shepherds have led them astray. They have made them turn aside on the mountains; they have gone along from mountain to hill and have forgotten their resting place" (Jeremiah 50:6).

In a culture where the pursuit of popularity and the practice of pastoral pragmatism threaten to replace personal holiness, the time has never been more urgent for the church and its leaders to make godliness a priority. To quote from M'Cheyne again, "It is not great talents God blesses so much as great likeness to Jesus."[2] True piety—the kind that God blesses—exhibits several characteristics, which might be expressed in the following ways: vision, love, purity, and prayer. While not an exhaustive list, these four categories provide markers for personal reflection and application.

Vision: A High View of God

A vision of God fuels godliness. It motivates a passion to live the genuine Christian life. I remember the first time I read *The Valley of Vision*, a collection of Puritan prayers and devotional writings, nearly 30 years ago.[3] I was immediately impressed with how sensitive the Puritans were to the reality of their sin. That sensitivity was fueled by a high view of God and His holiness, which in turn created a hatred for their own sinfulness. That same attitude is desperately needed in the church today. This perspective motivated the apostle Paul to describe himself as the worst of sinners while basking in the all-sufficient work of Christ (1 Timothy 1:15-16). However, this can only happen as we have a high view of the God we serve.

In Psalm 27:4, David wrote, "One thing I have asked from the LORD, that I shall seek: That I may dwell in the house of the LORD all the days of my life, to behold the beauty of the LORD and to meditate in His temple." More than anything else, David wanted to "behold the beauty" of God with a heart of worship. If the church is to recapture piety, it must desire divine beauty. The word "behold" carries the idea of fixation. David would not be satisfied with fleeting glances; he wanted to linger in the greatness of God. Those who would follow his example must take time daily, in the midst of their busy schedules, to set their hearts and minds to meditate on the reality of God's greatness.

Consider Paul's instruction to the believers in Colossae. He called them to seek and to set their minds on things above, where Christ is (Colossians 3:1-2). In other words, they were continually to contemplate the person and work of the Lord Jesus. The preeminent Christ is the solution to the impotent alternatives the false teachers offered (2:6-23). Temptation can be overcome only by focusing on Him, knowing that He is more satisfying than anything this world has to offer. The entire epistle places Christ as the central motivator, example, and means by which believers can live a victorious Christian life. Of the 95 verses in Colossians, 54 make reference to Christ, and 46 of those references occur in 1:1–3:4. This is significant because in Colossians 3:5, Paul transitioned to give his readers practical instruction for Christian living. In Paul's mind, the motivation for putting sin to death and living in God-honoring freedom is an accurate and exalted view of Christ. By considering the person of Christ, the Colossians were then prepared to submit to His precepts. An engaging vision of the Lord Jesus properly motivates a life of piety.

Often, believers fall away in their quest for godliness because they move their gaze away from Christ (cf. Hebrews 12:1-2). The church has gone astray because it is dining on a vision of the passing pleasures of sin instead of savoring the person and work of the Lord Jesus. The pursuit of piety begins by turning our eyes to behold the glory of our heavenly Lord, the only one who can truly satisfy the deepest longings and pangs of our hearts.

Love: An Affection for God and Others

The greatest duty and delight of the believer is to love God and His people. Jesus Himself explained that the foremost commandment is to "'love the Lord your God with all your heart, and with all your soul, and with all your mind, and with all your strength.' The second is this, 'You shall love your neighbor as yourself.' There is no other commandment greater than these" (Mark 12:30-31). In these verses, the Lord identified both the vertical relationship (our love for God) and the horizontal relationships (our love for others) that ought to characterize the life of every believer. When Christians prioritize their walk with God (the vertical relationship), their love for Him manifests itself in the way they interact with and show love to other people (the horizontal relationships). Put simply, the health of our relationships with others is dependent on the health of our relationship with God (cf. 1 John 4:7-12).

Love for God also motivates our pursuit of personal holiness, because love is the proper motivation for obedience. As Jesus told His disciples, "If you love Me, you will keep My commandments" (John 14:15). The apostle John reiterated this truth in his first epistle:

> By this we know that we have come to know Him, if we keep His commandments. The one who says, "I have come to know Him," and does not keep His commandments, is a liar, and the truth is not in him; but whoever keeps His word, in him the love of God has truly been perfected. By this we know that we are in Him: the one who says he abides in Him ought himself to walk in the same manner as He walked (1 John 2:3-6).

Those who love the Lord put Him first in everything. Out of love, they prioritize time spent in communion with Him, being characterized by a burning desire to know Him more deeply. Out of love, they seek to obey His commandments because their greatest ambition is to please Him in all things. And out of love for Him, they demonstrate love for other people, putting them first and seeking to serve them sacrificially. If the church today is to honor God in its pursuit of piety, it must begin by recovering its love for the Lord (cf. Revelation 2:4).

Purity: A Commitment to Personal Holiness

Purity, in both life and doctrine, ought to be a distinguishing mark of all believers. Again, the epistle of 1 John gives us timely words of admonition: "Do not love the world nor the things in the world. If anyone loves the world, the love of the Father is not in him. For all that is in the world, the lust of the flesh and the lust of the eyes and the boastful pride of life, is not from the Father, but is from the world" (1 John 2:15-16). Those who walk in purity are consistently distancing themselves from worldly desires. They fight temptations that seek to draw their fixation from God's beauty to the temporary attractions of the world. And they are sensitive to the varying manifestations of self-importance—pride is ugly to them even when cloaked as strength or conviction. Purity is not a burden for the person who is serious about godliness. There is great joy in discovering the many ways in which God is superior to "all that is in the world." That realization will motivate pure decisions.

Consider some of the ways in which believers ought to pursue purity:

- Purity in thought and action—winning the battle for the mind, and submitting our motives and priorities to the lordship of Christ

- Purity in entertainment—ensuring that our pastimes and pleasures are glorifying to the Lord and in keeping with biblical principles

- Purity in relationships—maintaining dignified and appropriate relationships, especially with members of the opposite sex

- Purity in speech—seasoning our words with the salt of God's grace, using language that is appropriate and honoring to Him

- Purity in ministry aspirations—cultivating a mindset of humility, as a loyal slave, instead of being motivated by selfish ambition and pride

Prayer: A Humble Dependence on the Lord

The call to prayer permeates Scripture. However, as evidenced by survey after survey, many believers fail to make prayer a priority. The Bible contains at least 139 prayers, ranging from expressions of praise to entreaties for the basic needs of life. This wide range of emphasis affords one of life's great privileges, to commune with the God of the universe in a way that is profoundly personal—extolling Him for His greatness, seeking help for daily needs, and standing in the gap for the concerns and cares of others.

Yet I have never met a person who said that they prayed too often or too passionately. Often, the response is, "I know I need to pray more. I feel convicted that I pray too little." Most Christians would agree that a vibrant prayer life produces many benefits, from equipping believers for spiritual battle (Ephesians 6:18-20) to alleviating feelings of worry and anxiety (Philippians 4:6). Yet they still struggle to pray consistently. Why is that? The answer may involve several factors.

First, many have an inadequate view of God. Those who truly understand His greatness as the glorious Sovereign of the universe recognize the high privilege of speaking to Him in prayer. Ironically, many Christians will linger in line to talk to a celebrity or political leader, but they will not take even a few minutes each day for the King of kings. A lofty view of God energizes a person's prayer life because it underscores the privilege afforded the creature to commune with his or her Creator.

Second, many believers do not know how to pray. Like Jesus' disciples, they need to be taught how to pray (cf. Luke 11:1-4). But they need look no further than the Scriptures. By following the pattern of biblical prayers, using the truth of God's Word to inform the words they speak back to God, they can faithfully fulfill their calling to be a praying people (Colossians 4:3; 1 Thessalonians 5:17, 25; 2 Thessalonians 3:1).

Third, some believers do not pray because they have allowed sin to go unchecked in their lives. Consequently, they feel a distance between themselves and God (cf. Psalm 66:18). That distance is removed when they confess their sin to the Lord and repent from it (1 John 1:9).

Fourth, some believers get their priorities turned around. They focus first on ministry tasks rather than prioritizing prayer. Sadly, they feel energized by engaging in ministry tasks, but there is not the same affection for God Himself. This can especially be a temptation for seminary students, who get so caught up in the rigors of theological study that their communion with God is, ironically, displaced by their study about Him.

Fifth, there are times when believers are simply too prideful to pray. Prayer is an act of humility. It is an acknowledgment that we are not sufficient in ourselves, and that we need God to intervene. Whereas pride convinces itself that it can manage on its own, humility falls to its knees in heartfelt dependence, recognizing that it must rely on the Lord for strength.

Believers cannot grow in godliness without the power of God working within them (Philippians 2:12-13). Consequently, for the pursuit of piety to be successful, it must be undergirded by a prayerful dependence on the Lord. Those who neglect the regular practice of prayer should not be surprised to find their spiritual growth significantly stunted.

Piety in Practice: Self-Evaluation

In concluding this chapter, here are a series of questions you can use to evaluate your personal piety:

Do I hunger for God and His Word?

In Psalm 42:1, the psalmist wrote, "As the deer pants for the water brooks, so my soul pants for You, O God." Does that kind of deep longing for God characterize your heart? (cf. Psalms 16:11; 21:6; 43:4). The apostle Peter instructed his readers to desire the Word of God like a newborn baby desires milk (1 Peter 2:1-3). It is through reading and meditating on the Word that we learn about our Savior and see His glory on display. And it is the truth about Christ, revealed in Scripture, that the Holy Spirit uses to mold us into His image (2 Corinthians 3:17-18).

Do I grieve over my sin?

A high view of God not only instills a greater desire to worship Him, it also increases a disdain for sin. Scripture is clear that God hates sin and executes judgment against sinners. Yet many in the church today ignore sin and react negatively toward those who preach against it. Privately, they glibly excuse worldly habits and even sinful practices. But those who are growing in Christlikeness take sin seriously, and they take serious measures to deal with it in their lives (cf. Matthew 5:29-30). When they fall, they are quick to confess their sin to the Lord and turn from it in heartfelt repentance.

Am I open to correction?

Those pursuing godliness understand their shortcomings and invite the correction of God's Word, the Spirit, and genuine counselors (Proverbs 11:14; 27:5-6; Hebrews 4:12). They respond in humility, seeing correction as an opportunity to confess sin and grow in spiritual maturity rather than becoming defensive, which is an indication of pride. Consequently, they welcome correction from others, even for seemingly small failures, because they recognize that small areas left untreated can lead to significant failures down the road.

Do I show genuine love to others?

Personal piety is often defined negatively as the avoidance of sin and ungodly behavior. But it is much more than that. Positively, it is the manifestation of our new life in Christ (2 Corinthians 5:17). This new life will evidence itself in the way we treat others, with love and kindness (John 13:34). As noted above, our vertical relationship with God is reflected in our horizontal relationships with one another. Stated another way, our love for other people serves as a barometer of our love for God (cf. 1 John 2:9-11; 3:14-18).

How do I respond when others do me wrong?

One of the greatest demonstrations of piety is a person's response to those who have offended them. A failure to forgive when wronged provides the backstory for some of the most life-shattering events in the church. How many church splits, conflicts, and wounded lives could be avoided if forgiveness had been extended? We are called to forgive "just as" He forgave us (Ephesians 4:32; Colossians 3:13). We are to be patient when wronged (2 Timothy 2:24) and to pray for our enemies (Matthew 5:44). When we respond to the attack of others with humility and gentleness, we follow in the footsteps of our Savior (1 Peter 2:21-24).

Does my life proclaim the truth of the gospel?

Having been saved by God's grace, believers ought to manifest the transforming truth of the gospel not just in what they say, but in how they live. They are to be lights shining brightly in the darkness (Matthew 5:14-16). They are to walk in a manner worthy of the gospel (Ephesians 4:1). And they are to be examples to other Christians of what godliness looks like (1 Corinthians 11:1; Philippians 3:17). Once more, the words of Robert Murray M'Cheyne carry a penetrating conviction and sweet encouragement: "The Christian is a person who makes it easy for others to believe in God." [4]

Those words bring us full circle in considering piety. The pursuit of personal piety has an evangelistic goal—to reflect an image of the Savior in the marketplace of life and allow others to see the glory of His transforming grace. Believers have the opportunity to represent the Lord Jesus Christ to a lost and dying world. Acts 11:26 reveals that the saints were "first called Christians" because they were bound to the One whom they represented.

If you are a follower of Jesus Christ, this privilege is yours. Cherish it, praise Him for it, and seek to serve Him with the utmost of your being. In pursuing a life of personal piety, your behavior will provide a compelling example to fellow believers, while also serving as a powerful witness to those who are lost. Your conduct will bring glory to the Lord Jesus, the One whom you love and long to please. And you "will be a vessel for honor, sanctified, useful to the Master, prepared for every good work" (2 Timothy 2:21).

CHAPTER 14

Global Risk Assessment

Threatening Trends Within Evangelical Missions

MARK TATLOCK

In order to fulfill the Great Commission, the church must send out workers into the harvest. Often, local churches have entrusted these workers to missions agencies, who oversee the sending process and supervise missionary work on the field. But unbeknown to many congregations, a number of dangerous trends are threatening the integrity of evangelical missions agencies. These trends need to be recognized so that church leaders can provide sound counsel to potential missionaries while also investing wisely in missions activities.

The state of the Western missionary enterprise has been threatened by a subtle yet significant philosophical shift over the last 30 years. This shift now threatens to become mainstream within the leadership circles of conservative missionary agencies and seminaries. While most pastors remain committed to preaching the great doctrines of Christ and salvation, they have often entrusted the oversight of the missions enterprise to well-intentioned but uninformed lay leaders and lay committees. These lay leaders are eager to support the missions enterprise, but rarely engage with scholarly missiological literature or conferences. This in turn leaves the church deaf to the leading voices shaping missions strategy, while pastors who possess theological discernment prove negligent in applying that discernment in the stewardship of their own church's missions programs.

At the same time, pastors are failing to stay alert on this front. Changing missions philosophies are being aggressively advanced by liberal seminaries, which now dominate the mission community.

Unsuspecting missions committee chairmen and elders, trusting the leadership of sending agencies through whom they have sent out earlier generations of missionaries, are ill-prepared to recognize and address the subtle changes afoot. In many cases, sound biblical churches are sending their best and brightest church members to join the ranks of missionary teams whose members would not be in agreement with the historic doctrinal views of their association or denomination.

Recently I had the opportunity to engage the full elder board of a large church on this subject. After a rich discussion about the biblical theology of missions, the role of the local church in the sending process, and the intentions of the elders to steward their oversight of their church's mission funding and personnel, I asked them a simple question: If you were to send out a couple from your own congregation to do Bible translation, which sending agency would you refer them to?

Hearing two or three agencies suggested, then I asked them the following questions: What is the basis for your recommendation? Do you as elders agree with the translation philosophy advocated by the current leadership of these agencies? And, how does each agency's philosophy of translation compare with your church's philosophy of Bible translation? To the credit and integrity of these men, they confessed none of them had ever thought about these issues. I could have continued asking about additional related issues, such as their church's view of church planting, indigenous leadership development, mercy ministry, business as missions, urban ministry, refugee ministry, short term missions, and so on.

Having spoken to many churches and missions committees, I have consistently found that very few pastors, elders, or missions committee members are able to articulate a biblically based philosophy of ministry in these categories of missions work. Instead, they trust the leadership of the mission agencies their church's missionaries have worked with historically. Unfortunately, this kind of trust should not be unquestionably extended. Elders are responsible for shepherding their missionaries, which includes possessing and cultivating discernment regarding the biblical soundness of the missions philosophy and strategy of those with whom they partner. Most importantly, this blind trust makes the spiritual lives, biblical convictions, and financial stewardship of their missionaries vulnerable. In many agencies, a subtle transfer of allegiance from a biblical philosophy of missions to a culturally acceptable model of ministry is currently taking place. Hence, church leaders must not be negligent in their role of shepherding the missionaries under their spiritual care.

A few key observations about missiology provide an insight into the shift that began occurring in the late 1980s. First, the discipline of missiology that is now entrenched in most seminaries and Christian universities was untethered from a core curriculum of biblical studies. A robust set of courses in doctrine, Bible interpretation, and exegesis was once required for missionary service. But as disciplines such as sociology, cultural anthropology, linguistics, and diversity studies came to dominate the missions curriculum, those trained in missions were no longer required to study theology, hermeneutics, and biblical languages. Without these foundational courses, missions students are left without a well-constructed biblical grid by which they can assess the influences of secular thinking on their philosophy of ministry.

Second, two major theological strains have been at work shaping today's missions movement: liberalism and Arminianism. Liberalism rejects a high view of the Bible and tends to elevate culture over Scripture as the ultimate authority in matters of knowledge, truth, and faith. This leads to an ecumenical tendency within missiological efforts. The result is an increasing tolerance for other religious systems that undermine the fundamental tenets of the gospel. This tolerant posture gives permission, if not openly advocates, an integration of Christianity with false religions, known as syncretism. In the end, the uniqueness of Christ and His gospel is corrupted by elements of superstitious folk religions, heretical state churches, or bankrupt mainline denominations. Where Scripture fails to reign as the authority, indigenous pastors and their disciples find a diminished lamp to guide them in their search for sound doctrine. Their churches, in turn, take on forms and functions that rarely align with the teachings of the New Testament.

The other dominant strain, Arminianism, is most often propagated by Baptistic ministries that share a key doctrinal flaw. This flaw exists in their anthropology, granting sinners a greater role in initiating and realizing their conversion than Scripture allows. The observable outcome of this flaw is an exaggerated pragmatism that governs most evangelistic, church planting, and Bible translation endeavors. Thinking that missionaries are able to entice, induce, or manipulate unbelievers to respond to the gospel leads to all sorts of "practical" strategies that give very little consideration to New Testament teaching on matters such as the lordship of Christ, separation from the world, or promises of persecution. Instead, Christianity is presented only in terms of man's self-interest. Evangelistic programs promise benefits and blessings keyed to the felt needs or fleshly desires of the lost. Borrowing from American marketing and media strategies, these missionary programs cycle through an endless pursuit of finding the most efficient way to manufacture converts.

While these realities have taken root, a generational transition among Western missionary leaders is occurring. An earlier generation that held its convictions tightly, especially as it related to the Gospel message itself, is being replaced by a younger generation. The earlier generation possessed a common commitment to the distinctiveness of the gospel message, which made the majority of denominational and faith mission agencies more alike than not. This gave assurance to churches that they could trust their young missionaries to these organizations, finding partners and teammates on the field who were more like them than not.

Today, however, the retiring generation of agency leaders is being replaced by those who received their graduate education in missions under liberal and/or Arminian missiologists. While not all schools or professors of missions have yielded to these influences, an increasingly vocal majority have embraced some elements of a heavily humanistic missiology. These leaders tolerate broader agendas and lesser doctrinal precision in their efforts to recruit the newest generation of missionaries. In addition, an increasing number of today's missionary candidates come bearing the marks of their own home churches, which also suffer the weakening influences within the American evangelical church at large.

Trends That Threaten Biblical Missions Efforts

In this changing landscape of missiology, there are five specific trends threatening the integrity of the evangelical missions enterprise. Church leaders who examine and understand the implications of these trends can better guide and counsel those in their church as to how they can either serve or invest in a wise manner.

Trend #1: Liberalization of International Theological Education

Where the church is established and biblical literacy is considered essential for its pastors, theological education emerges as a priority. This has always been true, especially within the annals of the modern missions movement. Many early missionaries, themselves graduates of universities with a strong foundation in theological studies, believed it was both necessary and loving to provide their disciples with a rigorous theological education. It is no wonder then that throughout Asia, Africa, and Europe missionary efforts in evangelism, discipleship, and church planting led to the establishment of seminaries and Bible colleges. Hundreds of such historic seminaries still exist around the world, and many more are being founded.

It can be generally observed that until the early 1980s, most of these institutions were still led and administered by conservative Western missionaries. As the missions movement matured to recognize that Western missionaries must shift their strategy and replace themselves with national leaders, a need was created to provide these national leaders with advanced degrees in order for them to assume the positions of faculty, deans, or presidents of their institutions. This need to provide national leaders with graduate degrees aligned with a growing vision among Western universities and seminaries eager to grow their enrollments while achieving greater cultural diversity among their student bodies. A significant increase in recruiting efforts and scholarships targeting international students became common practice by Western institutions, resulting in a significant number of faithful national church and denominational leaders traveling to the United States, Britain, and Australia to complete their graduate theological education.

As stated earlier, it was in this same window of time that secular humanism and pragmatism came to dominate the Western evangelical church, including its institutions of higher education. Seminaries and universities that had succumbed to these influences were also those most financially well-endowed and generous in terms of providing scholarships to international students. These same institutions were becoming the leading voices in missiology and in essence became first responders to the need for training national leaders. Most international students had come to faith and been discipled through the ministries of conservative missionaries. These conservative missionaries, distanced from their alma maters, had not experienced their theological erosion. And so they encouraged their disciples to come to the West to finish their theological education. This naiveté on the part of both missionaries and nationals eventually resulted in a majority of national leaders having their view of Scripture and historic doctrines questioned by their Western professors.

To the extent Western scholars undermined the faith of these leaders, multiple generations of national leaders adopted biblical skepticism and cultural hermeneutics, accepting liberal interpretations on issues such as the authority of Scripture, charismatic theology, and the role of women in the church. When retiring missionaries passed the mantle of leadership to these returning graduate students, the door for theological compromise was unlocked. Today, one will find the majority of international seminaries started by conservative missions agencies to be doctrinally unrecognizable from what their founders believed. The tragedy is that subsequent generations of national pastors have been trained by these seminaries. This doctrinal decline of historically conservative seminaries and Bible colleges is one of the greatest spiritual injustices perpetuated by the Western church.

Of course, it is important to note that many international students did study at sound schools and serve faithfully at home. In addition, a growing number of pastoral training ministries have arisen to provide biblically solid alternatives to these international seminaries and pose one of the most exciting and most needed opportunities in mission work today.

Trend #2: Hyper-Contextualization

For decades, the missions community has been focused on contextualizing its work. To avoid imposing extrabiblical preferences and practices on national churches, missionaries became self-critical. Missionaries were challenged to carefully assess how biblical mandates must be adhered to within a specific culture while refusing to impose Western cultural practices that have no biblical foundation. This was necessary where legalism and denominational policies that were not biblically supported had prescribed practices for newly evangelized communities of believers.

Over time, expanding theories of contextualization—as taught in Western seminaries—came to be advocated. These expanded theories led to an inversion of authority in determining how biblical truth and practice should be taught by missionaries. With the authority and inerrancy of Scripture under assault, the quest shifted to focus on being tolerant, relevant, and humble. As a result, culture came to be elevated above Scripture as the ultimate authority. And the trajectory for what can be termed *hyper-contextualization* was set. The Insider Movement methodology, increasingly adopted by those evangelizing Muslims, is one of the clearest examples of hyper-contextualization. As explained by Reverend Ayub Edward, a Presbyterian minister from Bangladesh,

> We have come to know that certain methodologies, which are very different from the historic mission methodologies, have started to be applied in Bangladesh. In fact, Bangladesh has become the "experiment field" of these types of methodologies. In the past it was known as the "C5" approach, and now it is more commonly known as the "Insider Movement." When the Insider Movement started working in our country,

its leaders said that a Muslim should not become Christian by identity, but if he believes Jesus as his Savior in his heart, that's all that is necessary. He can continue to practice all Islamic rituals. So by heart he is a Christian or a follower of Jesus, a "messianic Muslim," but externally, he is a Muslim: going to the mosque and praying with Muslims, fasting with the Muslims, sacrificing animals with the Muslims at their special feasts, and also practicing Islamic ethics.[1]

The allusion of the Insider Movement as the "C5 approach" is in reference to the scale of contextualization observed and defined by John Travis. He summarizes this spectrum as follows,

> The C1–C6 Spectrum compares and contrasts types of "Christ-centered communities" (groups of believers in Christ) found in the Muslim world. The six types in the spectrum are differentiated by language, culture, worship forms, degree of freedom to worship with others, and religious identity. All worship Jesus as Lord and core elements of the gospel are the same from group to group. The spectrum attempts to address the enormous diversity which exists throughout the Muslim world in terms of ethnicity, history, traditions, language, culture, and, in some cases, theology. This diversity means that myriad approaches are needed to successfully share the gospel and plant Christ-centered communities among the world's one billion followers of Islam. The purpose of the spectrum is to assist church planters and Muslim background believers to ascertain which type of Christ-centered communities may draw the most people from the target group to Christ and best fit in a given context. All of these six types are presently found in some part of the Muslim world.[2]

Hyper-contextualization, freed from the obligation to recognize the authority of Scripture, has matured into an aberrational mission practice that even Muslim-background believers reject. Most such believers recognize this pragmatic approach is inconsistent with authentic Christianity and is an accommodation based most often on the West's prioritization of personal safety over truth. For former Muslims who have counted the cost of following Christ as Lord, the offensiveness of Western missionaries advocating such accommodations is seen for the error that it is.

Trend #3: Expedited Bible Translation

For many American pastors, the process of Bible translation is quickly recognized as an essential task consistent with New Testament practice. For a disciple to mature, he must be able to read, memorize, meditate on, study, and in time, teach the Word of God.

The earliest of modern missionaries engaged both in teaching converts to read as well as cataloging and constructing alphabets and dictionaries to be used in creating accurate Bible translations. Their ambition was to assure the churches they planted were comprised of "Bereans"—those who were able to discern the faithfulness of their pastor's teaching with the clear language of the Scriptures (see Acts 17:10-11). This legacy in missions is due to the effects of the Reformation, which saw and confronted the abuse of congregations by priests not held accountable by parishioners possessing the Scriptures in an accessible and common language. But again, pragmatism (and hyper-contextualization) have begun to influence the methodology and philosophy currently applied by many Bible translation agencies.

Pragmatism, valuing quantity over quality, makes the noble goal of completing a Bible translation for every spoken language a slave to haste. Passionate statements made by leaders in translation work, such as, "We can complete the work of Bible translation in our lifetime," are compelling. Expediency, though, can begin to inform methodology in the work of translation. Accuracy must not be sacrificed and requires a diligence to understand unwritten languages and cultural meaning. When accuracy is sacrificed for expediency, it will lead to misinterpretations of key biblical doctrines. Adding to this threat to accuracy, today's missionary Bible translators usually hold degrees in linguistics and not biblical studies, and few possess graduate training in the biblical languages. D.A. Carson observes this reality in his critiques of SIL/Wycliffe:

> I am a huge admirer of their work, some of it undertaken in highly challenging circumstances. Some of them are linguistically well trained. But I have to say that rather few of them are trained in exegesis, biblical theology or systematic theology. Very few of them have an MDiv, let alone more advanced training. With rare exceptions, I have not found them to be deep readers of Scripture, with the result that their approaches to translation challenges tend to be atomistic. No one can be an expert in everything, of course—but if I have any hope for this book, it is that some of these diligent and learned workers will begin to see the importance for Bible translation of the considerations I am advancing here, and that more of them will pursue advanced theological training as part of their preparation for a life in translation.[3]

When coupled with the increasing acceptance of hyper-contextualization, biblical accuracy can be sacrificed on the altar of efficiency. Again the Insider Movement serves as an example. Reverend Edwards extends his statements about the concerns with this movement as it relates to Bible translation, stating,

> Since a key principle of the Insider Movement is to give Muslims what they want to hear, that means that if anything in the Bible is negative to a Muslim it should be left out. One of the dominant factors is using the phrase "Son of God" in reference to Jesus, which Muslims don't believe and don't accept. This translation has tried to replace "the Son of God" with "Messiah," and at the same time they also replace the word "Father" with "Guardian."
>
> This has come because of much scholarly study and thinking in the West. Local Bangladeshi people are hired to apply or implement these translations. Some of the guiding

factors coming out of the Insider methodology and translation argue that traditional, existing churches don't have an agenda to reach the Muslims; they see them as being a failure and unsuccessful, so they want to come up with some different ideas to reach Muslims. They also say that the methodologies of the Insider Movement are very effective. In fact, I know two groups of insiders in my country: one who has claimed they have 700,000 believers in their group, and another group claims to have 20 times the amount of followers as all the Protestant churches in Bangladesh. So when they claim these numbers, they want to justify that their methodology and their translation should be accepted.[4]

But truth must not be sacrificed in order to claim success. Clearly, careful consideration must be given to the future of translation work. Those going into this critical ministry must carefully consider how a high view of Scripture should inform their work. Opportunities to reunite theological training and Bible translation must be encouraged.

Trend #4: Rapid Church Planting Movements

Expediency and pragmatism have also led to the propagation of strategies like the rapid church planting movement. Claims of 10,000 or more churches being planted in one year raise serious questions regarding both legitimacy and logistics. Discerning evangelical missionaries who understand that the Great Commission's emphasis is on making mature disciples and not merely converts recognize the importance of establishing solid churches where qualified elders are developed and pastors are accountable for accurately teaching the Word. To hastily plant immature churches that are devoid of sound doctrine or strong spiritual leadership leaves congregants stunted in their spiritual growth and vulnerable to false teaching. Cautions have often been raised, even within conservative missionary circles, about inadequate follow-up for new converts. For those familiar with the common practice of syncretism—where immature converts simply add Christ to an already polytheistic religious worldview, or integrate folk or animistic superstitions into Christian practices such as prayer—rapid church planting poses a significant problem.

Greg Gilbert, in his review of David Garrison's book entitled *Church Planting Movements*, makes the effort to affirm the many good qualities emphasized within the International Mission Board's church planting program. He also helpfully observes the following concern:

> I am left with many unanswered questions from Garrison's description of the IMB vision. Most of those questions have to do with the development of strong leadership in an environment where rapidity is so prized. I worry that the push for speed may be cutting the feet out from under these many churches before they are even started. It is one thing to start a huge number of churches in a short time; it is quite another for those churches to remain healthy and sound witnesses for decades to come. For that, you need solid, well-grounded leadership...My concern is that they all be solidly instructed in the doctrines and beliefs of Christians, and be taught how to rightly divide the Word of truth. One section of the book is particularly disturbing. Garrison writes: "Church Planting Movements are driven by lay leaders. These lay leaders are typically bi-vocational and come from the general profile of the people group being reached. In other words, if the people group is primarily non-literate, then the leadership shared this characteristic...How is a Christian leader supposed to rightly divide the Word of truth if he is illiterate?" [5]

Keeping the emphasis on the critical need for qualified leaders to be developed and trained, Gilbert recommends,

> Let the explosion of new churches slow down for a few years because of a leadership deficit while these men are taught, at the very least, how to read. Otherwise, a decade from now, you will undoubtedly see a thousand indigenous churches with an orthodoxy-deficit. Wouldn't it be worth the time spent to teach these leaders how to read the Bible instead of

planting thousands of churches who claim to have the Bible as their authority but are utterly incapable of knowing what it says?[6]

Trend #5: Post-Colonialism

It has become popular in recent years in political, academic, and ministry contexts to embrace what has been termed *post-colonialism*. Many are advocating for a return to *pre-Constantinianism*, which rejects the concept of *Christendom*. Christendom is seen as the result of Constantine giving Christianity legal status in the Roman Empire by issuing the Edict of Milan in AD 313. (Christianity later became the official religion of the Roman Empire under Theodosius I in AD 380.)

By the time of the Reformation and Enlightenment, the nations of Europe were all characterized as having state churches (Anglican, Catholic, Lutheran, etc.). This historic era of exploration and subsequent colonization (in the fifteenth through early nineteenth centuries) saw the introduction and imposition of these churches upon the "uncivilized" pagans now under a sovereign European crown. This often led to the establishment of false faiths such as Catholicism in the Philippines or Anglicanism in Uganda, where native peoples were baptized in an effort to make them both converts and citizens. Many injustices were suffered throughout the Southern Hemisphere due to the cruel and exploitative practices of despotic governors and viceroys from Western Europe. Today, the memory of those historic injustices is being used both to fuel a sense of strong nationalistic pride and to throw off any semblances of Western influence.

In some places, this nationalistic emphasis has gained footing within churches that wish to do away with the influence of Western missionaries. The wholesale rejection of Western missionaries and their teaching often results in the baby (of biblical truth) being thrown out with the bathwater (of Western culture). Consequently, the influx of anti- or post-colonialism has rendered many national churches vulnerable to error and heresy.

One example of this is the growing popularity of vernacular theologies authored by national church leaders. Their anti-Western reaction, coupled with a weak hermeneutical approach to Scripture, can result in both syncretistic and liberal positions being widely distributed. This nationalistic approach to hermeneutics can be seen throughout the developing world. For example, in his article entitled "What Is African Biblical Hermeneutics?" David Adamo explains that this methodology

> reappraises ancient biblical tradition and African worldviews, cultures and life experiences, with the purpose of correcting the effect of the cultural, ideological conditioning to which Africa and Africans have been subjected in the business of biblical interpretation. It is the rereading of the Christian scripture from a premeditatedly African perspective...The analysis of the biblical text is done from the perspective of an African world-view and culture.[7]

In places where biblical discernment is undeveloped and spiritual resources are limited, these works find a trusting audience. Biblically sound positions and historically orthodox creeds are rejected because of their association with colonial Western powers. Conversely, their writings often reflect the influence of the theologically liberal institutions at which the proponents were trained. Clearly, those who are doctrinally unsound should not be encouraged to write just because they are nationals.

On the other hand, it is essential for national church leaders to write and publish for the benefit of their countrymen. This affirms the sufficiency and authority of Scripture for every people and every culture. The church is not only American or Dutch or German, it is Nigerian and Indian and Brazilian too. Western missionaries must ensure that they in no way convey the cultural superiority of one people group over another. All must be done to lend the biblically sound convictions and resources to their national colleagues and denomination leaders. Every effort must be made to equip and train leaders in every country to lead and serve their churches, guiding them to a full confidence in the authority of Scripture as God's Word to all peoples. A strong and growing development in missions is the authoring of theological resources by national church leaders. This is good and necessary, provided the authors are doctrinally sound.

We end this chapter where it began. If you are a pastor or elder at a local church committed to missionary work, would you be prepared to lead your missions committee in a discussion about which agencies to work with? Would you be able to counsel would-be missionaries about how best to proceed? Below are seven practical recommendations to guide you in developing a more informed pastoral staff and missions leadership team.

Recommendations to Affirm Biblical Missions Efforts

1. Conduct training for elders and lay leaders in the theology of missions.

2. Develop a biblically informed position on the following areas:
   - church planting
   - discipleship
   - evangelism
   - Bible translation
   - pastoral training

3. Define a set of critical questions prospective missionaries should ask sending agencies.

4. Investigate and establish a list of mission agencies with whom your church can partner.

5. Investigate and establish a list of recommended seminaries and Christian universities whose mission programs affirm your church's convictions.

6. Identify the best resources that address current trends in missions for your missions committee to review.

7. Conduct annual training sessions to stay current with new developments within missiology.

CHAPTER 15

To the Praise of His Glory

A Call to Remember the Church's Ultimate Priority

JAMES MOOK

If the church is to be faithful to her Lord, she must not forget the primary reason for which she was redeemed. When Christians lose sight of this ultimate priority, the church inevitably begins to go astray. Hence, this chapter serves as a fitting conclusion to this book because it calls believers to embrace the purpose for which God redeemed the church.

What is the ultimate purpose for the church? Many answers have been proposed. Here is a small sampling from evangelical sources:

- "The purpose of the church is to join people of different backgrounds and talents and provide them training and opportunities for God's work." [1]

- "The purpose of the church is to be the believer's spiritual family...We were not meant to live the Christian life alone; surrounded by the biblical teaching and loving community of the church, together we find our own purpose in life." [2]

- "And when we go to Scripture, what do we find is God's purpose for His church? We find two things, and two things only: God's enduring purpose for His church is to proclaim the Gospel to the unbelieving world, and to build up the saints in sound doctrine...Proclaim the Gospel to the world, and build up the saints in sound doctrine. That's it. Nothing else." [3]

In the 1970s, I was a member of a conservative Presbyterian church in a theologically liberal denomination. In those days, the liberal theologians were saying that the purpose of the church is to engage in societal liberation. The conservatives in the denomination always responded by saying that the purpose is to evangelize the lost in order to win people to Christ.

In the mid-1990s, Rick Warren published *The Purpose Driven Church*.[4] He claimed that the church must balance five purposes (worship, ministry, evangelism, fellowship, and discipleship) with an orientation toward the felt needs of people in the congregation. According to Warren's seeker-sensitive approach, the purpose of the church revolves around methods that appeal to the target audience.

Clearly, a wide spectrum of opinions exist—from social action to personal evangelism to market-driven pragmatism. But what really is the ultimate purpose for the church? To answer that question, we need to look at what the New Testament specifically presents as the church's highest priority.

The Highest Priority: To Glorify God

God has eternally ordained the church to glorify Him, especially through the worship of the redeemed. That this is the church's ultimate priority can be discerned from a number of New Testament passages. For example, in John 4:23-24, Jesus explained that God the Father seeks "true worshipers." Genuine worshipers are those who worship Him "in spirit and truth."

In 1 Peter 2:9, the apostle Peter describes believers as "a chosen race, a royal priesthood, a holy nation, a people for God's own possession" whom God has called "out of darkness into His marvelous light." Peter said that God's purpose in choosing and calling Christians to belong to Him is that they "may proclaim" His "excellencies." God's purpose for Christians, and therefore their duty and destiny, is to praise Him for the wonders of His grace.

Arguably, the most extensive statement of God's ultimate priority for the church is in Ephesians 1:3-14. This text surveys God's eternal plan for the church to glorify Him, with the entire Trinity in mind.

To the Praise of the Glory of the Father's Grace

In Ephesians 1:3-7, Paul explained that God the Father has "blessed" believers with "every spiritual blessing in the heavenly places in Christ" based on His electing choice "before the foundation of the world." The Father "predestined us to adoption as sons" to Himself "through Jesus Christ." This eternal plan was "according to the kind intention of His will." The end goal of the Father's plan is stated in verse 6: "to the praise of the glory of His grace." His ultimate priority for the church is that, having put His infinite grace on display through the plan of redemption, the glory of that grace would be forever praised by His people. For all of eternity in heaven, the redeemed will proclaim the wonders of God's essential glory, especially in response to His grace toward His elect.

To the Praise of the Glory of His Grace, Given Through the Son

Believers are called to praise God for His grace because by His grace He has granted them "redemption" and "forgiveness" in His Son, the Lord Jesus Christ (verses 7-8). This bestowal of grace has an eternal view to the future. As Paul explained, "With a view to an administration suitable to the fullness of the times, that is, the summing up of all things in Christ, things in the heavens and things on the earth" (verse 10).

This future gathering of the redeemed in Christ is assured to them as an inheritance based on the eternal predestination of the Father: "In Him also we have obtained an inheritance, having been predestined according to His purpose who works all things after the counsel of His will, to the end that we who were the first to hope in Christ would be to the praise of His glory" (verses 10-12). Again, the ultimate goal is that God the Father will receive praise from the elect for the glory of His grace in salvation (verse 12). In the future "administration" in "the fullness of the times" (verse 10), believers will praise God's glorious bestowal of His grace on His elect, given to them in and through Christ.

To the Praise of the Glory of His Grace, Guaranteed by the Holy Spirit

The Father's ultimate purpose for the church is that believers would praise the glorious gift of His grace extended to them through the redeeming work of His Son. But the third person of the Trinity is also involved, guaranteeing that God's ultimate purpose for the church will come to fruition (cf. Ephesians 1:13-14). At the point of saving faith, the elect were "sealed" with the Holy Spirit. The concept of sealing here indicates that God owns the redeemed, and the Spirit's presence is a "guarantee," "pledge," "down payment," and "initial installment" of the believer's inheritance (cf. Ephesians 4:30; 2 Corinthians 1:21-22). This sealing occurs at the moment of conversion. It is a permanent, uninterrupted ministry of the Spirit.

The Holy Spirit is given to the elect at the moment of saving faith to guarantee their inheritance will be realized. He ensures that the golden chain of Romans 8:29-30 will not be broken: "For those whom He [God the Father] foreknew, He also predestined to become conformed to the image of His Son, so that He would be the firstborn among many brethren; and these whom He predestined, He also called; and these whom He called, He also justified; and these whom He justified, He also glorified." The Holy Spirit was given as a guarantee that those whom the Father elected and the Son redeemed would receive their heavenly inheritance, including the resurrection of their bodies (Romans 8:23; 2 Corinthians 5:5). In Ephesians 1:14, Paul stated for the third time that the purpose of God's saving activity is "to the praise of His glory." The Father's glory will be praised fully and perfectly when those in Christ, who were sealed by the Holy Spirit, have received the fullness of their inheritance in Him.

So, what is the church's ultimate priority? According to Ephesians 1:3-14, the eternal purpose for which God predestined the church to salvation is that believers might eternally worship Him—to the praise of His glory (verses 6, 12, 14). The Father's glory is specifically manifested through His grace, on account of which He sent His Son to redeem His elect. And having redeemed them, He sent His Spirit to seal them until the reception of their inheritance in Christ is complete. The response of the redeemed, then, is to glorify the Triune God on account of this marvelous work of redemption.

Creation's Chief End

In 1765, Jonathan Edwards wrote *The End for Which God Created the World*. In it, Edwards set forth an excellent case from Scripture showing that God's "last end" for creation is Himself.[5] So God's ultimate priority for creation is that it should manifest Him in His essence, which is His perfections/attributes, and that creatures should worship and praise Him for His glory (His essence) and all the ways in which He manifests His glory by His works.

As His creatures, the praise of the glory of God is our chief end. Consider the following truths, each of which gives us reason to respond to Him in worship.

God is the first and last cause of all things.

God is "the first" and "the last" (Isaiah 44:6; 48:12), and so He is, in Himself, the beginning and end of all things outside Him. He is the "ultimate cause" and the "final cause" of all creation. All things were created "from Him and through Him and to Him" (Romans 11:36; see also Hebrews 2:10).

God acts for His own sake, which is for His glory.

After stating that all things are "from Him and through Him and to Him," Paul said, "To Him be the glory forever" (Romans 11:36). In all His acts, God has manifested His glory so that people will glorify Him, praising Him for His mighty works. God's acts are all God-centered, intended to cause people to exalt Him alone as having glory.

God will regather and redeem Israel for His own glory.

This point will not be found in Edwards, but is derived from a literal interpretation of biblical passages denoting Israel and the church as distinct entities in God's program for the ages. God promised that He would regather Israel as a saved people in their promised land of Canaan. And His motive for this future redemption of the nation of Israel is His own glory.

Psalm 79 reflects the cry of Israel for salvation as an act of vindication in the face of the nations who had invaded and shamed God's nation. The motive for this cry is seen in verse 9: "Help us, O God of our salvation, for the glory of Your name; and deliver us and forgive our sins for Your name's sake." The name represents God's person, so the glory of His name is the glory inherent in His person. In this psalm, the people of Israel cry out for national redemption not for their sake, but to uphold God's glory as revealed in His name. And God will bring glory to Himself by fulfilling His promises to Israel, including the future salvation of the nation (cf. Isaiah 42:8-12; 43:1-7; 44:23; 48:10-11; 49:3; 60:19-21; 61:3; 66:19; Romans 11:26).

God's purpose is to be glorified in the holy lives of Christians.

In the church age, God intends believers to be "sincere and blameless until the day of Christ…to the glory and praise of God" (Philippians 1:10-11). The Holy Spirit uses their spiritual gifts with the strength that He supplies so that "in all things God may be glorified" (1 Peter 4:11).

The one who offers thanksgiving "honors" (or glorifies) God (Psalm 50:23). By "good works" people are caused to "glorify your Father who is in heaven" (Matthew 5:16; see 1 Peter 2:12). By being "strong in faith" in believing God's promise, Abraham was "giving glory to God" (Romans 4:20). Believers are commanded, "Glorify God in your body" (1 Corinthians 6:20). Giving money to God is "for the glory of the Lord" (2 Corinthians 8:19). Scripture repeatedly makes it clear that the duty of believers is to give God glory in everything they do (1 Chronicles 16:28-29; Psalms 29:1-2; 57:5; 69:7-8; 72:18-19; 115:1; Romans 11:36; 16:27; 1 Corinthians 10:31; 2 Corinthians 4:14-15; Galatians 1:4-5; Ephesians 3:21; Philippians 4:20; 2 Timothy 4:18; Hebrews 13:21; 1 Peter 4:11; 2 Peter 3:18; Jude 25; Revelation 1:5-6).

Saints and angels in heaven continually give glory to God.

In heaven, before the throne of God, the seraphim cry, "Holy, holy, holy, is the LORD of hosts, the whole earth is full of His glory" (Isaiah 6:2-3). The angels in heaven "give glory and honor and thanks to Him who sits on the throne" (Revelation 4:9; cf. 5:11-14; 7:11-12), praising

Him as the Creator of all things. They proclaim, "Worthy are You, our Lord and our God, to receive glory and honor and power; for You created all things, and because of Your will they existed, and were created" (Revelation 4:11).

During His earthly ministry, Christ glorified God the Father.

Angels announced that the birth of Christ was to bring "glory to God in the highest" (Luke 2:14). Jesus said that He came to glorify the name of God the Father, climactically through His death, resurrection, and ascension (John 12:27-28; 13:31-32; 17:1-5). The apostle Paul said that Christ "emptied Himself" in becoming incarnate and "humbled Himself" to die on the cross and has been "highly exalted" so that one day "every tongue" will "confess that Jesus Christ is Lord, to the glory of God the Father" (Philippians 2:6-11). Paul's point was that Christ's purpose in accepting His humiliation and subsequent exaltation was to cause all people to glorify God the Father.

God is glorified in the natural world.

God's "splendor" is "displayed" "above the heavens" (Psalm 8:1). God's "glory" will "endure forever" in His created works (Psalm 104:31; cf. 148:13). "The whole earth is full of His glory" (Isaiah 6:3). God's perfections are everywhere manifested in creation.

God states throughout Scripture that His ultimate purpose, His "last end" for the created order, is that it should manifest Him in all His essence, and that people should worship and praise Him for His glory (His essence). The Bible also declares that in all His works in creation, God's purpose is to manifest His perfect attributes.

Psalm 145 is a helpful example to illustrate this point. This passage from the Word of God declares that He is "highly to be praised" because His "greatness is unsearchable" (verse 3), meaning that it cannot be fully searched out by people. The psalm goes on to show how God's greatness consists of His perfect attributes (the essence of His glory, see verses 5, 12), and they are manifested by His mighty deeds and awesome acts (cf. verses 4-6, 9, 12, 17). In this psalm, God's works include His powerful rule ("kingdom") and His merciful provision for those who "call upon Him in truth," "fear Him," and "love Him" (verses 11-20). God's works reveal His goodness (verse 7), grace (verse 8), love (verse 8), mercy (verse 9), power (verses 11-13), and righteousness (verse 17). No wonder this psalm repeatedly resounds with worship and praise to God (verses 1-3, 10, 21), since the point is to motivate God's people to worship Him for His glory manifested in His works.

For the Sake of His Name

As we have seen, God elicits the praises of His people, in response to His mighty works, so that they might glorify Him. This is what Scripture means when it says that God acts "for His name's sake." God's "name" (His reputation, His person) is exalted by Him in creation (Psalms 8:1, 9; 148:13). It is for the glory of His name that He demonstrates His perfect attributes of mercy, grace, righteousness, and faithfulness (1 Samuel 12:22; Psalms 23:3; 25:11; 31:3; 79:9; 109:21; Jeremiah 14:7; 1 John 2:12). God's deliverance of the nation of Israel, both in the past and in the future, is assured because God's name is at stake (cf. Joshua 7:8-9; 2 Samuel 7:23; Psalm 106:8; Isaiah 48:9-10; 63:12; Ezekiel 20:34-38, 42, 44; 29:9-22; 36:21-23; 39:25; Daniel 9:15, 19). God's salvation of the church is also for His name's sake (Acts 15:14; Romans 1:5; 3 John 7; Revelation 2:3). Moreover, it is for the sake of His name that He brings judgment on the wicked (Exodus 9:16; Nehemiah 9:10; Isaiah 64:4; Daniel 4:17; Romans 9:22-23).

Worshipers that the Father Desires

The edification of the saints and the evangelization of the lost are obviously important. But the church's ultimate priority is to praise and worship God for His essential glory as manifested in His mighty works of creation and redemption. As believers gather in local congregations, they must be taught about the character and work of the Triune God as He has revealed Himself in His Word. As noted earlier, Jesus told the Samaritan woman, "True worshipers will worship the Father in spirit and truth" (John 4:23). The clear implication is that worship which is devoid of truth is not true worship. So, it is essential to ground people in the truth about God revealed in the Scriptures.

Romans 12:1-2 indicates that worship consists of far more than singing hymns or praise songs on a Sunday morning. It is a lifestyle that is committed to glorifying God in everything (1 Corinthians 10:31). Whether our worship expresses itself in song (Ephesians 5:19-20), or in a life of loving obedience (Mark 12:29-30), it is motived by a recognition of who God is and what He has done in both creation and redemption.

Worship includes the believer's future hope in Christ. The believer's praise should be filled with confident expectation regarding the full inheritance that awaits those who have placed their hope in Christ (cf. Romans 8:17). Because worship is the primary activity of heaven (cf. Revelation 4–5), to engage in worship here on earth is simply a foretaste of the profound joy that will enthrall the hearts of believers for all of eternity.

The teaching of Scripture is clear: God's ultimate priority for the church is to praise His essential glory in all His perfections as He manifests them in His works. One day, believers will praise Him in His glorious presence without compromise (Revelation 22:3-5). But in this life, we must seek to worship the Triune God in spirit and in truth by responding to His Word concerning His person and work.

If we would be the worshipers that the Father desires, let us cast our eyes on Him in Scripture. Let us become increasingly God-focused by seeking to know Him as He has revealed Himself in His Word. And as we look ahead to the future, let us yearn for the day when our Lord Jesus will break through the clouds, rid us of our indwelling sin, change our bodies to be like His, and free our hearts to delight solely in our great and awesome God—so that for all of eternity we might live to the praise of His glory.

TOPICAL
REFERENCE
GUIDE

Topical Reference Guide

Though not an exhaustive list of relevant Scripture verses, our hope is that this appendix will help guide you in developing right thinking about the following topics:

Authority and Sufficiency of Scripture

Psalm 19:7-11—The law of the LORD is perfect, restoring the soul; the testimony of the LORD is sure, making wise the simple. The precepts of the LORD are right, rejoicing the heart; the commandment of the LORD is pure, enlightening the eyes. The fear of the LORD is clean, enduring forever; the judgments—of the LORD are true; they are righteous altogether. They are more desirable than gold, yes, than much fine gold; sweeter also than honey and the drippings of the honeycomb. Moreover, by them Your servant is warned; in keeping them there is great reward.

Psalm 119:105—Your word is a lamp to my feet and a light to my path.

Isaiah 40:8—The grass withers, the flower fades, but the word of our God stands forever.

Isaiah 66:2—"My hand made all these things, thus all these things came into being," declares the LORD. "But to this one I will look, to him who is humble and contrite of spirit, and who trembles at My word."

Jeremiah 23:29—"Is not My word like fire?" declares the LORD, "and like a hammer which shatters a rock?"

Matthew 5:18—Truly I say to you, until heaven and earth pass away, not the smallest letter or stroke shall pass from the Law until all is accomplished.

Matthew 24:35—Heaven and earth will pass away, but My words will not pass away.

John 17:17—Sanctify them in the truth; Your word is truth.

2 Timothy 3:16-17—All Scripture is inspired by God and profitable for teaching, for reproof, for correction, for training in righteousness; so that the man of God may be adequate, equipped for every good work.

2 Peter 1:2-3, 19-21—Grace and peace be multiplied to you in the knowledge of God and of Jesus our Lord; seeing that His divine power has granted to us everything pertaining to life and godliness, through the true knowledge of Him who called us by His own glory and excellence...So we have the prophetic word made more sure, to which you do well to pay attention as to a lamp shining in a dark place, until the day dawns and the morning star arises in your hearts. But know this first of all, that no prophecy of Scripture is a matter of one's own interpretation, for no prophecy was ever made by an act of human will, but men moved by the Holy Spirit spoke from God.

Care and Compassion

Romans 12:9-21—Let love be without hypocrisy. Abhor what is evil; cling to what is good. Be devoted to one another in brotherly love; give preference to one another in honor; not lagging behind in diligence, fervent in spirit, serving the Lord; rejoicing in hope, persevering in tribulation, devoted to prayer, contributing to the needs of the saints, practicing hospitality. Bless those who persecute you; bless and do not curse. Rejoice with those who rejoice, and weep with those who weep. Be of the same mind toward one another; do not be haughty in mind, but associate with the lowly. Do not be wise in your own estimation. Never pay back evil for evil to anyone. Respect what is right in the sight of all men. If possible, so far as it depends on you, be at peace with all men. Never take your own revenge, beloved, but leave room for the wrath of God, for it is written, "Vengeance is Mine, I will repay," says the Lord. "But if your enemy is hungry, feed him, and if he is thirsty, give him a drink; for in so doing you will heap burning coals on his head." Do not be overcome by evil, but overcome evil with good.

James 1:27—Pure and undefiled religion in the sight of our God and Father is this: to visit orphans and widows in their distress, and to keep oneself unstained by the world.

James 2:15-17—If a brother or sister is without clothing and in need of daily food, and one of you says to them, "Go in peace, be warmed and be filled," and yet you do not give them what is necessary for their body, what use is that? Even so faith, if it has no works, is dead, being by itself.

1 John 3:17-18—Whoever has the world's goods, and sees his brother in need and closes his heart against him, how does the love of God abide in him? Little children, let us not love with word or with tongue, but in deed and truth.

1 John 4:20—If someone says, "I love God," and hates his brother, he is a liar; for the one who does not love his brother whom he has seen, cannot love God whom he has not seen.

Hebrews 13:1-3—Let love of the brethren continue. Do not neglect to show hospitality to strangers, for by this some have entertained angels without knowing it. Remember the prisoners, as though in prison with them, and those who are ill-treated, since you yourselves also are in the body.

Creationism Versus Evolution

Genesis 1:1—In the beginning God created the heavens and the earth.

Genesis 1:24-27—Then God said, "Let the earth bring forth living creatures after their kind: cattle and creeping things and beasts of the earth after their kind"; and it was so. God made the beasts of the earth after their kind, and the cattle after their kind, and everything that creeps on the ground after its kind; and God saw that it was good. Then God said, "Let Us make man in Our image, according to Our likeness; and let them rule over the fish of the sea and over the birds of the sky and over the cattle and over all the earth, and over every creeping thing that creeps on the earth." God created man in His own image, in the image of God He created him; male and female He created them.

Genesis 1:31–2:2—God saw all that He had made, and behold, it was very good. And there was evening and there was morning, the sixth day. Thus the heavens and the earth were completed, and all their hosts. By the seventh day God completed His work which He had done, and He rested on the seventh day from all His work which He had done.

Exodus 20:11—In six days the LORD made the heavens and the earth, the sea and all that is in them, and rested on the seventh day; therefore the LORD blessed the sabbath day and made it holy.

Exodus 31:17—It is a sign between Me and the sons of Israel forever; for in six days the LORD made heaven and earth, but on the seventh day He ceased from labor, and was refreshed.

Nehemiah 9:6—You alone are the LORD. You have made the heavens, the heaven of heavens with all their host, the earth and all that is on it, the seas and all that is in them. You give life to all of them and the heavenly host bows down before You.

Psalm 53:1—The fool has said in his heart, "There is no God." They are corrupt, and have committed abominable injustice; there is no one who does good.

Isaiah 45:11-12, 18—Thus says the LORD, the Holy One of Israel, and his Maker: "Ask Me about the things to come concerning My sons, and you shall commit to Me the work of My hands. It is I who made the earth, and created man upon it. I stretched out the heavens with My hands and I ordained all their host...For thus says the LORD, who created the heavens (He is the God who formed the earth and made it, He established it and did not create it a waste place, but formed it to be inhabited), "I am the LORD, and there is none else."

John 1:1-3—In the beginning was the Word, and the Word was with God, and the Word was God. He was in the beginning with God.

All things came into being through Him, and apart from Him nothing came into being that has come into being.

Acts 17:24-27—The God who made the world and all things in it, since He is Lord of heaven and earth, does not dwell in temples made with hands; nor is He served by human hands, as though He needed anything, since He Himself gives to all people life and breath and all things; and He made from one man every nation of mankind to live on all the face of the earth, having determined their appointed times and the boundaries of their habitation.

Romans 1:20-22—Since the creation of the world His invisible attributes, His eternal power and divine nature, have been clearly seen, being understood through what has been made, so that they are without excuse. For even though they knew God, they did not honor Him as God or give thanks, but they became futile in their speculations, and their foolish heart was darkened. Professing to be wise, they became fools.

Evangelism and the Great Commission

Psalm 105:1—Oh give thanks to the LORD, call upon His name; make known His deeds among the peoples.

Matthew 5:13-16—You are the salt of the earth; but if the salt has become tasteless, how can it be made salty again? It is no longer good for anything, except to be thrown out and trampled under foot by men. You are the light of the world. A city set on a hill cannot be hidden; nor does anyone light a lamp and put it under a basket, but on the lampstand, and it gives light to all who are in the house. Let your light shine before men in such a way that they may see your good works, and glorify your Father who is in heaven.

Matthew 28:18-20—And Jesus came up and spoke to them, saying, "All authority has been given to Me in heaven and on earth. Go therefore and make disciples of all the nations, baptizing them in the name of the Father and the Son and the Holy Spirit, teaching them to observe all that I commanded you; and lo, I am with you always, even to the end of the age."

Romans 1:16-17—I am not ashamed of the gospel, for it is the power of God for salvation to everyone who believes, to the Jew first and also to the Greek. For in it the righteousness of God is revealed from faith to faith; as it is written, "But the righteous man shall live by faith."

Romans 10:9-15—If you confess with your mouth Jesus as Lord, and believe in your heart that God raised Him from the dead, you will be saved; for with the heart a person believes, resulting in righteousness, and with the mouth he confesses, resulting in salvation. For the Scripture says, "Whoever believes in Him will not be disappointed." For there is no distinction between Jew and Greek; for the same Lord is Lord of all, abounding in riches for all who call on Him; for "Whoever will call on the name of the Lord will be saved." How then will they call on Him in whom they have not believed? How will they believe in Him whom they have not heard? And how will they hear without a preacher? How will they preach unless they are sent? Just as it is written, "How beautiful are the feet of those who bring good news of good things!"

1 Corinthians 1:18; 2:14—The word of the cross is foolishness to those who are perishing, but to us who are being saved it is the power of God...But a natural man does not accept the things of the Spirit of God, for they are foolishness to him; and he cannot understand them, because they are spiritually appraised.

1 Peter 3:14-16—Even if you should suffer for the sake of righteousness, you are blessed. And do not fear their intimidation, and do not be troubled, but sanctify Christ as Lord in your hearts, always being ready to make a defense to everyone who asks you to give an account for the hope that is in you, yet with gentleness and reverence; and keep a good conscience so that in the thing in which you are slandered, those who revile your good behavior in Christ will be put to shame.

Gender Roles in Home and Church

Ephesians 5:22-27—Wives, be subject to your own husbands, as to the Lord. For the husband is the head of the wife, as Christ also is the head of the church, He Himself being the Savior of the body. But as the church is subject to Christ, so also the wives ought to be to their husbands in everything. Husbands, love your wives, just as Christ also loved the church and gave Himself up for her, so that He might sanctify her, having cleansed her by the washing of water with the word, that He might present to Himself the church in all her glory, having no spot or wrinkle or any such thing; but that she would be holy and blameless.

Colossians 3:18-19—Wives, be subject to your husbands, as is fitting in the Lord. Husbands, love your wives and do not be embittered against them.

1 Timothy 2:9-15—I want women to adorn themselves with proper clothing, modestly and discreetly, not with braided hair and gold or pearls or costly garments, but rather by means of good works, as is proper for women making a claim to godliness. A woman must quietly receive instruction with entire submissiveness. But I do not allow a woman to teach or exercise authority over a man, but to remain quiet. For it was Adam who was first created, and then Eve. And it was not Adam who was deceived, but the woman being deceived, fell into transgression. But women will be preserved through the bearing of children if they continue in faith and love and sanctity with self-restraint.

Titus 2:3–5—Older women likewise are to be reverent in their behavior, not malicious gossips nor enslaved to much wine, teaching what is good, so that they may encourage the young women to love their husbands, to love their children, to be sensible, pure, workers at home, kind, being subject to their own husbands, so that the word of God will not be dishonored.

1 Peter 3:1-2, 7—In the same way, you wives, be submissive to your own husbands so that even if any of them are disobedient to the word, they may be won without a word by the behavior of their wives, as they observe your chaste and respectful behavior...You husbands in the same way, live with your wives in an understanding way, as with someone weaker, since she is a woman; and show her honor as a fellow heir of the grace of life, so that your prayers will not be hindered.

Harsh Language and Pastoral Propriety

Matthew 15:18-19—The things that proceed out of the mouth come from the heart, and those defile the man. For out of the heart come evil thoughts, murders, adulteries, fornications, thefts, false witness, slanders.

Ephesians 4:29—Let no unwholesome word proceed from your mouth, but only such a word as is good for edification according to the need of the moment, so that it will give grace to those who hear.

Ephesians 5:3—Immorality or any impurity or greed must not even be named among you, as is proper among saints; and there must be no filthiness and silly talk, or coarse jesting, which are not fitting, but rather giving of thanks. For this you know with certainty, that no immoral or impure person or covetous man, who is an idolater, has an inheritance in the kingdom of Christ and God.

Colossians 3:8—Now you also, put them all aside: anger, wrath, malice, slander, and abusive speech from your mouth.

1 Timothy 4:12—Let no one look down on your youthfulness, but rather in speech, conduct, love, faith and purity, show yourself an example of those who believe.

Titus 2:6-8—Likewise urge the young men to be sensible; in all things show yourself to be an example of good deeds, with purity in doctrine, dignified, sound in speech which is beyond reproach, so that the opponent will be put to shame, having nothing bad to say about us.

Headship of Christ over His Church

Matthew 16:18b—[Jesus said,] I will build My church; and the gates of Hades will not overpower it.

Ephesians 1:19-22—These are in accordance with the working of the strength of His [God the Father's] might which He brought about in Christ, when He raised Him from the dead and seated Him at His right hand in the heavenly places, far above all rule and authority and power and dominion, and every name that is named, not only in this age but also in the one to come. And He put all things in subjection under His feet, and gave Him as head over all things to the church, which is His body, the fullness of Him who fills all in all.

Ephesians 4:15-16—Speaking the truth in love, we are to grow up in all aspects into Him who is the head, even Christ, from whom the whole body, being fitted and held together by what every joint supplies, according to the proper working of each individual part, causes the growth of the body for the building up of itself in love.

Colossians 1:16-20—By Him [Jesus Christ] all things were created, both in the heavens and on earth, visible and invisible, whether thrones or dominions or rulers or authorities—all things have been created through Him and for Him. He is before all things, and in Him all things hold together. He is also head of the body, the church; and He is the beginning, the firstborn from the dead, so that He Himself will come to have first place in everything. For it was the Father's good pleasure for all the fullness to dwell in Him, and through Him to reconcile all things to Himself, having made peace through the blood of His cross; through Him, I say, whether things on earth or things in heaven.

Colossians 2:9-10—In Him all the fullness of Deity dwells in bodily form, and in Him you have been made complete, and He is the head over all rule and authority.

Revelation 1:12-20—I turned to see the voice that was speaking with me. And having turned I saw seven golden lampstands; and in the middle of the lampstands I saw one like a son of man, clothed in a robe reaching to the feet, and girded across His chest with a golden sash. His head and His hair were white like white wool, like snow; and His eyes were like a flame of fire. His feet were like burnished bronze, when it has been made to glow in a furnace, and His voice was like the sound of many waters. In His right hand He held seven stars, and out of His mouth came a sharp two-edged sword; and His face was like the sun shining in its strength. When I saw Him, I fell at His feet like a dead man. And He placed His right hand on me, saying, "Do not be afraid; I am the first and the last, and the living One; and I was dead, and behold, I am alive forevermore, and I have the keys of death and of Hades. Therefore write the things which you have seen, and the things which are, and the things which will take place after these things. As for the mystery of the seven stars which you saw in My right hand, and the seven golden lampstands: the seven stars are the angels of the seven churches, and the seven lampstands are the seven churches."

Homosexuality

Genesis 19:4-7—Before they lay down, the men of the city, the men of Sodom, surrounded the house, both young and old, all the people from every quarter; and they called to Lot and said to him, "Where are the men who came to you tonight? Bring them out to us that we may have relations with them." But Lot went out to them at the doorway, and shut the door behind him, and said, "Please, my brothers, do not act wickedly."

Leviticus 18:22-23—You shall not lie with a male as one lies with a female; it is an abomination. Also you shall not have intercourse with any animal to be defiled with it, nor shall any woman stand before an animal to mate with it; it is a perversion.

Leviticus 20:13—If there is a man who lies with a male as those who lie with a woman, both of them have committed a detestable act; they shall surely be put to death. Their bloodguiltiness is upon them.

Deuteronomy 22:5—A woman shall not wear man's clothing, nor shall a man put on a woman's clothing; for whoever does these things is an abomination to the LORD your God.

Matthew 19:4-6 (regarding the properness of heterosexual marriage)—[Jesus] answered and said, "Have you not read that He who created them from the beginning made them male and female, and said 'For this reason a man shall leave his father and mother and be joined to his wife, and the two shall become one flesh'? So they are no longer two, but one flesh. What therefore God has joined together, let no man separate."

Romans 1:26-27—For this reason God gave them over to

degrading passions; for their women exchanged the natural function for that which is unnatural, and in the same way also the men abandoned the natural function of the woman and burned in their desire toward one another, men with men committing indecent acts and receiving in their own persons the due penalty of their error.

1 Corinthians 6:9-11—Do you not know that the unrighteous will not inherit the kingdom of God? Do not be deceived; neither fornicators, nor idolaters, nor adulterers, nor effeminate, nor homosexuals, nor thieves, nor the covetous, nor drunkards, nor revilers, nor swindlers, will inherit the kingdom of God. Such were some of you; but you were washed, but you were sanctified, but you were justified in the name of the Lord Jesus Christ and in the Spirit of our God.

1 Timothy 1:8-11—We know that the Law is good, if one uses it lawfully, realizing the fact that law is not made for a righteous person, but for those who are lawless and rebellious, for the ungodly and sinners, for the unholy and profane, for those who kill their fathers or mothers, for murderers and immoral men and homosexuals and kidnappers and liars and perjurers, and whatever else is contrary to sound teaching, according to the glorious gospel of the blessed God, with which I have been entrusted.

Hope and Confidence in God

Genesis 50:20a—As for you, you meant evil against me, but God meant it for good.

Psalm 42:5—Why are you in despair, O my soul? And why have you become disturbed within me? Hope in God, for I shall again praise Him for the help of His presence.

Psalm 130:5-7—I wait for the LORD, my soul does wait, and in His word do I hope. My soul waits for the Lord more than the watchmen for the morning; Indeed, more than the watchmen for the morning. O Israel, hope in the LORD; for with the LORD there is lovingkindness, and with Him is abundant redemption.

Lamentations 3:21-24—This I recall to my mind, therefore I have hope. The LORD's lovingkindnesses indeed never cease, for His compassions never fail. They are new every morning; great is Your faithfulness. "The Lord is my portion," says my soul, "Therefore I have hope in Him."

Micah 7:7—As for me, I will watch expectantly for the Lord; I will wait for the God of my salvation. My God will hear me.

Romans 8:31, 38-39—What then shall we say to these things? If God is for us, who is against us?...For I am convinced that neither death, nor life, nor angels, nor principalities, nor things present, nor things to come, nor powers, nor height, nor depth, nor any other created thing, will be able to separate us from the love of God, which is in Christ Jesus our Lord.

1 Thessalonians 4:13-14, 18—We do not want you to be uninformed, brethren, about those who are asleep, so that you will not grieve as do the rest who have no hope. For if we believe that Jesus died and rose again, even so God will bring with Him those who have fallen asleep in Jesus...Therefore comfort one another with these words.

1 Timothy 6:17—Instruct those who are rich in this present world not to be conceited or to fix their hope on the uncertainty of riches, but on God, who richly supplies us with all things to enjoy.

Love, Tolerance, and Truth

John 14:6, 15—Jesus said to him, "I am the way, and the truth, and the life; no one comes to the Father but through Me...If you love Me, you will keep My commandments."

Romans 12:9—Let love be without hypocrisy. Abhor what is evil; cling to what is good.

1 Corinthians 13:6—[Love] does not rejoice in unrighteousness, but rejoices with the truth.

Ephesians 5:2-3—Walk in love, just as Christ also loved you and gave Himself up for us, an offering and a sacrifice to God as a fragrant aroma. But immorality or any impurity or greed must not even be named among you, as is proper among saints.

James 3:17—The wisdom from above is first pure, then peaceable, gentle, reasonable, full of mercy and good fruits, unwavering, without hypocrisy. And the seed whose fruit is righteousness is sown in peace by those who make peace.

1 Peter 1:22—Since you have in obedience to the truth purified your souls for a sincere love of the brethren, fervently love one another from the heart.

2 John 1:4-6—I was very glad to find some of your children walking in truth, just as we have received commandment to do from the Father. Now I ask you, lady, not as though I were writing to you a new commandment, but the one which we have had from the beginning, that we love one another. And this is love, that we walk according to His commandments. This is the commandment, just as you have heard from the beginning, that you should walk in it.

Pastoral Qualifications

1 Timothy 3:1-7—It is a trustworthy statement: if any man aspires to the office of overseer, it is a fine work he desires to do. An overseer, then, must be above reproach, the husband of one wife, temperate, prudent, respectable, hospitable, able to teach, not addicted to wine or pugnacious, but gentle, peaceable, free from the love of money. He must be one who manages his own household well, keeping his children under control with all dignity (but if a man does not know how to manage his own household, how will he take care of the church of God?), and not a new convert, so that he will not become conceited and fall into the condemnation incurred by the devil. And he must have a good reputation with those outside the church, so that he will not fall into reproach and the snare of the devil.

1 Timothy 4:16—Pay close attention to yourself and to your teaching; persevere in these things, for as you do this you will ensure salvation both for yourself and for those who hear you.

2 Timothy 2:15—Be diligent to present yourself approved to God as a workman who does not need to be ashamed, accurately handling the word of truth.

2 Timothy 2:21-26—If anyone cleanses himself from these things, he will be a vessel for honor, sanctified, useful to the Master, prepared for every good work. Now flee from youthful lusts and pursue righteousness, faith, love and peace, with those who call on the Lord from a pure heart. But refuse foolish and ignorant speculations, knowing that they produce quarrels. The Lord's bond-servant must not be quarrelsome, but be kind to all, able to teach, patient when wronged, with gentleness correcting those who are in opposition, if perhaps God may grant them repentance leading to the knowledge of the truth, and they may come to their senses and escape from the snare of the devil, having been held captive by him to do his will.

2 Timothy 4:1-5—I solemnly charge you in the presence of God and of Christ Jesus, who is to judge the living and the dead, and by His appearing and His kingdom: preach the word; be ready in season and out of season; reprove, rebuke, exhort, with great patience and instruction. For the time will come when they will not endure sound doctrine; but wanting to have their ears tickled, they will accumulate for themselves teachers in accordance to their own desires, and will turn away their ears from the truth and will turn aside to myths. But you, be sober in all things, endure hardship, do the work of an evangelist, fulfill your ministry.

Titus 1:5-9—For this reason I left you in Crete, that you would set in order what remains and appoint elders in every city as I directed you, namely, if any man is above reproach, the husband of one wife, having children who believe, not accused of dissipation or rebellion. For the overseer must be above reproach as God's steward, not self-willed, not quick-tempered, not addicted to wine, not pugnacious, not fond of sordid gain, but hospitable, loving what is good, sensible, just, devout, self-controlled, holding fast the faithful word which is in accordance with the teaching, so that he will be able both to exhort in sound doctrine and to refute those who contradict.

1 Peter 5:1-4—I exhort the elders among you, as your fellow elder and witness of the sufferings of Christ, and a partaker also of the glory that is to be revealed, shepherd the flock of God among you, exercising oversight not under compulsion, but voluntarily, according to the will of God; and not for sordid gain, but with eagerness; nor yet as lording it over those allotted to your charge, but proving to be examples to the flock. And when the Chief Shepherd appears, you will receive the unfading crown of glory.

Personal Holiness (Piety)

Leviticus 19:2—Speak to all the congregation of the sons of Israel and say to them, "You shall be holy, for I the Lord your God am holy."

Psalm 139:23-24—Search me, O God, and know my heart; try me and know my anxious thoughts; and see if there be any hurtful way in me, and lead me in the everlasting way.

Matthew 5:29-30—If your right eye makes you stumble, tear it out and throw it from you; for it is better for you to lose one of the parts of your body, than for your whole body to be thrown into hell. If your right hand makes you stumble, cut it off and throw it from you; for it is better for you to lose one of the parts of your body, than for your whole body to go into hell.

2 Corinthians 7:1—Having these promises, beloved, let us cleanse ourselves from all defilement of flesh and spirit, perfecting holiness in the fear of God.

Ephesians 5:3—Immorality or any impurity or greed must not even be named among you, as is proper among saints.

1 Thessalonians 4:3—This is the will of God, your sanctification; that is, that you abstain from sexual immorality.

Hebrews 12:14—Pursue peace with all men, and the sanctification without which no one will see the Lord.

1 Peter 1:14-16—As obedient children, do not be conformed to the former lusts which were yours in your ignorance, but like the Holy One who called you, be holy yourselves also in all your behavior; because it is written, "You shall be holy, for I am holy."

1 John 3:2-3—Beloved, now we are children of God, and it has not appeared as yet what we will be. We know that when He appears, we will be like Him, because we will see Him just as He is. And everyone who has this hope fixed on Him purifies himself, just as He is pure.

Pride and Humility

Proverbs 11:2—When pride comes, then comes dishonor, but with the humble is wisdom.

Proverbs 16:5, 18—Everyone who is proud in heart is an abomination to the LORD; assuredly, he will not be unpunished...Pride goes before destruction, and a haughty spirit before stumbling.

Proverbs 26:12—Do you see a man wise in his own eyes? There is more hope for a fool than for him.

Proverbs 29:23—A man's pride will bring him low, but a humble spirit will obtain honor.

Isaiah 66:1-2—Thus says the LORD, "Heaven is My throne and the earth is My footstool. Where then is a house you could build for Me? And where is a place that I may rest? For My hand made all these things, thus all these things came into being," declares the LORD. "But to this one I will look, to him who is humble and contrite of spirit, and who trembles at My word."

Matthew 23:12—The greatest among you shall be your servant. Whoever exalts himself shall be humbled; and whoever humbles himself shall be exalted.

Romans 12:3, 16—Through the grace given to me I say to everyone among you not to think more highly of himself than he ought to think; but to think so as to have sound judgment, as God has allotted to each a measure of faith...Be of the same mind toward one another; do not be haughty in mind, but associate with the lowly. Do not be wise in your own estimation.

Philippians 2:1-5—If there is any encouragement in Christ, if there is any consolation of love, if there is any fellowship of the Spirit, if any affection and compassion, make my joy complete by being of the same mind, maintaining the same love, united in spirit, intent on one purpose. Do nothing from selfishness or empty conceit, but with humility of mind regard one another as more important than yourselves; do not merely look out for your own personal interests, but also for the interests of others. Have this attitude in yourselves which was also in Christ Jesus.

James 4:6—He gives a greater grace. Therefore it says, "God is opposed to the proud, but gives grace to the humble."

1 Peter 5:5-6—You younger men, likewise, be subject to your elders; and all of you, clothe yourselves with humility toward one another, for God is opposed to the proud, but gives grace to the humble. Therefore humble yourselves under the mighty hand of God, that He may exalt you at the proper time.

Separation from False Teachers

Matthew 7:15-17—Beware of the false prophets, who come to you in sheep's clothing, but inwardly are ravenous wolves. You will know them by their fruits. Grapes are not gathered from thorn bushes nor figs from thistles, are they? So every good tree bears good fruit, but the bad tree bears bad fruit.

Acts 20:28-30—Be on guard for yourselves and for all the flock, among which the Holy Spirit has made you overseers, to shepherd the church of God which He purchased with His own blood. I know that after my departure savage wolves will come in among you, not sparing the flock; and from among your own selves men will arise, speaking perverse things, to draw away the disciples after them.

2 Corinthians 6:14-18—Do not be bound together with unbelievers; for what partnership have righteousness and lawlessness, or what fellowship has light with darkness? Or what harmony has Christ with Belial, or what has a believer in common with an unbeliever? Or what agreement has the temple of God with idols? For we are the temple of the living God; just as God said, "I will dwell in them and walk among them; and I will be their God, and they shall be My people. Therefore, come out from their midst and be separate," says the Lord. "And do not touch what is unclean; and I will welcome you. And I will be a father to you, and you shall be sons and daughters to Me," says the Lord Almighty.

Ephesians 4:14—As a result, we are no longer to be children, tossed here and there by waves and carried about by every wind of doctrine, by the trickery of men, by craftiness in deceitful scheming.

2 Peter 2:1-3—False prophets also arose among the people, just as there will also be false teachers among you, who will secretly introduce destructive heresies, even denying the Master who bought them, bringing swift destruction upon themselves. Many will follow their sensuality, and because of them the way of the truth will be maligned; and in their greed they will exploit you with false words; their judgment from long ago is not idle, and their destruction is not asleep.

2 John 7-11—Many deceivers have gone out into the world, those who do not acknowledge Jesus Christ as coming in the flesh. This is the deceiver and the antichrist. Watch yourselves, that you do not lose what we have accomplished, but that you may receive a full reward. Anyone who goes too far and does not abide in the teaching of Christ, does not have God; the one who abides in the teaching, he has both the Father and the Son. If anyone comes to you and does not bring this teaching, do not receive him into your house, and do not give him a greeting; for the one who gives him a greeting participates in his evil deeds.

Jude 3-4—Beloved, while I was making every effort to write you about our common salvation, I felt the necessity to write to you appealing that you contend earnestly for the faith which was once for all handed down to the saints. For certain persons have crept in unnoticed, those who were long beforehand marked out for this condemnation, ungodly persons who turn the grace of our God into licentiousness and deny our only Master and Lord, Jesus Christ.

Sexual Purity

Job 31:1—I have made a covenant with my eyes; how then could I gaze at a virgin?

Psalm 119:9-11—How can a young man keep his way pure? By keeping it according to Your word. With all my heart I have sought You; do not let me wander from Your commandments. Your word I have treasured in my heart, that I may not sin against You.

Proverbs 6:32—The one who commits adultery with a woman is lacking sense; he who would destroy himself does it.

Matthew 5:27-30—You have heard that it was said, "You shall not commit adultery"; but I say to you that everyone who looks at a woman with lust for her has already committed adultery with her in his heart. If your right eye makes you stumble, tear it out and throw it from you; for it is better for you to lose one of the parts of your body, than for your whole body to be thrown into hell. If your right hand makes you stumble, cut it off and throw it from you; for it is better for you to lose one of the parts of your body, than for your whole body to go into hell.

Romans 6:12-14—Do not let sin reign in your mortal body so that you obey its lusts, and do not go on presenting the members of your body to sin as instruments of unrighteousness; but present yourselves to God as those alive from the dead, and your members as instruments of righteousness to God. For sin shall not be master over you, for you are not under law but under grace

Romans 13:12-14—The night is almost gone, and the day is near. Therefore let us lay aside the deeds of darkness and put on the armor of light. Let us behave properly as in the day, not in carousing and drunkenness, not in sexual promiscuity and sensuality, not in strife and jealousy. But put on the Lord Jesus Christ, and make no provision for the flesh in regard to its lusts.

1 Corinthians 6:15-18—Do you not know that your bodies are members of Christ? Shall I then take away the members of Christ and make them members of a prostitute? May it never be! Or do you not know that the one who joins himself to a prostitute is one body with her? For He says, "The two shall become one flesh." But the one who joins himself to the Lord is one spirit with Him. Flee immorality. Every other sin that a man commits is outside the body, but the immoral man sins against his own body.

1 Thessalonians 4:3-6—This is the will of God, your sanctification; that is, that you abstain from sexual immorality; that each of you know how to possess his own vessel in sanctification and honor, not in lustful passion, like the Gentiles who do not know God; and that no man transgress and defraud his brother in the matter because the Lord is the avenger in all these things, just as we also told you before and solemnly warned you.

Hebrews 13:4—Marriage is to be held in honor among all, and the marriage bed is to be undefiled; for fornicators and adulterers God will judge.

1 Peter 2:11—Beloved, I urge you as aliens and strangers to abstain from fleshly lusts which wage war against the soul.

Trials, Persecution, and Suffering

Matthew 5:10-12—Blessed are those who have been persecuted for the sake of righteousness, for theirs is the kingdom of heaven. Blessed are you when people insult you and persecute you, and falsely say all kinds of evil against you because of Me. Rejoice and be glad, for your reward in heaven is great; for in the same way they persecuted the prophets who were before you.

Acts 5:40-42—After calling the apostles in, [the religious leaders] flogged them and ordered them not to speak in the name of Jesus, and then released them. So they went on their way from the presence of the Council, rejoicing that they had been considered worthy to suffer shame for His name. And every day, in the temple and from house to house, they kept right on teaching and preaching Jesus as the Christ.

Romans 5:2b-5—We exult in hope of the glory of God. And not only this, but we also exult in our tribulations, knowing that tribulation brings about perseverance; and perseverance, proven character; and proven character, hope; and hope does not disappoint, because the love of God has been poured out within our hearts through the Holy Spirit who was given to us.

James 1:2-4—Consider it all joy, my brethren, when you encounter various trials, knowing that the testing of your faith produces endurance. And let endurance have its perfect result, so that you may be perfect and complete, lacking in nothing.

1 Peter 1:6-9—In this you greatly rejoice, even though now for a little while, if necessary, you have been distressed by various trials, so that the proof of your faith, being more precious than gold which is perishable, even though tested by fire, may be found to result in praise and glory and honor at the revelation of Jesus Christ; and though you have not seen Him, you love Him, and though you do not see Him now, but believe in Him, you greatly rejoice with joy inexpressible and full of glory, obtaining as the outcome of your faith the salvation of your souls.

1 Peter 2:20—What credit is there if, when you sin and are harshly treated, you endure it with patience? But if when you do what is right and suffer for it you patiently endure it, this finds favor with God.

Worldliness

Matthew 5:13-16—You are the salt of the earth; but if the salt has become tasteless, how can it be made salty again? It is no longer good for anything, except to be thrown out and trampled under foot by men. You are the light of the world. A city set on a hill cannot be hidden; nor does anyone light a lamp and put it under a basket, but on the lampstand, and it gives light to all who are in the house. Let your light shine before men in such a way that they may see your good works, and glorify your Father who is in heaven.

Matthew 13:22—The one on whom seed was sown among the thorns, this is the man who hears the word, and the worry of the world and the deceitfulness of wealth choke the word, and it becomes unfruitful.

John 17:14-17 (in Jesus' High Priestly prayer)—I have given them Your word; and the world has hated them, because they are not of the world, even as I am not of the world. I do not ask You to take them out of the world, but to keep them from the evil one. They are not of the world, even as I am not of the world. Sanctify them in the truth; Your word is truth.

Romans 12:2—Do not be conformed to this world, but be transformed by the renewing of your mind, so that you may prove what the will of God is, that which is good and acceptable and perfect.

Philippians 3:18-21—For many walk, of whom I often told you, and now tell you even weeping, that they are enemies of the cross of Christ, whose end is destruction, whose god is their appetite, and whose glory is in their shame, who set their minds on earthly things. For our citizenship is in heaven, from which also we eagerly wait for a Savior, the Lord Jesus Christ; who will transform the body of our humble state into conformity with the body of His glory, by the exertion of the power that He has even to subject all things to Himself.

2 Timothy 2:22—Now flee from youthful lusts and pursue righteousness, faith, love and peace, with those who call on the Lord from a pure heart.

2 Timothy 3:1-5—Realize this, that in the last days difficult times will come. For men will be lovers of self, lovers of money, boastful, arrogant, revilers, disobedient to parents, ungrateful, unholy, unloving, irreconcilable, malicious gossips, without self-control, brutal, haters of good, treacherous, reckless, conceited, lovers of pleasure rather than lovers of God, holding to a form of godliness, although they have denied its power; Avoid such men as these.

James 4:4—You adulteresses, do you not know that friendship with the world is hostility toward God? Therefore whoever wishes to be a friend of the world makes himself an enemy of God.

1 John 2:15-17—Do not love the world nor the things in the world. If anyone loves the world, the love of the Father is not in him. For all that is in the world, the lust of the flesh and the lust of the eyes and the boastful pride of life, is not from the Father, but is from the world. The world is passing away, and also its lusts; but the one who does the will of God lives forever.

Worship and Glorifying God

Psalm 29:1-2—Ascribe to the Lord, O sons of the mighty, ascribe to the Lord glory and strength. Ascribe to the Lord the glory due to His name; worship the Lord in holy array.

Psalm 95:1-3, 6-7—O come, let us sing for joy to the Lord, let us shout joyfully to the rock of our salvation. Let us come before His presence with thanksgiving, let us shout joyfully to Him with psalms. For the Lord is a great God and a great King above all gods...Come, let us worship and bow down, let us kneel before the LORD our Maker. For He is our God, and we are the people of His pasture and the sheep of His hand.

Psalm 150:1-6—Praise the LORD! Praise God in His sanctuary; praise Him in His mighty expanse. Praise Him for His mighty deeds; praise Him according to His excellent greatness. Praise Him with trumpet sound; praise Him with harp and lyre. Praise Him with timbrel and dancing; praise Him with stringed instruments and pipe. Praise Him with loud cymbals; praise Him with resounding cymbals. Let everything that has breath praise the LORD. Praise the LORD!

John 4:21-24—Jesus said to her, "Woman, believe Me, an hour is coming when neither in this mountain nor in Jerusalem will you worship the Father. You worship what you do not know; we worship what we know, for salvation is from the Jews. But an hour is coming, and now is, when the true worshipers will worship the Father in spirit and truth; for such people the Father seeks to be His worshipers. God is spirit, and those who worship Him must worship in spirit and truth."

Romans 12:1—I urge you, brethren, by the mercies of God, to present your bodies a living and holy sacrifice, acceptable to God, which is your spiritual service of worship.

1 Corinthians 10:31—Whether, then, you eat or drink or whatever you do, do all to the glory of God.

Philippians 2:9-11—For this reason also, God highly exalted Him, and bestowed on Him the name which is above every name, so that at the name of Jesus every knee will bow, of those who are in heaven and on earth and under the earth, and that every tongue will confess that Jesus Christ is Lord, to the glory of God the Father.

Hebrews 13:15-16—Through Him then, let us continually offer up a sacrifice of praise to God, that is, the fruit of lips that give thanks to His name. And do not neglect doing good and sharing, for with such sacrifices God is pleased.

Revelation 4:9-11—When the living creatures give glory and honor and thanks to Him who sits on the throne, to Him who lives forever and ever, the twenty-four elders will fall down before Him who sits on the throne, and will worship Him who lives forever and ever, and will cast their crowns before the throne, saying, "Worthy are You, our Lord and our God, to receive glory and honor and power; for You created all things, and because of Your will they existed, and were created."

Revelation 5:11-14—I looked, and I heard the voice of many angels around the throne and the living creatures and the elders; and the number of them was myriads of myriads, and thousands of thousands, saying with a loud voice, "Worthy is the Lamb that was slain to receive power and riches and wisdom and might and honor and glory and blessing." And every created thing which is in heaven and on the earth and under the earth and on the sea, and all things in them, I heard saying, "To Him who sits on the throne, and to the Lamb, be blessing and honor and glory and dominion forever and ever." And the four living creatures kept saying, "Amen." And the elders fell down and worshiped.

Contributors

William D. Barrick
Professor of Old Testament
(emeritus), The Master's Seminary

Nathan Busenitz
Dean of Faculty,
The Master's Seminary

Irv Busenitz
Vice President for Academic
Administration,
The Master's Seminary

Abner Chou
Professor of Bible,
The Master's University

Carl Hargrove
Director of Placement and Alumni
Relations, The Master's Seminary

Jesse Johnson
Lead Teaching Pastor,
Immanuel Bible Church

Michael Mahoney
Pastor of Administration,
Grace Community Church

Alex Montoya
Senior Pastor,
First Fundamental Bible Church

James Mook
Associate Professor of Theology, The
Master's Seminary

Tom Patton
Pastor of Congregational Care,
Grace Community Church

Michael Riccardi
Pastor of Local Outreach Ministries,
Grace Community Church

Mark Tatlock
President, The Master's
Academy International

Notes

Chapter 1—When the Church Goes Astray

1. This chapter is derived from a seminar delivered at the 2016 Shepherds' Conference. In putting together the material for this chapter, I am indebted to Dr. Larry Pettegrew, who taught a contemporary evangelicalism class that I took nearly two decades ago. I am also grateful for the work of Iain Murray in *Evangelicalism Divided* (Edinburgh: Banner of Truth Trust, 2000).

2. W. Robert Godfrey, "The Myth of Influence," Westminster Seminary, California (March 31, 2006). Online at: http://wscal.edu/resource -center/resource/the-myth-of-influence. Accessed March 2016.

3. Godfrey, "The Myth of Influence."

4. George Marsden, *Reforming Fundamentalism* (Grand Rapids: Eerdmans, 1987), 13-14.

5. Charles Fuller, as cited in Ken Ellingwood, "Religion's Caltech," *The Los Angeles Times* (October 17, 1997). Online at http://articles.latimes .com/1997/oct/17/local/me-43716/2.

6. Godfrey, "The Myth of Influence."

7. Marsden, *Reforming Fundamentalism*, 250, 52.

8. Murray, *Evangelicalism Divided*, 190.

9. D. Martyn Lloyd-Jones, *What Is an Evangelical?* (Edinburgh: Banner of Truth Trust, 1993), 47-48.

10. Mark A. Noll, *The Scandal of the Evangelical Mind* (Grand Rapids: Eerdmans, 1994), 109.

11. "The church has lost the ability to tell a coherent story about the relationship between its history and convictions and empirical discoveries of the modern sciences. We have lost the credibility of witness even to those who receive [our] charity." See at http://www.biologos.org/blog/the-biologos-foundation-and-darwins-pious-idea/.

12. Murray, *Evangelicalism Divided*, 210.

13. Mark Noll and Carolyn Nystrom, *Is the Reformation Over?* (Grand Rapids: Baker Academic, 2005), 69-70.

14. Cal Thomas and Ed Dobson, *Blinded by Might* (Grand Rapids: Zondervan, 1999), 26-27.

15. Christian Smith, *Christian America?* (Los Angeles: University of California Press, 2000), 1.

16. Godfrey, "The Myth of Influence."

17. Murray, *Evangelicalism Divided*, 58.

18. Cf. Jon M. Sweeney, "Billy Graham and the Catholics," *The Huffington Post* (Nov. 4, 2014). Online at http://www.huffingtonpost.com/jon-m-sweeney/billy-graham-catholics-_b_6100092.html. Accessed October 2016.

19. Billy Graham, as cited from Iain Murray, *Evangelicalism Divided*, 74.

20. David Wells, "Foreword" in *Reforming or Conforming?* eds. Gary L.W. Johnson and Ronald N. Gleason (Wheaton, IL: Crossway, 2008), 11.

21. Mark Dever, "Improving the Gospel: Exercises in Unbiblical Theology," 99-120 in *Proclaiming a Cross-Centered Theology*, eds. Mark Dever, J. Ligon Duncan III, C.J. Mahaney, R. Albert Mohler, Jr. (Wheaton, IL: Crossway, 2009), 109-110.

Chapter 2—Rock-Star Religion

1. Jordan Runtagh, "When John Lennon's 'More Popular Than Jesus' Controversy Turned Ugly," *Rolling Stone* (July 29, 2016), online at http://www.rollingstone.com/music/features/when-john-lennons-jesus-controversy-turned-ugly-w431153. Accessed October 2016.

2. Jake Halpern, *Fame Junkies: The Hidden Truths behind America's Favorite Addiction* (New York: Houghton Mifflin, 2007), 162.

3. "National Church of Bey," online at http://national-church-of-bey.tumblr.com/. Accessed October 2016. It should be noted that some have interpreted this movement as intending to be tongue-in-cheek. But even so, it still illustrates the great lengths to which some people are willing to go in order to elevate their favorite celebrities.

4. Daniel Boorstin, *The Image: A Guide to Pseudo-Events in America* (New York: Harper and Row, 1961), 47.

5. Neil Gabler, "Toward a New Definition of Celebrity," The Norman Lear Center, 2. Online at https://learcenter.org/images/event_uploads/Gabler.pdf. Accessed October 2016.

6. Gabler, "Toward a New Definition of Celebrity," 4.

7. Deena Weinstein and Michael Weinstein, "Celebrity Worship as Weak Religion," *Word & World* 23/3 (Summer 2003), 298.

8. John Calvin, *Commentary on the Epistles of Paul the Apostle to the Corinthians* (Grand Rapids: Baker, 1999), 1:125.

Chapter 3—The Crescent and the Cross

1. Samuel Shahid, "Christianity Vis-à-vis Islam," *Southwestern Journal of Theology* 44/2 (Spring 2002): 73.

2. Len Sherman, "Abandon All Hope: Welcome to Afghanistan" (Zia Home Entertainment, 2001), VHS.

3. A number of books are recommended for those interested in studying more about Islam from a Christian perspective: Frederick Mathewson

Denny, *An Introduction to Islam*, 2nd ed. (New York: Macmillan Collier, 1994). Norman L. Geisler and Abdul Saleeb. *Answering Islam: The Crescent in Light of the Cross*, 2nd ed. (Grand Rapids: Baker, 2002). Bruce Green, *Islam & Christianity* (Torrance, CA: Rose Publishing, Inc., 2013), PowerPoint, handouts, and worksheets.

Chapter 4—When Truth Meets Love

1. This chapter is adapted from Alex D. Montoya, "The Church's Response to Homosexuality," *The Master's Seminary Journal* 19/2 (Fall 2008): 233-248.

2. Tim Wilkins, "Preaching on Homosexuality/Taking the Road Less Traveled," *Preaching* 23/6 (January/February 2008): 13.

3. Cited in Wilkins, "Preaching on Homosexuality," 14.

4. Cf. Stanton L. Jones and Mark A. Yarhouse, *Ex-Gays?* (Downers Grove, IL: InterVarsity, 2007), 16.

5. Mark Christopher, *Same-Sex Marriage: Is It Really the Same?* (Constantia, South Africa: The Voice of Hope, 2007), 44.

6. Horace L. Griffin, *Their Own Received Them Not* (Cleveland: Pilgrim, 2006), 74.

7. Louis P. Sheldon, *The Agenda* (Lake Mary, FL: Frontline, 2005), 9.

8. David Kupelian, *The Marketing of Evil* (Washington, DC: WND Books, 2015), chapter 1.

9. Cited in Sheldon, *The Agenda*, 48.

10. It might be noted that such a lifestyle is most harmful to homosexuals themselves, evidenced by the diseases spread by homosexual on homosexual, and by the emotional and physical harms homosexuals bring on themselves.

Chapter 5—Is This Jesus Calling?

1. Sarah Young, *Jesus Calling* (Nashville, TN: Thomas Nelson, 2011), vii.

2. Young, viii.

3. Young, xi.

4. Young, xi.

5. Young, xi.

6. Young, xii.

7. Young, xiii.

8. Young, xii.

9. Young, xii.

10. Young, January 9.

11. Young, xiv.

12. Young, January 20.

13. Young, January 10.

14. Young, January 26.

15. Young, February 17.

16. Young, March 8.

17. Young, March 16.

18. Young, xiii.

19. Young, xii.

20. Sarah Young, *Jesus Calling*—Women's Edition (Nashville, TN: Thomas Nelson Publishers, 2011), xii.

21. Young, *Jesus Calling*, xiv.

22. Young, xiv.

23. Young, xii. Young is quoting from J.I. Packer, *Your Father Loves You* (Wheaton, IL: Harold Shaw, 1986).

24. Packer, *Your Father Loves You*, 12.

25. Young, *Jesus Calling*, xii, 2004 edition.

Chapter 6—Who's in Charge of Your Church?

1. For example, see Richard S. Cervin, "Does *kephale* Mean 'Source' or 'Authority' in Greek Literature? A Rebuttal," *Trinity Journal* 10 NS (1989):85-112.

2. John Piper and Wayne Grudem, *Recovering Biblical Manhood & Womanhood* (Wheaton, IL: Crossway, 1991) 467-78.

3. Cf. Harold W. Hoehner, *Ephesians, an Exegetical Commentary* (Grand Rapids: Baker Academic, 2002), 290.

4. John Huss, *De Ecclesia* (New York: Charles Scribner's Sons, 1915), 28.

5. Huss, *De Ecclesia*, 29.

6. "13 Christians Everyone Should Know," *Christian History* (Nashville, TN, 2000), 371.

7. From the hymn "A Mighty Fortress Is Our God," written by Martin Luther in 1529.

8. Charles Spurgeon, "The Head of Church," sermon no. 839 delivered on November 1, 1868, by C.H. Spurgeon at the Metropolitan Tabernacle, Newington.

9. William G. Blaikie, *The Preachers of Scotland* (Edinburgh, UK: T. & T. Clark, 1888), 97.

10. Blaikie, *The Preachers of Scotland*.

11. John Stott, as cited from Frank E. Gaebelein, *The Expositor's Bible Commentary* (Grand Rapids: Zondervan, 1981), 12:430.

12. John MacArthur, *Ephesians* (Chicago: Moody, 1986), Ephesians 1:21-23.

13. D. Martyn Lloyd-Jones, *God's Ultimate Purpose: An Exposition of Ephesians 1:1 to 23* (Grand Rapids: Baker, 1979), 420.

14. William H. Goold, ed., *The Works of John Owen* (Edinburgh: Banner of Truth Trust, 1980), 2:70-71.

15. Abraham Kuyper, "Sphere Sovereignty," in *Abraham Kuyper: A Centennial Reader,* ed. James D. Bratt (Grand Rapids: Eerdmans, 1998), 488.

16. Kuyper, "Sphere Sovereignty."

17. David Prince, "Don't Theologize or Spiritualize Ministry Mediocrity," Prince on Preaching (Jan. 28, 2016), online at http://www.davidprince. com/2016/01/28/dont-theologize-or-spiritualize-ministry-mediocrity. Accessed October 2016.

Chapter 7—Nothing But the Truth

1. David Wells, *The Courage to Be Protestant: Truth-Lovers, Marketers, and Emergents in the Postmodern World* (Grand Rapids: Eerdmans, 2008), 1-21.

2. Gerald Hiestand and Todd Wilson, *The Pastor Theologian: Resurrecting an Ancient Vision* (Grand Rapids: Zondervan, 2015), 7-20.

3. Rob Bell, *Love Wins: A Book About Heaven, Hell, and the Fate of Every Person Who Ever Lived*, rep. ed. (New York: HarperOne, 2012). Bell's work is a clear example of how a low view of Scripture leads to a different gospel.

Chapter 8—The Hallmarks of Heresy

1. Albert Mohler, "A Call for Theological Triage and Christian Maturity," online at http://www.albertmohler.com/2005/07/12/a-call-for-theolog ical-triage-and-christian-maturity/. Accessed September 29, 2016.

2. Though *pneuma*, the Greek word translated "Spirit," is grammatically neuter, the apostle John uses a *masculine* pronoun to refer to the Holy Spirit in John 16:8, intentionally employing poor Greek grammar to ensure that his readers accurately understand the theological point: the Holy Spirit is a *person*—a "He" and not an "it."

Chapter 9—The Charismatic Question

1. Parts of this chapter are adapted from Nathan Busenitz, "Addressing the Charismatic Question," *Voice* magazine 91/6 (Nov/Dec 2012): 11-21.

2. Continuationist author Sam Storms expresses the position this way: "When I speak of signs, wonders, and miraculous phenomena available to the church today, I have in mind not the mere potential for rare supernatural activity or surprising acts of providence, but the actual operation of those miraculous gifts listed in 1 Corinthians 12:7-10." C. Samuel Storms, "A Third Wave View," 175-223 in *Are Miraculous Gifts for Today?*, ed. Wayne A. Grudem (Grand Rapids: Zondervan, 1996), 186.

3. For a list of cessationist quotes from leading historical figures, see John MacArthur, *Strange Fire* (Nashville, TN: Thomas Nelson, 2013), 251-261.

4. Continuationist author Wayne Grudem clearly affirms the cessation of apostleship. He writes, "It seems that no apostles were appointed after Paul, and certainly, since no one today can meet the qualification of having seen the risen Christ with his own eyes, there are no apostles today." Wayne Grudem, *Systematic Theology* (Grand Rapids: Zondervan, 1994), 911.

5. As cessationist author Richard Gaffin points out, "Many continuationists are in fact cessationists, in that they recognize there are no apostles today." Richard B. Gaffin, Jr., "A Cessationist View," 25-64 in *Are Miraculous Gifts for Today?*, ed. Wayne A. Grudem (Grand Rapids: Zondervan, 1996), 45. For more on this point, see Samuel E. Waldron, *To Be Continued?* (Merrick, NY: Calvary Press, 2005). Also, see John MacArthur, *Strange Fire* (Nashville, TN: Thomas Nelson, 2013), 85-104.

6. The primary proponent of this two-tier understanding of prophecy is Wayne Grudem. Cf. Wayne Grudem, *The Gift of Prophecy in the New Testament and Today* (Wheaton, IL: Crossway, 2000). Grudem

acknowledges that modern prophecy is fallible and full of mistakes. He writes, "There is almost uniform testimony from all sections of the charismatic movement that prophecy is imperfect and impure, and will contain elements which are not to be obeyed or trusted" (Grudem, *The Gift of Prophecy in the New Testament and Today*, 110). Elsewhere, he acknowledges that modern prophecy is nonauthoritative: "Prophecies in the church today should be considered merely human words, not God's words, and not equal to God's words in authority" (Grudem, *Systematic Theology*, 1055).

7. For example, continuationist author Jack Deere admits that modern prophets are prone to errors and mistakes. He says, "Prophets are really messy. Prophets make mistakes. And sometimes when a prophet makes a mistake, it's a serious mistake. I mean, I know prophets just last year that cost people millions of dollars with a mistake they made. I talked to people who made the wrong investments, actually moved their homes, spent tons of money..." (Jack Deere, National School of the Prophets, "Mobilizing the Prophetic Office," May 11, 2000, 11:30 AM tape #3). Wayne Grudem similarly writes, "[P]rophecy in the Church age is not the word of God [i.e. the Bible], and can frequently contain errors" (Wayne Grudem, "Should Christians Expect Miracles Today? Objections and Answers from the Bible," 55-110 in Gary S. Greig and Kevin N. Springer, *The Kingdom and the Power* (Ventura, CA: Regal Books, 1993), 84.

8. Continuationist author Sam Storms argues that the kind of tongues in Acts 2 was categorically different than the tongues of 1 Corinthians 12–14. He writes, "Acts 2 is the only text in the New Testament where tongues-speech consists of foreign languages not previously known by the speaker" (Sam Storms, *The Beginner's Guide to Spiritual Gifts* [Ventura, CA: Regal Books, 2012], 180). Storms is convinced that passages like 1 Corinthians 14 describe a type of tongues that produced something other than human languages, and that such passages provide the precedent for contemporary charismatic practice. As Storms explains, "There is no reason to think Acts 2, rather than, say, 1 Corinthians 14, is the standard by which all occurrences of tongues-speech must be

judged" (Storms, *The Beginner's Guide*, 180). For a response to Storms's arguments, see Nathan A. Busenitz, "Are Tongues Real Foreign Languages? A Response to Four Continuationist Arguments," *The Master's Seminary Journal* 25/2 (Fall 2014), 63-84.

9. D.A. Carson, who holds continuationist views, articulates the difference between modern tongues and the New Testament precedent. Regarding modern tongues, he writes, "Modern tongues are lexically uncommunicative and the few instances of reported modern xenoglossia [speaking foreign languages] are so poorly attested that no weight can be laid on them" (D.A. Carson, *Showing the Spirit* [Grand Rapids: Baker, 1987], 84). Later, he adds this important delineation: "How... may tongues be perceived? There are three possibilities: [1] disconnected sounds, ejaculations, and the like that are not confused with human language; [2] connected sequences of sounds that appear to be real languages unknown to the hearer not trained in linguistics, even though they are not; [3] and real language known by one or more of the potential hearers, even if unknown to the speaker...[T]he biblical descriptions of tongues seem to demand the third category, but the contemporary phenomena seem to fit better in the second category; and never the twain shall meet" (*Showing the Spirit*, 85). As Carson's explanation rightly demonstrates, the modern gift of tongues does not match the New Testament description of the gift.

10. Thus, continuationist Jack Deere tries to distance modern charismatic "healings" from the biblical precedent. He writes, "It is wrong to insist that the apostolic ministry of signs and wonders is the standard for the gifts of healing given to the average New Testament Christian. We have vivid descriptions of the apostles' ministry in signs and wonders, but apart from the ministry of the apostles there are few if any descriptions of the average Christian who had healing gifts, or examples of how the miraculous gifts operated in the local church. It is simply not reasonable to insist that all miraculous spiritual gifts equal those of the apostles in their intensity or strength in order to be perceived as legitimate gifts of the Holy Spirit" (Jack Deere, *Surprised by the Power of the Spirit* [Grand Rapids: Zondervan, 1993], 66-67). In other words,

Deere recognizes that modern healings simply do not measure up to the healing ministries of Christ and the apostles.

11. Sam Storms illustrates the way that continuationists redefine the New Testament gift of healing so as to distance contemporary charismatic practice from the biblical reality. He writes, "When asked to pray for the sick, people are often heard to respond: 'I can't. I don't have the gift of healing.' But if my reading of Paul [in 1 Cor. 12] is correct, there is no such thing as the gift of healing, especially if it is envisioned as a God-given ability to heal every one of every disease on every occasion. Rather, the Spirit sovereignly distributes a charisma of healing for a particular occasion, even though previous prayers for physical restoration under similar circumstances may not have been answered, and even though subsequent prayers for the same affliction may not be answered. In sum, 'gifts of healings' are occasional and subject to the sovereign purposes of God" (Storms, *The Beginner's Guide to Spiritual Gifts*, 70).

12. For an in-depth discussion of the New Testament gift of prophecy from a cessationist perspective, see Thomas R. Edgar, *Satisfied by the Promise of the Spirit* (Grand Rapids: Kregel, 1996), 52-88. Also see John MacArthur, *Strange Fire*, 105-132. And also the multipart series by David F. Farnell, "Is the Gift of Prophecy for Today?" in *Bibliotheca Sacra*, 1992-1993.

13. For an in-depth defense of cessationist understanding of the gift of tongues, see Thomas R. Edgar, *Satisfied by the Promise of the Spirit*, 120-200. Also see John MacArthur, *Strange Fire*, 133-154. For a look at how the church fathers understood the gift of tongues, see Nathan A. Busenitz, "The Gift of Tongues: Comparing the Church Fathers with Contemporary Pentecostalism," *The Master's Seminary Journal* 17/1 (Spring 2006): 61-78.

14. For a book-length treatment of the gift of healing, see Richard Mayhue, *The Healing Promise* (Fearn, Ross-shire: Mentor/Christian Focus, 2001). Also see, Thomas R. Edgar, *Satisfied by the Promise of the Spirit*, 89-119; and John MacArthur, *Strange Fire*, 155-178.

15. Continuationists often point to James 5:13-16 to support their view

of healing. Cessationists agree that James 5:13-16 is an important passage of Scripture. However, they contend that it describes providential answers to prayer, not the miraculous gift of healing.

16. Cessationist author Thomas Edgar makes this point forcefully: "Modern charismatics also no longer argue for the gifts that were exhibited in the book of Acts by the apostles. They do maintain, however, that the Holy Spirit distributed gifts among believers of the early church, but these gifts were not of the same qualitative level as those of the apostles. They were the same as the charismatic gifts of today, such as gifts of healing that often fail…In other words, 'responsible' charismatics are conceding that the apostolic gifts and the power exhibited in the book of Acts did cease with the apostolic age and are not seen today. They have conceded the basic cessationist argument…The theory of lesser quality or defective gifts not only serves to explain why the charismatic gifts of today do not meet the standards of those in the New Testament, but it also helps to overcome the historical problem. Clearly, the gifts mentioned in the book of Acts did not continue; however, there is more possibility for them to claim that defective gifts such as those in the charismatic movement do occur in history. The charismatic movement gained credence and initial acceptance by claiming their gifts were the same as those in Acts. For most people this is why they are credible today. Yet now one of their primary defenses is the claim that they are not the same. Faced with the facts, they have had to revoke the very foundation of their original reason for existence." Thomas R. Edgar, *Satisfied by the Promise of the Spirit*, 31-32.

17. Some continuationists also appeal to 1 Corinthians 1:4-9. Although gifts (in a general sense) and the return of Christ are both mentioned in this passage (verse 7), the text does not state that the miraculous gifts will be in operation until the Parousia.

18. Douglas Oss argues for this position in "A Charismatic/Pentecostal View," 239-283 in *Are Miraculous Gifts for Today? Four Views*, ed. Wayne Grudem (Grand Rapids: Zondervan, 1996).

19. Cf. Robert L. Thomas, *Understanding Spiritual Gifts* (Grand Rapids: Kregel, 1999), 76–83.

20. Cf. R. Bruce Compton, "1 Corinthians 13:8-13 and the Cessation of Miraculous Gifts," *Detroit Baptist Seminary Journal* 9 (2004), 97-144.

21. Cf. Richard Gaffin, "A Cessationist View," 55.

22. Cf. John MacArthur, *Strange Fire*, 148-149. Also, Thomas R. Edgar, *Satisfied by the Promise of the Spirit*, 243-246.

23. Anthony C. Thiselton, *The First Epistle to the Corinthians*, NIGTC (Grand Rapids: Eerdmans, 2000), 1063, emphasis original.

24. For a more thorough exegetical treatment of Ephesians 2:20, see Thomas R. Edgar, *Satisfied by the Promise of the Spirit*, 76-79.

25. For more on the importance of this passage, see Samuel E. Waldron, *To Be Continued?*, 75-79.

26. Cf. Daniel B. Wallace, "Hebrews 2:3-4 and the Sign Gifts," *Bible. org.* Online at https://bible.org/article/hebrews-23-4-and-sign-gifts. Accessed October 2016.

27. Richard Gaffin, "Where Have All the Spiritual Gifts Gone? A Defense of Cessationism," *Modern Reformation* 10/5 (Sept/Oct 2001), 20-24. Online at http://www.modernreformation.org/default.php?page=artic ledisplay&var2=422. Accessed October 2016.

28. Continuationists often appeal to 1 Corinthians 14:4 to justify using devotional tongues for self-edification. But, in context, it is clear that Paul is not condoning such a practice. Rather, he is correcting it, explaining that prophecy is superior to tongues because it immediately edifies others, whereas tongues requires translation in order to accomplish the intended purpose of edification (verse 5).

29. Thomas Edgar, *Satisfied by the Promise of the Spirit*, 39-40.

Chapter 10—Things That Should Not Be Forgotten

1. This chapter was originally posted as a series of articles on *Preachers and Preaching*, the blog of The Master's Seminary.

2. Carl Trueman, "Teaching Historical Sense to a Sophisticated and Discerning Lady (Aged 7)," *Postcards from Palookaville*, Alliance of Confessing Evangelicals (Jan. 21, 2013). Online at http://www.alliance net.org/mos/postcards-from-palookaville/teaching-historical-sense-to-a-sophisticated-and-discerning-lady-age.

3. John MacArthur, *Matthew 16–23*, The MacArthur New Testament Commentary (Chicago: Moody, 1988), Matthew 16:18.

4. Trueman, "Teaching Historical Sense to a Sophisticated and Discerning Lady (Age 7)."

5. C.S. Lewis, *Mere Christianity* (New York: Macmillan, 1952), 104.

6. If you are interested in in a brief survey of church history, you may be interested in Christopher Catherwood's short book *Church History: A Crash Course for the Curious*. Longer church history textbooks (like the multivolume set by Nicholas R. Needham, *2000 Years of Christ's Power*) can also be excellent places to start. Steven Lawson's *Pillars of Grace* and Gregg Allison's *Historical Theology* are also great resources that approach church history topically.

Chapter 11—To the Ends of the Earth

1. This chapter is adapted from Irv Busenitz, "Reaching the World: God's Global Agenda," *MSJ* 22/2 (Fall 2011), 235-257.

2. Peter Kline, "Is God Missionary? Augustine and the Divine Missions," *Princeton Theological Review* (Spring 2010), XVI:1:32.

3. The ongoing revelation of man as one who flees from and even disdains the presence of God (e.g., Genesis 3:7-8; 4:16) is repeatedly contrasted by God's pursuit of man (e.g., Genesis 3:8-9; 4:9; 12:1-3; Acts 7:2; 9:1-9) and His intervention on man's behalf (e.g., Genesis 3:21, 22-24; 4:15; 6:1–9:17; 11:1-9).

4. Walter C. Kaiser, *Mission in the Old Testament: Israel as a Light to the Nations* (Grand Rapids: Baker, 2000), 10.

5. Kaiser, *Mission in the Old Testament*, 9.

6. Isaiah 61:7 and Zechariah 9:12 leave no doubt that a double portion of blessing is promised for Israel nationally in the future (cf. Isaiah 54:1).

7. Abraham and his descendants repeatedly attempted to choose an alternative plan, an action that would have derailed this integral part of God's design (e.g., Genesis 15:2; 16:2; 17:18; cf. 25:23 with 27:4; Numbers 25). Each attempt is decisively rebuffed by God, revealing His unequivocal intentionality.

8. Kaiser, *Mission in the Old Testament*, 22. Later he comments: "All were to be agents of God's blessing to all on earth. Nothing could be clearer from the missionary and ministry call issued in Exodus 19:4-6" (24).

9. U. Cassuto, *A Commentary on the Book of Exodus*, trans. Israel Abrahams (Jerusalem: Magnes Press, 1997), 227.

10. G.W. Grogan, "Isaiah," *Expositor's Bible Commentary*, Volume 6, ed. Frank E. Gaebelein (Grand Rapids: Zondervan, 1986), 260.

11. Mitch Glaser, *To the Jew First: The Case for Jewish Evangelism in Scripture and History*, eds. Darrell Bock & Mitch Glaser (Grand Rapids: Kregel Publications, 2008), 16. C.E.B. Cranfield concurs: "At the same time, 'first' indicates that there is a certain priority of the Jew" (*Romans* [Grand Rapids: Eerdmans, 1985], 20).

12. Wayne A. Brindle, "'To the Jew First:' Rhetoric, Strategy, History, or Theology?" *BSac* (April-June, 2002), 159:226.

13. Moo, *Romans 1–8*, Wycliffe Exegetical Commentary (Chicago: Moody, 1991), 64.

14. Brindle, "To the Jew First," 233.

15. For a more thorough discussion on this point, see Irv Busenitz, "Reaching the World: God's Global Agenda," 243-246.

16. John Murray, *The Epistle to the Romans* (Grand Rapids: Eerdmans, 1968; reprint 1997), 40.

17. As Isaiah vividly illustrates, his sinful condition made him utterly useless (6:5-8) as God's missionary herald. In the vision of Ezekiel, the prophet was exhorted to eat the scroll, thereby picturing God's requirement to live according to His word and speak His message to the Israelites (2:8–3:4, 10).

18. That is David's point in Psalm 19. Having noted how physical creation (1–6) and special revelation (7–11) both testify with perfection the revelations of God, he sees the imperfections of his own life and cries out for mercy and forgiveness (12–14; cf. Psalm 51; 1 Peter 2:12).

19. Annie Johnson Flint, "The World's Bible," *Home Missions Monthly* 22 (January 1918), 3:66.

20. The passion of the Father is reflected in Jesus' parable of the banquet (Luke 14:16-24), where, after some invited guests turn down the invitation, the slaves are exhorted to invite still others and to persuasively urge them to attend.

21. Elsewhere, Paul reiterated this vital link between prayer and evangelism (1 Timothy 2:1-2, 8; 2:4-7; cf. Colossians 4:2).

22. Acts 15:3; 20:38; 21:5; Romans 15:24; 1 Corinthians 16:6, 11; 2 Corinthians 1:16; Titus 3:13; 3 John 6.

23. Tom Steller, "Afterword: The Supremacy of God in Going and Sending," *Let the Nations Be Glad* (Grand Rapids: Baker, 2010), 262.

24. Carl F.H. Henry, "The Renewal of Theological Education," *Vocatio* (Summer 1989), 4.

25. The account of the rich man and Lazarus (Luke 16:19-31) vividly illustrates the power and preeminence of the Word.

26. As Peter O'Brien argues, the phrase "of the Spirit" is best understood as a genitive of source, "indicating that the Spirit makes the sword powerful and effective, giving to it its cutting edge (cf. Heb. 4:12)" (*The Letter to the Ephesians*, Pillar New Testament Commentary, ed. D.A. Carson [Grand Rapids: Eerdmans, 1999], 481-482).

27. O'Brien, *Ephesians*, 482.

28. S.R. Hirsch, *The Psalms* (New York: Scribners Publishing, 1966), 388.

29. UN Declaration of Human Rights Article 18 "protects 'teaching, practice, worship and observance,' but overtly and explicitly fails to protect public preaching. The UN's 1981 Declaration on the Elimination of All Forms of Intolerance uses the same approach on matters of religion. Article 9 of the European Convention for the Protection of Human Rights and Fundamental Freedoms allows evangelism to be banned to protect 'public order'" (Craig L. Parshall, "Tampering with Freedom of Religion," *Israel My Glory* [November/December 2010], 31).

30. Parshall, "Tampering with Freedom of Religion," 27; emphasis his.

31. Moo, *Romans 1-8*, 101.

Chapter 12—Compassion Without Compromise

1. For example, Norm Geisler claims, "The economic disparity among mankind is a type of social injustice." Norman Geisler, *Love Your Neighbor* (Wheaton, IL: Crossway, 2007), 75.

2. For more development on this, see Kevin DeYoung and Greg Gilbert, *What Is the Mission of the Church?* (Wheaton, IL: Crossway, 2011), 179-181.

3. See Wayne Grudem and Barry Asmus, *The Poverty of Nations* (Wheaton, IL: Crossway, 2013), 65ff for detailed explanation of why these approaches do more harm than good. The authors make a compelling point that economic systems that create wealth—and thus create economic winners and losers—actually do more to eliminate social injustice than any culture which pursues economic equality.

4. As John Wesley said in his *Explanatory Notes on the New Testament* on Luke 7:22, "'To the poor the gospel is preached'—which is the greatest mercy, and the greatest miracle of all."

5. "U.S. Abortion Statistics." Online at: http://www.abort73.com/abortion_facts/us_abortion_statistics. Accessed October 2016.

Chapter 13—Fit for the Master's Use

1. Robert Murray M'Cheyne as cited in D.A. Carson, *A Call to Spiritual Reformation* (Grand Rapids: Baker Academic, 1992), 16.

2. Robert Murray M'Cheyne. *Memoir and Remains of the Rev. R.M. M'Cheyne* (Dundee: William Middleton, 1852), 243.

3. Arthur Bennett, ed. *The Valley of Vision: A Collection of Puritan Prayers & Devotions* (Edinburgh: Banner of Truth Trust, 1975).

4. Robert Murray M'Cheyne as cited in George Sweeting, *Who Said That?* (Chicago: Moody, 1995), section on "Christian Living."

Chapter 14—Global Risk Assessment

1. *Ayub Edward.* "Inside the Insider Movement." July 2, 2013. Westminster Theological Seminary. Online at http://www.wts.edu/stayinformed/view.html?id=1579. Accessed October 2016.

2. John Travis, *Evangelical Missions Quarterly* (October 1998): 407-408.

3. D.A. Carson, *Jesus the Son of God* (Wheaton, IL: Crossway, 2012), 107-108.

4. Edwards, "Inside the Insider Movement," online at www.wts.edu/stay informed/view.html?id=1579.

5. Greg Gilbert, "Book Review: *Church Planting Movements*, by David Garrison," Online at https://9marks.org/review/church-planting-move ments-david-garrison. Accessed October 2016.

6. Gilbert, "Book Review."

7. David Adamo, "What is African Biblical Hermeneutics?" *Black Theology: An International Journal* 13/1 (April 2015): 70.

Chapter 15—To the Praise of His Glory

1. "What was God's purpose in establishing the church?" Online at https://compellingtruth.org/purpose-church.html. Accessed October 2016.

2. "What was God's purpose in establishing the church?"

3. Paul M. Elliott, "What Is God's Purpose for His Church?" Online at http://www.teachingtheword.org/apps/articles/?columnid=5449&artic leid=67131. Accessed October 2016.

4. Rick Warren, *The Purpose Driven Church* (Grand Rapids: Zondervan, 1995).

5. John Piper, *God's Passion for His Glory: Living the Vision of Jonathan Edwards, with the Complete Text of* The End for Which God Created the World (Wheaton, IL: Crossway, 1998).

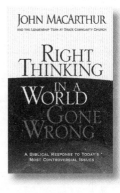

Right Thinking in a World Gone Wrong

One of the greatest challenges facing Christians today is the powerful influence of secular thinking. From all directions we're fed a constant barrage of persuasive—yet unbiblical—worldviews. This makes it difficult to know where to stand on today's most talked-about issues.

The leadership team at Grace Community Church, along with their pastor, John MacArthur, provide much-needed discernment and clarity in the midst of rampant confusion. Using the Bible as the foundation, you'll learn how to develop a Christian perspective on key issues—including...

political activism	environmentalism
homosexual marriage	abortion and birth control
euthanasia and suicide	immigration
disasters and epidemics	God and the problem of evil

This guide will arm you with right thinking and biblical answers to challenging questions.